THE COMPLETE IDIOT'S GUIDE® TO

Getting Government Contracts

John C. Lauderdale III

ALPHA

A member of Penguin Group (USA) Inc.

ALPHA BOOKS

Published by the Penguin Group

Penguin Group (USA) Inc., 375 Hudson Street, New York, New York 10014, USA

Penguin Group (Canada), 90 Eglinton Avenue East, Suite 700, Toronto, Ontario M4P 2Y3, Canada (a division of Pearson Penguin Canada Inc.)

Penguin Books Ltd., 80 Strand, London WC2R 0RL, England

Penguin Ireland, 25 St. Stephen's Green, Dublin 2, Ireland (a division of Penguin Books Ltd.)

Penguin Group (Australia), 250 Camberwell Road, Camberwell, Victoria 3124, Australia (a division of Pearson Australia Group Pty. Ltd.)

Penguin Books India Pvt. Ltd., 11 Community Centre, Panchsheel Park, New Delhi—110 017, India

Penguin Group (NZ), 67 Apollo Drive, Rosedale, North Shore, Auckland 1311, New Zealand (a division of Pearson New Zealand Ltd.)

Penguin Books (South Africa) (Pty.) Ltd., 24 Sturdee Avenue, Rosebank, Johannesburg 2196, South Africa

Penguin Books Ltd., Registered Offices: 80 Strand, London WC2R 0RL, England

International Standard Book Number: 978-1-59257-944-0
Library of Congress Catalog Card Number: 2009924931

11 10 09   8 7 6 5 4 3 2 1

Interpretation of the printing code: The rightmost number of the first series of numbers is the year of the book's printing; the rightmost number of the second series of numbers is the number of the book's printing. For example, a printing code of 09-1 shows that the first printing occurred in 2009.

Printed in the United States of America

Note: This publication contains the opinions and ideas of its author. It is intended to provide helpful and informative material on the subject matter covered. It is sold with the understanding that the author and publisher are not engaged in rendering professional services in the book. If the reader requires personal assistance or advice, a competent professional should be consulted.

The author and publisher specifically disclaim any responsibility for any liability, loss, or risk, personal or otherwise, which is incurred as a consequence, directly or indirectly, of the use and application of any of the contents of this book.

Most Alpha books are available at special quantity discounts for bulk purchases for sales promotions, premiums, fundraising, or educational use. Special books, or book excerpts, can also be created to fit specific needs.

For details, write: Special Markets, Alpha Books, 375 Hudson Street, New York, NY 10014.

Publisher: *Marie Butler-Knight*
Editorial Director: *Mike Sanders*
Senior Managing Editor: *Billy Fields*
Acquisitions Editor: *Tom Stevens*
Development Editor: *Ginny Bess Munroe*
Senior Production Editor: *Megan Douglass*
Copy Editor: *Nancy Wagner*

Contributing Editor: *Michelle Tullier*
Cartoonist: *Steve Barr*
Cover Designer: *Kurt Owens*
Book Designer: *Trina Wurst*
Indexer: *Angie Bess*
Layout: *Ayanna Lacey*
Proofreader: *John Etchison*

Contents at a Glance

Contents

17 Creating Management Volumes · 211

18 Creating Cost/Price Volumes · 223

19 Clean-Up and Improvement Tasks · 233

Introduction

In recent times, our nation and the world, for that matter, has experienced a high degree of uncertainty in just about every aspect of our lives, especially financial and political. Some institutions we've long regarded as "steady as the rock of Gibraltar" have not only lost that steady grip but have even gone away entirely. Who would have wagered, or even imagined, that Merrill Lynch would be sold at garage sale prices to avoid a complete collapse; that Lehman Brothers would be dissolved; that the Yankees would finish third in the American League East?!

Thomas Paine captured it well more than 200 years ago when he said, "These are the times that try men's souls." In tough times in our personal and business lives, we seek assurance through institutions and relationships that we can count on being there when all else fails. As business people, we want to do business with customers who do have that steady hand—who need our products and services, can and will pay our bills on time, and, ideally, keep coming back for more. We want stable, secure, and steady customers over the long term. That's where government contracting comes in.

Regardless of your political party affiliation—if any—and no matter what your view is of big government versus small, one thing you can be certain of is that in difficult economic times, there will be increased spending by governments. The composition of the spending in the second decade of the twenty-first century may be quite different from that of the first decade. The only certainty is that it will be greater in total.

If you're already a part of the government contracting world, then you're already on board and this book may teach you some new strategies. If you're thinking, as many are, "Okay, but how do I take full advantage of the coming wave of government contracts?" then you've also come to the right place.

How to Use This Book

The Complete Idiot's Guide to Getting Government Contracts teaches businesses large and small what to do, how to do it, and why do it that way for all aspects of seeking government contracts. The chapters follow a logical sequence of events from identifying a product or service that a government can use and that you can provide, to the details of a successful offering, to the award and execution of a specific contract. Feel free to skip around, though, and read the chapters out of order if you have a specific need and want to zero in on the section most relevant for you.

I've organized the chapters into six parts:

Part 1, "What Successful Contractors Know"—To know what succeeds, just look at the successful. Here's where you can start to determine if investing your company's scarce time and money to bid on government contracts is likely to result in enough success to justify the investment.

Part 2, "The Government Contracting Landscape"—Before focusing on the trees (opportunities), you need to know the forest (how contracts are awarded).

Part 3, "Choosing Your Targets"—Choosing the right customer and the right opportunity are your simple keys to success.

Part 4, "Kicking Off the Proposal Process"—Getting off to a quick start and sticking to your proposal plan increases the chance your proposal will result in a contract.

Part 5, "Creating a Winning Response by the Volumes"—Winning proposals follow instructions and provide a solution that is not only different from, but also better than, those of your competitors.

Part 6, "Starting and Remaining Strong After You Win (or Lose)"—Holding on to your government contracts is almost as important as getting new contracts. Here's how.

You'll come across lots of standard industry vocabulary, so if you see an unfamiliar term or acronyms that look like alphabet soup, look them up in Appendix A. If you want to know more about a particular topic, look for resources for further advice among the people, places, and things listed in Appendix B. Appendixes C, D, and E offer supplementary materials, such as sample documents and documents on training your team.

Extras

Along the way, you'll see sidebars throughout the chapters. These point out special tips, insider information, common pitfalls, and government contracting jargon.

> **Government Insider**
>
> These are tips shared from over four decades of involvement with government contracts.

> **Beltway Buzz**
>
> These are insights into how things work—or don't work—in the world of government contracting.

Red Flag

These alert you to potential problems. If you choose to ignore these red flags, you could find danger ahead.

def•i•ni•tion

Government contracting is like a subculture with its own language. Become fluent with the definitions offered in these boxes!

Acknowledgments

A word of thanks goes to Michelle Tullier for her special role as contributing editor. Her experience with the *Complete Idiot's Guide* series, and her broader experience as an author of many books and professional papers, was of exceptional help to me as a rookie in the book-writing business. Her patience and skill, delivered with both precision and clarity, made my creation task much less anxiety-producing than it would have, and should have, been.

Another special thanks to my colleague, Jay Richman, for providing incisive comments and suggestions on the content of the manuscript.

Special Thanks to the Technical Editor

The Complete Idiot's Guide to Getting Government Contracts was reviewed by an expert who double-checked the accuracy of what you learn here, to help us ensure that this book gives you everything you need to know about getting government contracts. Special thanks are extended to Jay Richman.

Trademarks

All terms mentioned in this book that are known to be or are suspected of being trademarks or service marks have been appropriately capitalized. Alpha Books and Penguin Group (USA) Inc. cannot attest to the accuracy of this information. Use of a term in this book should not be regarded as affecting the validity of any trademark or service mark.

Part 1

What Successful Contractors Know

How do you make your business stand out from the pack to emerge the winner? You'll get off to the right start in these chapters with an overview of the factors that separate the winners from the losers—and the winners from the runners-up. Cultivating relationships with government entities even before a contract opportunity is announced, scoping out your competition, and detecting ethical and legal landmines to avoid are all important first steps to take. And you'll explore whether you should even take a first step at all by looking at who can and should bid and why you should bid only to win.

Critical Elements of Success

In This Chapter

- Bidding: who can and should

- The three playing fields: federal, state, local

- Fitting government contracts into your strategic plan

- The importance of top management involvement

- Financial staying power

- Practicing patience

Close your eyes, and think about your company's best customer or handful of customers. What do they have in common? Are they long-standing clients who send a steady stream of good business your way? Do they pay on time? Does "net 30 days" really mean 30 days to them, not 60 or 75? Are they rock-solid and stable, with good credit ratings and not likely to go into liquidation before honoring your invoices? Are they open in their communications, sharing news of opportunities to do more business with them?

These typical attributes of a good customer fit just about any type of business and also describe the attributes of the government as a customer. When government entities find reliable contractors, they tend to stay with those contractors for a long time. They're required by law to pay their bills on time or face strict penalties, and they must share their opportunities publicly, except where limited by national security issues. So doesn't this sound like a good customer worth going after?

If you've picked up this book, you are at least mildly interested in how you can get government contracts. Your company is probably already doing business in the commercial arena (private sector) but hasn't yet ventured into government contracting. Or maybe you've gone after some government (public sector) business but haven't been successful and want to learn how to get it right the next time. This chapter focuses on the keys to success in getting government contracts.

Understanding Who Can and Should Bid

If you and your organization know you're going to go after government contracts or if you just want to explore the options, then you probably have one or more of these logical questions:

♦ What do successful government contractors have in common?

♦ How do I know whether government contracts are for me and my company without wasting a lot of money?

♦ What are the differences between contracting with the federal government (the United States government) and state and local governments?

Beltway Buzz

The federal government has about 1,200 agencies and 3,200 individual customers within those agencies. Add the number of state governments (50 plus the District of Columbia) and a boatload of local governments, and you have a huge number of potential customers for your products or services.

♦ How would the addition of government business affect my existing strategic and tactical plans?

♦ What does it take to submit the winning *bid* (also called a *proposal* or *response)*?

♦ How can our business develop a solution that will meet the government customer's needs and requirements?

def•i•ni•tion

The **bid** is an offer in response to an Invitation for Bid (IFB).

Normally a written offer by you, as a seller, the **proposal** describes the offering terms. Proposals may be issued in response to a specific request; for example, a Request for Proposal (RFP).

The **response** is a general term for the material you, as an offeror, provide to the customer, consistent with the customer's description of what he requires. The responses from all offerors will be evaluated, and a contract awarded (or not) in accordance with the terms of the customer's solicitation.

The heart of your response should be the **solution** to the customer's problem described in the solicitation and as you have determined from the solicitation and other relevant sources.

Do Your Products Distinguish Your Business from Others?

A first element of success is simply knowing if you should bid on a particular *opportunity* or *solicitation*. One way to know this is to assess whether you have products that not only the customer wants but are also different in some way. Ideally, your product(s) should be different from and better than that of your competition. It's even more ideal if your product has high value to the customer. It does little good to be better than the competition if the product still offers little value to the customer. When you read a solicitation in detail, you'll be able to see what counts as good in the mind of the customer.

def•i•ni•tion

A government entity identifies a need it has for a specific product or service and seeks offers from suppliers who can fulfill that need. That need is an **opportunity** for those who wish to secure a contract to fulfill the need.

A **solicitation** is a document requesting or inviting offerors to submit offers. A formal announcement of an opportunity, solicitations typically include a draft contract and provisions on preparing and submitting offers.

The government has the ability to invest in new technology. The Department of Energy (DoE) national laboratories, for example, have been investing in new technologies for seven decades. The Department of Defense (DOD) is consistently investing in new hardware and software to defend our nation. Lesser known, but also powerful, are other government agencies' activities that sponsor innovative products. There are contract research and development opportunities for innovative ideas. The government is always interested in products that can help it better do its job. So evaluate if you might have a product that meets a technology need or innovative idea.

In addition, the budgets of all agencies in all governments are always under pressure to do more with less, and the only way they can do that is through increased productivity. So consider whether you have something that can increase the productivity of a government agency.

The bottom line is if you can show that what you're offering is significantly different from and better than the products they are now buying, you have a very good chance of succeeding in getting a government contract.

Are You a Good Fit for the Government?

If your company is successful in business development in the commercial world, you know what processes work in that arena. Unfortunately, you'll find that those processes do not necessarily translate directly into the world of government contracting. For example, governments have their own peculiar rules on accounting that have no direct counterpart in the commercial world. Because you must conform to these government rules, for a while you'll be on a learning curve to get comfortable with the new and different requirements.

Beltway Buzz
Creating winning proposals can take a long time. It's not unusual for large, high-value government contracts to take years between the identification of a need and an award. For example, the large contracts for telecommunications services often run more than five years between identification of need and award of contracts.

Assuming you and your colleagues are adaptable and are willing and able to learn the ropes quickly, you might still wonder if your company is the government contracting type. Well, there is no such thing, so you can relax. Sure, you must meet certain standards. You have to offer a quality product or service at a good price that helps a government entity do something better, faster, smarter, or more cost-effectively. You must be reliable and dependable, getting projects done on time and within budget. But, beyond that, companies doing business with the government come in all shapes and sizes, and that's not so different from the commercial world.

Why You Should Bid Only to Win

While you're deciding whether government contracting makes sense for your organization and if you have any business getting into the game, you might wonder if you have to make a firm decision. You might think you can just toss out a bid and see what happens, like flinging spaghetti on the wall and wondering if it will stick. That's a perfectly normal, natural thought process, but one that could end up getting you into trouble.

One of the most important lessons to learn from this book is that you should bid *only* to win. Too often I've heard my own clients say, "Well, we won't win this one, but we'll establish a name for ourselves with the customer." Again, this may seem like a perfectly logical way to approach things, but this can be counterproductive. Let's not even delve into the issue of why you have a negative attitude about your work. Setting that aside, we come to the reality that if you bid and lose, you *will* have a name with this particular government customer, but, sorry to tell you, that name will be *loser!* No one wants that.

Winning is difficult enough when you think you *can* win, so don't stack the odds against yourself by assuming you'll lose. Remember, by the end of the process, you and your team will have invested a lot of time and money into this project that, if you lose, you could have used elsewhere, possibly in a more profitable endeavor.

Throughout this book we give you more information to help you make an informed decision, so don't decide just yet. But if you do end up realizing you have no products that governments can use or that are any different from what they already have, then a no-go decision might be the way to go. And as you learn more about the long, involved process of responding to government solicitations and decide you're satisfied with the nongovernment work you have, then it's a further indicator that deciding not to bid may be the best way to go.

If you reach that decision, well, at least you haven't wasted more money than the price of this book or transportation costs getting to the local library to read it!

Beltway Buzz

The cost of getting government contracts is highly variable. Large companies, such as Boeing, General Dynamics, Northrop Grumman, Computer Sciences, and SAIC spend millions of dollars to submit proposals each year. A very large proposal, such as the United States Air Force's Tanker Replacement Program, can run into the tens or even hundreds of millions of dollars. At the other end of the spectrum, small businesses may spend only a few hundred dollars to submit winning proposals. The only constant is that the cost of getting government contracts is roughly proportional to the value of those contracts.

Deciding the Time Isn't Now, But Maybe Later

Just because today's answer or the answer you come to in the near future is "no-go," this doesn't mean that's the right answer forever. Change is the only constant in today's business and government worlds. So as your company develops new products or perhaps merges into another company with such products or you yourself change jobs or careers, any one of these changes could require a re-evaluation of the situation.

In addition, government requirements or needs evolve over time. For example, few would've thought the United States government would ever buy American technical services to go to the former republics of the Soviet Union to assist in, and monitor, the de-commissioning of nuclear weapons! Virtually no one thought that in 1970 or 1980, but in the mid-2000s, that requirement became obvious and necessary.

> ### Red Flag
>
> Getting government contracts is hard, focused, intelligent, and disciplined work. Anyone who tries to sell you a magic potion, a cure-all for your business development, is a charlatan, a huckster. Beware of those people who claim they can get you a winning contract without meeting the solicitation's requirements or by doing only half the work.

Government Opportunities at the Federal, State, and Local Levels

Another early step to take in your process to ensure success down the road is to understand the three levels of government opportunities and which might be the best fit for your business. This book covers the three major categories of government contracts within the United States: federal, state (50, plus the District of Columbia), and local (all the cities, counties, and regional authorities). However, covering in great detail the many different agencies within those three levels is far beyond the scope of this book.

We focus primarily on United States federal government processes and how to get federal government contracts. So throughout the book, most references to "government" will mean federal government, but you'll see a number of instances where we offer specific information about state and local (S & L) contracts as well.

When dealing with the different levels of government, remember that they don't work under all of the same rules. Here are some ways state and local contracting differs from federal contracts:

♦ Each S & L has its own peculiar procurement rules, which may vary a little or a lot from federal government rules.

♦ If your business is based outside of the S & L locality offering the contract, you must have a strong in-locality partner to overcome the carpetbagger image.

♦ S & Ls do not stick as strictly to the rules—even their own rules—in making contract awards. Sometimes their decisions are not subject to the same transparency required by the federal government. (One exception to this is a contract offered though the General Services Administration [GSA], which we describe in Chapter 10.)

How Government Contracts Fit in Your Strategic Plan

Before deciding to pursue government contracts, you should know whether such contracts fit into your company's strategic plan. At this point, you may be saying to yourself, "Say what? I didn't know I had to have a strategic plan, I just want to know how to get government contracts." Best business practice says you can't carry out business without a good plan, and best government contracting practice says you start with a good business plan and then see how contracting fits into it or enhances it.

Red Flag

The basis of a successful business is a strategic plan. If you've been successful to this point in your business life without such a plan, you are outstandingly lucky. Or maybe you inherited a lot of money and don't have to worry about profit margins. If you're now venturing into government contracting, you're about to add a whole new layer of complexity to your company's financial, operational, and business development structure. Don't venture down this path without a strategic business plan!

Building Your Strategic Plan

If you do an Internet search for "strategic planning process," you'll get oodles of hits. Though detailed discussions on how to create strategic plans are beyond the scope of this book, if you don't have one, here's a suggested high-level outline of a strategic plan courtesy of NetMBA (www.netmba.com/strategy/process) to get you started:

♦ Mission—This statement establishes the reason for the organization's existence.

♦ Objectives—These concrete goals should be operationally defined and verifiable.

- Situation Analysis—This includes plans to reach those objectives.

- Strategy Formulation—Here you consider alternative paths to the objectives.

- Implementation—This lists detailed policies, down to the functional level.

- Control—Here you keep track of your progress toward your goals and objectives, and make appropriate mid-course corrections.

Using Your Strategic Plan

The important thing about any strategic plan is that you must not only create one but also continuously revisit the elements of the plan. Doing annual strategic planning and then allowing it to become *shelfware* is not the best use of the plan. Consider the plan a living document and have a specific mechanism to keep it current.

def•i•ni•tion

Shelfware is the practice of creating great documents (policy manuals, procedure manuals, ethics manuals) and then putting them on the shelf while you calmly await the next your-hair's-on-fire crisis.

Government agencies establish a set of criteria on which they will evaluate how well a response to that agency's solicitation meets that agency's requirements or needs. These evaluation criteria (that is, what counts as being "good" in the eyes of the customer) typically contain many evaluation factors, and vary from contract to contract. But the contract is most often awarded to either the company with the lowest offered price (among otherwise-acceptable offers) or the company that is sufficiently better than other companies though its price might be higher. It is important to know where, from a strategic standpoint, you and your company seek to be.

You can think of your company's positioning as fitting somewhere in a competitive triangle, as shown in the following figure. The place for your company in that triangle depends on the circumstances of that competition. You may want to be toward one corner on Competition A and toward another corner in Competition B depending on what you think the customer's evaluation criteria are for each competition. However, your company is most likely to pursue a consistent strategy in most of its offers. So whatever else is a part of your strategic plan, you should decide where, in the triangle shown in the following figure, you typically strive to be.

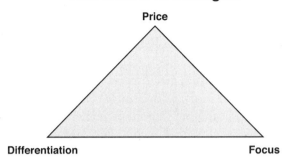

Pure Business Strategies   *Competitive Triangle.*

The three pure business strategies are price, differentiation, and focus.

Each corner of the triangle in the figure represents a pure strategy. The upper corner (#1) is clear. Companies in that corner are competing only on price. A handful of companies, some rather large, feature one of their divisions (usually, for support services and at the *low* end of the technological spectrum) with rock-bottom labor rates and barebones compliance with the solicitation requirements. The company strategy is to price its services at such a low rate that the customer is almost forced to choose that bid over others, even if they judge competing bids superior. In the industry, this is called, "Pass/Fail for other evaluation factors, and award to the lowest price bid."

Corner #2 at the bottom left is also clear. "Differentiation" means that a company's strategy is to offer solutions different from those of the competition. An example is to offer a Macintosh platform, when all other offers feature PC platforms. However, to be successful, this difference must also be judged "better" in the eyes of the customer.

The meaning of Corner #3 is perhaps the least obvious. "Focus" describes the case in which a company goes after a market that is so specialized, and in some cases so small, that other potential offerors are simply not attracted to that line of product or service. Most of the time, these markets have relatively high barriers to entry.

A good example of this type of strategy is Dr. Scholl's foot care products. That market is so small (in relation, for example, to the personal care products sector) that Dr. Scholl's has enjoyed a dominating role in that market segment. Other than house brands, Dr. Scholl's has no significant competition.

Few strategies are absolutely pure strategies that would put your company in the extreme corners. However, the danger is that your strategy will be in what we call the "Bermuda Triangle of Losing," which means stuck in the middle. The center strategies appeal to almost no buyers as the criteria for what counts as good tends to be in one of those corners. By default, your proposition is, "We certainly are another offeror!" and rarely wins the contract.

Clear Exit Strategy

Despite your own best efforts at acquiring government business, you may reach the point that the logical (if unfortunate) conclusion is that government business is not for your company. So an *exit strategy* is another important element of a strategic business plan because the lack of a clear exit strategy is a common cause of business failure. Even surviving businesses can look back to a time where the warning signs were clear that exiting was the best, if not only sensible, strategy, but they ignored the signs.

If you see signs that your future efforts are not likely to produce contracts, then your best strategy is to cut your losses and exit the government contracting arena.

def•i•ni•tion

The policy of having pre-established criteria for deciding to discontinue efforts you've started is your **exit strategy**. Only by leaving some efforts can you have enough resources to pursue new, more appealing avenues.

Top Management Involvement

Of all the elements of success, this is the most important: the number-one reason for losing competitions for government contracts is the lack of top management involvement in the process. The participation of top management is a key to winning. This might be one person or a small group of people, and it's typically senior officers in your organization. This involvement makes a difference for many reasons.

The Customer Notices

The customer can tell if top management is truly involved. For example, has the top management visited the customer's place of business? The customer typically knows top management by face and name and tends to award government contracts to people with positive name and face recognition. For example, if the highest-ranking person in your company known by the customer is the local program manager, the conclusion drawn by the customer is that no one above the program manager cares about the program. This is probably not true, but why let your customer guess wrong? Make it a point to be present on some occasion to make yourself known to the customer.

The Proposal Team Notices

Your proposal team knows whether top management cares about this opportunity or not. If top management has given the personal stamp of approval to the team's leadership and assigned the right priority, staff members know it and will work harder because of that commitment. Who wants to work on a proposal and requirements for a contract if management doesn't support the company's winning it?

Top Management Knows How to Make a Difference

Business development is too important to be left to the marketers. Good marketing people come to rely on top management and use those individuals to speak to their counterparts in the customer's organization. We discuss more about proposal team roles and responsibilities in Chapter 5.

Top Management Can Build Relationships

Only top managers can build certain relationships. Confidence and a feeling of well-being is just as important in government work as it is in commercial work. Winning depends on the customer having the confidence and good feeling that either the customer *wants* your company to win or at least *doesn't mind* if your company wins.

Government Insider _____

For a more detailed discussion of top management's involvement in the contracting process, see Chapter 5, where you'll find specific ways to get top management involved.

Having Financial Staying Power

Financial staying power is the ability to fund marketing and sales efforts and to keep on doing so until you are successful in getting that government contract. As you might imagine, this is an important key to success.

The battlefield for government contracts is littered with companies who came to the arena without the financial backing to stay on the field long enough to be successful. Regardless of how well prepared you are, success comes only after much hard work and the focused effort of many people, all of which you must fund with money. This endeavor is not for companies with shallow pockets.

However, deep pockets are not enough. Just throwing money at the problem will not ensure success. You must have realistic expectations about how quickly your marketing success will translate into revenues and how quickly these contracts will show a positive cash flow. So having the money is not enough; you must have good financial planning, forecasting, and budgeting as well.

Make Patience Pay Off

In addition to financial staying power, successful contractors have another kind of staying power, which involves waiting and waiting and waiting to see your efforts finally pay off. Patience means doing it with a sense of calm. At one time in my government contracting career, the John Lauderdale Standard Prayer was, "Lord, give me patience, but give it to me *now!*" Fortunately, I've learned to muster up patience without having to demand it *now*, but I keep the old prayer on hand just in case!

The history of government contracting is replete with examples of successful commercial companies who attempt to enter the government market without patience. A typical and, sadly, often repeated scenario is this: a Silicon Valley company, very successful in the commercial market, believes the government market is its Next Best Thing. So the company takes a successful (usually relatively junior) person from the sales or marketing ranks, who has zero experience in selling to the government, and transplants that seller to the Washington, D.C., area.

The charter is to "go get government business." The title is "Director of Government Marketing and Sales." After two weeks, the director's immediate superior gets on the phone and asks, "Well, you've been there two weeks. Where's your first contract?" This is a disaster in the making, as neither the director nor the immediate boss has a clue that patience is an absolute requirement. It may be months or quarters or more likely years before the first contract comes in and even longer before net earnings appear.

Beltway Buzz

A single-award opportunity is likely to have two or three, no more than four, bidders with a reasonable chance of winning. Rarely are there more than four truly viable contenders. So you typically have at least a 25 percent chance of winning, maybe even 50 percent or better. That's not too bad! Of course, to win, you must submit a compliant and convincing response.

People experienced in the ways of government procurement process (described in detail in Chapter 5) know it is long and complex and not readily understood by the general public. Like the proverbial battleship, the process is difficult to get started and once underway, almost impossible to turn about quickly. It takes a mighty, focused effort to turn the ship. That's the bad news. The good news is that, once underway, the ship tends to go in the same direction for a very long time. It's slow to get started but can be a reliable source of revenues and profits, often for years and years.

The Least You Need to Know

◆ Government is a very good customer and offers many different opportunities to sell your products.

◆ Your products should be different from and better than those of your competition.

◆ Your efforts at getting government contracts must be consistent with and a part of your company's strategic plan.

◆ Your organization's top management must be involved in the process of getting government contracts.

◆ You must have both patience and financial staying power to succeed in this market.

Taking the First Steps Toward a Win

In This Chapter

- ◆ Cultivate customer relationships
- ◆ Know your competition
- ◆ Have a solid marketing plan
- ◆ Make careful staffing decisions

Now that you have an idea of the critical elements of success in winning government contracts, you're ready to start taking action toward that win. The process of writing proposals to respond to a government contract opportunity is a long and winding road—as in expensive—so we devote several later chapters to the details necessary to help you navigate that road. For now, let's look only at the highlights of some initial steps you should take as you set out.

This chapter focuses on several important things to do from the get-go. We discuss building relationships with customers and gaining an awareness of your competition. You must do a lot of sleuthing of your customer and competition before you and your team can identify a specific target to market your products or services to. This target is called an opportunity.

Once you identify an opportunity, you need a marketing plan to put into writing how you're going to work with the customer, even though you might not yet know of a specific opportunity the customer will offer. Then, you need to start identifying potential staff to work as a team committed to getting the contract.

Building Relationships

You need to cultivate relationships with your customer. What kind of relationships? Both good and long-term ones. But what do these qualities really mean?

Good relationships mean having positive name and face recognition with your customer. Good relationships mean your customer has faith, trusts in what you say, and relies on your word being your bond.

Good relationships don't happen overnight; the best ones are built not only over the long haul but also in advance of the identification of a specific opportunity. Building these relationships is neither easy nor cheap, so be prepared to invest your dollars in this effort. The ability and willingness to spend money to build these relationships are the true marks of *commitment*.

def•i•ni•tion

Commitment is the ability and willingness to spend your own money to help solve the customer's problems. This investment includes, but exceeds, the cost of submitting a proposal. This term is often misused, when a claim of "commitment" is confined to just submitting a proposal.

What is the size of your investment as measured by time and money? That's a valid question. The short answer is, "It depends." I know that's not very helpful, but it truly does depend on the size of the customer, the size of the product stream you hope to capture, and your own resources. In an urban myth, a business leader observed, "I know that half of my advertising isn't paying off. The problem is, I don't know *which* half." Similarly, you're going to have to use that old reliable business judgment to decide both when it's the right time and place to start and when it's the right time and place to stop building relationships with a specific customer.

As you develop relationships with customers, you have a number of choices for places and occasions to meet the customer. Some are official events where you, your customer, and even your competition congregate. Others are informal occasions, such as birthday gatherings or going-away celebrations for individuals at the customer's organization. Receiving these invitations tells you that you have a good relationship! Here's a short list of some likely venues:

◆ Social events, such as golf tournaments and softball games. (Attendance by government employees at these events is within the procurement rules, as the values are typically low, and under any regulated limits.)

◆ Professional meetings, such as the meeting of the local chapters of AFCEA (the Armed Forces Communications and Electronics Association).

◆ Industry Days when the government opens its facilities to allow contractors and potential contractors typically to discuss a specific upcoming competition, and to get industry input helpful to the government competition managers.

◆ Formal meetings between your people and the corresponding government people. These are described in Chapter 6. During these, you have a chance to not only give but also get information.

At any and all of these occasions to meet with the customer, let common sense be your behavioral guide. Dress appropriately. Refrain from discussing specific topics that the government person could find out of place in the workplace. And, of course, avoid heavy drinking and other behavior you might regret the next day.

Red Flag

If you're targeting a particular government agency as a likely customer for your business, use good judgment about the frequency of contact you have with people at that agency. More meetings are better than fewer as you cultivate a solid relationship, but be careful not to wear out your welcome. And make each meeting friendly, professional, and to the point. Avoid wasting the customer's time or giving him a feeling of dread when seeing you.

Find Out What the Competition Is Doing

You must know the competition for the type of products you wish to sell to the government. Usually, this information is readily available from the competition's public documents, which give you easy access to the types of products it is already providing to its government customers, with the exception of any *classified contracts*. Your competitors' sales and marketing people are always eager to tout their company's products, so plenty of information should be available on the companies' websites and in any publicly accessible marketing materials.

def•i•ni•tion

> Contracts with the intelligence agencies, such as the Central Intelligence Agency (CIA), the National Security Agency (NSA), and other agencies doing work that must be hidden from public view, are **classified contracts**. You cannot expect to learn about these contract opportunities unless you have the proper government clearances.

You also have access to information on government contracts your competitors may have secured when you take advantage of the Freedom of Information Act (FOIA).

FOIA opens up government documents to the public. Sunshine is a great disinfectant, and provides public access to public documents, without the requirement to justify the request. Early in the Obama administration, the new president ordered a turn-about in the mechanics of agency compliance with the Act by changing the default from favoring non-disclosure to favoring disclosure. Under the now-current rules, agencies must present convincing reasons for failure to comply with a FOIA request. Find more information about FOIA in Chapter 8.

Most companies are not particularly skilled at employing FOIA to their greatest advantage. Most companies are not satisfied with the results obtained by trying to get good information on the competition, and on the processes of the government. So after you and your company reach the conclusion that this game is not for amateurs, you will probably want to engage one or more fee-for-service companies to provide more specific information about your competition.

These companies are the professionals, and can achieve much better results for you, because of their experience and expertise. For example, you may be able to obtain a copy of the current contract in hours, rather than in either months or not at all. See Appendix B for references to these companies.

As a Boy Scout responsible for managing waterfront activities, you learn this sequence for rescuing another swimmer in trouble: reach, throw, row, and go.

The first thing you try is to reach your hand to the swimmer. If that doesn't work, throw a rope. Next, go after him in a rowboat. Only as a last resort do you swim after him. This sequence starts with the simplest, most basic, least costly, and most readily at hand. You risk something important, such as your life, if and only if everything that's less risky has failed.

Similarly, with competitor knowledge, start with the simplest and least costly source, such as newspapers, professional journals, advertising of all types, and personal contact you can easily do. Move up to using more sophisticated and costly methods, such as your own Internet searches, and as the last resort use professional services. This is not to downplay the value of these services, but you should see what's readily available for free, or nearly free, before you move up to more costly methods.

Your Marketing Plan

When you identify a specific target to bid on, you'll need to create an opportunity-specific marketing plan. At this point, you may not have a target identified and might need the advice offered in Chapters 7 and 8, on targeting a specific customer and a specific opportunity. You are probably not ready to put together a full marketing plan tailored to one opportunity; however, at this early stage, you should know what goes into a plan and even start developing a basic template. This will keep you from being caught off guard at the eleventh hour when you do need a plan and find yourself having to start from scratch with no template and no forethought.

Common elements of a marketing plan include:

- ◆ Executive Summary—Presents a brief summary, suitable for a high-level review of your plan.

- ◆ Situation Analysis—Describes the total situation: the timing of the solicitation, the size of the opportunity, the competition, and your knowledge of the customer's real wants.

- ◆ Marketing Strategy—Describes a plan to call on the customer's important people before there is a prohibition against such contact; explains where you plan to be strategically. For example, are you planning to win on your low price?

- ◆ Financials—Explains how you plan to make money on this opportunity and may discuss the size of your up-front investment (including proposal costs and all the others required to stay competitive) to win this contract.

- ◆ Controls—Explains what plans you have for controlling the program during the running of the contract, especially the costs of the program.

We provide a sample capture plan in Appendix C so you can see how these elements are fleshed out to form a strong capture plan that you can customize for a particular opportunity.

Getting Help Writing a Capture Plan

You will want to develop a capture plan template for the type of market you're in and the types of products you sell or services you offer. Do an online search to find templates for "capture plans," or for "marketing plans." The difference is that a capture plan focuses on a single opportunity, and a marketing plan may focus on a broader field, such as a set of opportunities.

KnowThis.com (www.knowthis.com) is a useful site that focuses on marketing basics. This site includes about 50 different plans for a variety of industries and products, so you are likely to find a sample for your type of business.

Use Your Capture Plan Effectively

Until you have a specific customer and opportunity in your sights, you might wonder how much time you should spend on a capture plan and what you should do with the template or rough plan you put together.

Do spend a significant amount of time on this plan. A good plan prevents you from being unprepared, for example, for the release of the solicitation. Realize, however, that the capture plan is a living, evolving document. You'll develop an initial version and then revisit the plan often, revising it accordingly. When you've begun to execute a specific capture plan, you'll find that a few minutes each week or so will verify that you really are getting smarter about the information in that plan.

Assembling a Winning Team

Chapter 6 focuses on how to assemble a winning proposal team, outlining all the roles that you must fill from top management down through every aspect of the management, technical, pricing, and proposal creation processes. For now, start thinking about how you will staff your team.

Every company that goes after government contracts faces this question: do we use only in-house (permanent) staff or do we outsource some of the work using temporary resources? This question is especially important to government bidders, partly because preparing winning proposals often requires a large effort, and you may not have enough people on staff to handle it or at least not enough people who can take time away from their regular jobs. So the ultimate question you need to ask within your organization is, "What is the best way to invest our company's precious *Bid & Proposal (B&P) dollars?*"

def•i•ni•tion

Bid and proposal dollars (B&P) is the amount of money your company intends to spend on bids and proposals. You should set a budget every year and monitor the rate of expenses to keep your actual costs in line with your budget. Don't spend all your B&P money in the first quarter of your fiscal year, or you'll have to pass up opportunities later in the year.

The question is the same for both small and large companies. The answers range from keeping proposal preparation totally in-house to outsourcing the entire proposal preparation process.

Few companies choose only one or the other strategy; most fall somewhere in between these two extremes. The question becomes, "What is the right mix of permanent resources and temporary resources?" The decision of where your business should be along this spectrum depends on two factors:

1. Are your opportunities relatively small and arrive at a more-or-less steady and predictable rate, or large and arrive sporadically?

2. What are your business development goals?

Because every solicitation is different, and every company is different, there are no immutable rules for determining the best mix of permanent and temporary staff. But we can look at what these factors entail and how you might make your decision.

Steady and Predictable or Large and Sporadic?

The difference is dramatic between companies with a steady workload for proposal creation and those with workloads that swing wildly from almost no activity to such a high level of activity as to require a great deal of work on nights and weekends to meet the solicitations' delivery schedules. A simplifying description of the differences is to look at the variance in the level of workloads.

Business Development Goals

Let's assume your goal is to develop $40 million in new business during the next year. Let's further assume that you usually have a 50 percent win rate and that you usually bid on contracts either in the $5 to $10 million range or in the $20 to $30 million range. Arithmetic tells how many bids you will need to win to reach your goal, and by applying your recent experience to the ratio of wins to bids, therefore how many bids you will need to submit. Your recent experience should help you estimate the quantity of skills and personnel hours needed to get the work done.

Although business development goals help define the quantity of effort you need to prepare your proposals, the frequency with which proposals hit your desk is also important in determining whether you require outside help. A company bidding on a large number of smaller contracts may be able to spread the effort so that the permanent staff has the ability to handle all of its proposals. In contrast, if your company submits proposals for a few large programs with gaps of inactivity between proposals, using temporary resources is often the best answer.

For many companies, the issue of whether to use temporary resources (and if so, how many) is not clear cut. Given the uncertainty of solicitation releases, for example, it is impossible to predict the timing of proposal talent. Consequently, you may have good luck in the release schedules, so you can then reach your goals using only permanent staff. However, when too many opportunities arrive at the same time due to simultaneous release dates, the only solution may be to use temporary resources.

The use of temporary resources is an excellent methodology to manage surges in solicitations you plan to work. The ability to ramp up to meet demand as well as to ramp down when demand slows is a cost-effective way to manage your B&P dollars.

Use mostly permanent staff solutions when …

- bids are highly regularly spaced so that it's easy to maintain a steady proposal preparation operation.

- the group has valuable trade secrets that would be compromised by using temporary personnel.

- business development goals are modest and the permanent approach used in the past has been satisfactory.

Use mostly temporary staff solutions when …

- the company typically bids a few large programs, producing a peak-and-valley workload in proposal preparation.

- the company is bidding programs in which the specialized expertise needed to win the contract is not available.

- the company has a sudden peak in the workload due to simultaneous releases of several solicitations.

- the company wishes to make a large, dramatic increase in the number and size of contract wins.

Nearly all federal bidders (excluding small businesses) maintain some level of a permanent proposal staff. In the case of those firms bidding large opportunities infrequently, the permanent staff may be just for proposal coordination and to provide an "institutional memory" that temporary resources cannot provide. A more common situation is for a firm to maintain at least the staff needed to pursue just one medium-size proposal at a time. This typically includes at a minimum a proposal manager, technical writer, editor, and combined coordinator/desktop publisher/graphic artist. A few robust divisions of Fortune 500 firms still maintain large departments with 30, 40, or more personnel.

Some companies, even large ones, with modest business development goals choose to use little temporary help in the belief that they can achieve their goals with permanent resources only. Sadly, many of those companies could grow faster and achieve greater profits by using temporary assistance to bid and win additional programs. This is always a tough judgment call, usually reserved for top management.

The Least You Need to Know

- Continuous relationships with your customers are an absolute necessity for success.

- Your marketing plan, consistent with your strategic plan, addresses a specific opportunity.

- You must decide on in-house versus outsourced personnel resources based on your (dynamic) business development goals.

- Because you are in a competitive market, you must be aware of the strengths and weaknesses of your competition.

Avoiding Ethical and Legal Landmines

In This Chapter

- ◆ Avoiding common pitfalls
- ◆ Sources of general legal and ethical guidance
- ◆ Understanding the Federal Acquisition Regulation
- ◆ Learning from case law
- ◆ Things allowed and not allowed
- ◆ Assuring compliance

It's your worst nightmare. You and your proposal team are plugging away, working long and hard to create a winning proposal for a government contract that would be huge for your company. Your own top management has built a strong team with your company as the prime contractor and including a group of subcontractors known to be "in tight" with the customer. The customer loves you and your team, so you're whistling while you work and are confident this one is just about in the bag. Then listening to the radio on the way into work one morning, you hear that another division of your company, two time zones away from your location, has been charged with massive irregularities in time accounting, meaning your entire company is now threatened with debarment from government contracting.

In other words, through no fault of your own, for something that has (allegedly) happened in another time zone, there's now a real possibility that your division will suffer by no longer being eligible to get the contract you're seeking. Your subcontractors will suffer as well through even less fault of their own.

What's the lesson here? You cannot be successful in government contracting for long unless you know and adhere to the ethical and legal restrictions in this field. Failure to abide by "the rules" can sink your ship quickly and permanently. On the other hand, if you know and obey those rules, you and your company have the opportunity to have successful business relationships with the public sector.

This chapter gives you guidance on how to avoid the described contractor's nightmare by focusing on common pitfalls and how to stay away from them. We also cover the sources of general guidance, an acquaintance with the Federal Acquisition Regulation (FAR), highlights of case law, a short list of what's okay and what's not okay, and end with suggestions on how to be assured you're in compliance with government rules.

Common Pitfalls and How to Avoid Them

Markets have their own special vocabulary, practices, and conventions, and the government market is no different. If you're coming from the commercial world (the nongovernment world), you must acquaint yourself with the practices that apply to dealing with governments.

Red Flag

This book contains no legal advice. If you're uncertain how any of the general guidelines and other material provided here apply to your specific situation, consult an attorney. Choose an attorney familiar with the "tribal customs" of whichever government you're dealing with, not just general contracting law. There is no substitute for competent, relevant legal advice.

This chapter focuses on the federal government rules and regulations. S&Ls (state and local governments) have corresponding and analogous rules and regulations, but each government has somewhat different rules. If you're going after S&L work, your best guidance is to rely first on your in-locality partner and the contracts and legal staff of that company for any differences between federal laws and regulations and S&L laws and regulations.

If you're new to getting government contracts, you may sometimes feel as if you're a stranger in a strange land. But don't worry; everyone was new once. Experienced hands come to know what's permissible and what's not, and in time you will, too. Until that time comes, consider this book, especially this chapter, as a chance to learn from the mistakes of others and not have to make your own.

Common pitfalls to watch out for include:

- You don't understand that you can't speak to anyone in the customer community involved in any way in the selection process after the solicitation is released. The exception is that you may communicate with the customer's Contracting Officer (KO).

- You are not aware that some customers impose that "cone of silence" even *before* the final solicitation comes out.

- You don't understand that you cannot give anyone in the customer community anything of value (certain low-value items are excluded). This applies regardless of the intent of that gift.

- You don't understand that you are not allowed to collude with other offerors to fix prices or to limit competition.

These are just a handful of the potential pitfalls that could trip you up, but they are the most common, so if you can avoid these, you're a big step ahead. It's impossible to anticipate every potential misstep you could make, but you can get yourself much closer to a smooth road by following trusted sources of guidance on ethical and legal issues in contracting.

Sources of General Guidance

Before turning to any official sources, look within yourself and your own sense of good judgment to guide you. You are already equipped to do three things:

- Do what's right because it's right.

- If you would not want what you are about to do to appear in the front section of tomorrow morning's *Washington Post* (and then all over the Internet, too), don't do it.

- In the words of Jiminy Cricket, from Walt Disney's *Pinocchio* " ... always let your conscience be your guide."

Office of Government Ethics (OGE)

Okay, so you want something a little more official than Jiminy Cricket? Maybe some place where people have diplomas on the wall or papers published? I can understand that. So let me suggest the Office of Government Ethics (OGE), established in 1978 by The Ethics in Government Act. Although this office was established as a part of the Office of Personnel Management (OPM), the Office of Government Ethics Reauthorization Act of 1988 made it a separate agency.

The OGE's charter is to prevent conflicts of interest by government employees and to resolve those conflicts when they do happen. OGE establishes policy and provides guidance about ethics issues. It is unlikely that you, as a government contractor, would have occasion to contact this office. However, it does exist and does help determine what is and is not acceptable practice.

The Federal Acquisition Regulation

The FAR is the government-wide procurement regulation mandated by Congress and issued by the Department of Defense (DOD), the General Services Administration (GSA), and the National Aeronautics and Space Administration (NASA). All federal agencies are authorized to issue regulations implementing the FAR.

> **Government Insider**
>
> You can read the complete Federal Acquisition Regulation at www.acqnet.gov/Far.

def•i•ni•tion

> **Debarment** is an official action taken to exclude a contractor from contracting and subcontracting for a reasonable, specified period because of actions so serious or compelling in nature that it affects the present responsibility of a government contractor or subcontractor.

Typically, the FAR clauses are written to describe what is absolutely prohibited or to state what is permitted up to a certain limit. For example, anything given to a government employee for influencing that employee to give something of value in return, such as awarding your company a contract, is strictly prohibited and punishable by fines and imprisonment. Doing other things that are prohibited can result in *debarment*, which is the act of shutting out (that is, preventing) you and perhaps your company from winning future government contracts.

The relevant clauses in the FAR are in Part 3—Improper Business Practices and Personal Conflicts of Interest. You and your company staff members should review this information. The best way to avoid running afoul of the regulation is to know what the FAR says. The clauses are within Part 52 of the FAR, specifically at 52.203.1 through 52.203.14. Part 3 provides the policy and guidance.

 Red Flag

> Many large agencies, most prominently the Department of Defense, have agency-specific supplements to the FAR (see www.acq.osd.mil/dpap/dars/index.html).
>
> If you're dealing with one of these agencies, you must also be aware of those regulations. If in doubt about whether the agency you're dealing with has supplemental regulations to FAR, go to the agency's website and search for "FAR Supplements."

Case Law Made Simple

Not only laws and regulations set the limits on ethical behavior. *Case law* also helps dictate appropriate behavior.

A great deal of case law has been recorded as a result of legal questions about government procurements. Again, you must seek competent, relevant legal advise on how, if at all, the case law applies to your situation. With any luck, you won't find yourself appearing in any future case law!

def•i•ni•tion

> **Case law** is the body of legal opinions of various courts from individual legal actions, such as criminal and civil suits.

Case law has motivated changes in the FAR and other governing regulations. For example, if the outcome of a specific case results in the court deciding that something is not illegal but the government believes it should be illegal, the response is to put into place new regulations or pass new laws to apply to future such acts.

Government Insider

> Many useful white papers on legal and ethical issues are available to the general public through the National Contract Management Association (NCMA) website (www.ncmahq.org). The NCMA is a highly respected professional organization. It provides research and training programs, thereby lifting the performance standards and the actual performance, of individuals with the government having contract management responsibilities. These activities also assist in raising the performance standards and the performance of those in the private sector with corresponding responsibilities for contract management.

What Is Permissible and What Is Not

Remember that this chapter emphasizes only the highlights of some of the most common aspects of government regulations for contractors. This list of acceptable and not acceptable actions is a good starting point, covering some common situations you are likely to find yourself in, but don't forget to read the FAR and confer with legal counsel when you need to know about situations we've not covered here.

Permissible Conduct

Several years ago, a Washington Redskins quarterback beat his own head against a concrete block wall after a particularly pivotal play. The player injured his neck and missed several games. When asked, the Redskins coach said he never thought to tell his players not to beat their head against a block wall.

The same holds true with ethical guidelines when dealing with the government in contracting situations. It's not accurate to say, "If it's not prohibited, then it's permissible." Similarly, it's not a worthwhile exercise to try to list everything that's permissible. It's not wise to conduct relations with your government customer on the basis that you've never seen it on a list of prohibited actions.

The best guidance we can give is to proceed with care in any relations you have with your government customer personnel. And here are two examples of reasonable things you *can* do for and with government employees:

 ◆ Taking a government employee out to lunch or giving gifts, subject to a limit of $20 on any one occasion and $50 in a calendar year (see 5 CFR Para 2635.204(a).) So as a contractor or an offeror or prospective offeror, it's acceptable to buy a government employee a sandwich once in a while.

 ◆ Inviting a government employee having procurement responsibilities for an outing, as long as the employee pays a fair share of the costs associated with that outing.

Conduct That Is Not Permissible

Here's a short list of sample conduct not permissible by government contractors:

 ◆ Providing bribes to government officials.

 ◆ Giving a gratuity (value not stated) to a government official or employee and intended to obtain a contract or favorable treatment under a contract as a result of providing that gratuity.

◆ Hiring a government employee if the prospective employer (you as the contractor) has interests that could be affected by performance or nonperformance of the government employee's current duties (Procurement Integrity Act—PIA). This addresses the problem of the "revolving door" of government employees taking jobs with the very contractors they previously were responsible for evaluating or managing. Recent history has a half dozen individuals—some from government and some from private industry—convicted of conflicts of interest. These individuals and their companies paid heavy fines, and the individuals were guests of the government in involuntary confinement.

◆ Hiring former federal officials within a period of one year (subject to detailed qualifications). (See the PIA.)

Compliance, Integrity, and Ethics

Many companies doing business with the federal government set their own rules and regulations, a code of conduct that details permissible behaviors as well as nonpermissible behaviors. You and your company should have a program in place to ensure compliance with, at minimum, the government's rules and regulations. Here are four simple suggestions for how to do that:

◆ Include a specific section in your policies and procedures (P&P) manuals covering these issues. Make sure it's up-to-date with the latest rules and regulations. The principles remain largely unchanged, but the detailed interpretations do change, and often, various government agencies promulgate new regulations to prevent newly discovered loopholes in the current ones.

◆ Make training in ethics a part of all new employees' (and contractors'!) orientations. All employees need to understand the important elements of your company's own policies and procedures, and how your own company seeks to avoid ethics violations.

> **Beltway Buzz**
>
> Some people on your proposal team have an even greater need to know about ethical and legal expectations. These include relationship managers, marketing managers, program managers (particularly those working at a customer site, where daily contact is expected, and where violations—however innocent—are most likely to occur), and even support personnel working on a customer site.

◆ Make ethics training a part of your annual retraining and updating. Believe it or not, the ethics rules change from time to time.

◆ Have a clear path for all employees and contractors to report any instance of a possible ethics violation. This path should allow individuals to report suspected violations without fear of retaliation, under protection as a whistleblower.

Over and above these guidelines, FAR, Part 3.1002, states, in part:

◆ Government contractors must conduct themselves with the highest degree of integrity and honesty.

◆ Contractors should have a written code of business ethics and conduct. To promote compliance with such code of business ethics and conduct, contractors should have an employee business ethics and compliance training program and an internal system that:

   ◆ Are suitable to the size of the company and extent of its involvement in government contracting;

   ◆ Facilitate timely discovery and disclosure of improper conduct in connection with government contracts; and

   ◆ Ensure corrective measures are promptly instituted and carried out."

The Least You Need to Know

◆ The Federal Acquisition Regulation (FAR) is your primary source of general guidance on legal and ethical issues in government contracting, especially Part 3 of FAR.

◆ Some government agencies have additional rules and regulations specific to them that are supplements to FAR and are usually available on the agency's website.

◆ Find reliable sources within your company to turn to for advice on any contemplated action that might be outside the laws and regulations.

◆ You must have an ethics program appropriate to your level of government contracting, whether federal, state, or local.

◆ Everyone in your company must know where to go within your company to report any perceived ethics problems.

◆ There is no substitute for focused, competent expert legal advice in specific situations.

Part 2

The Government Contracting Landscape

In this part you'll explore the government market—how to find out what products and services are needed, who is already supplying them, and where your business might fill a gap. You'll also get a short course in procurement—the chain of events that stretches from the President of the United States and the Congress who set the budgets that fund the government agencies that offer the contracts that companies like you can bid on. No one individual can make it in this process alone, so building a winning team that can research the market, influence the procurement process, and submit the winning bid is covered as well.

Chapter 4

Collecting Important Market Data

In This Chapter

- ◆ Matching your products to government wants
- ◆ Finding data on the market for your products
- ◆ Finding data on the competition
- ◆ Bid Decision Point #1

It's time to put your research hat on—or make someone else on the proposal team wear the funny hat. This chapter is all about getting information on what the government wants to buy and who else is trying to sell it to them. By collecting good data on the market for your products or services and on what the competition has to offer, you can start to build a solid case for why your organization best fits the government's needs.

Making Sure You Have What the Government Wants

We use the word "wants" more than the word "needs" in this chapter and book for a reason. Sure, it *is* all about what the government needs. Governments need all types of products and services. From soup to nuts (literally), governments need radios, airplanes, coffee makers, hand tools, and heavy earthmoving equipment. They need wedding cakes, left-handed *framazoids*, janitorial services, bomb detection machines, and hand soap. No joke!

def•i•ni•tion

A **framazoid** is a mythical device, of questionable origin and unknown use. (It's the only product mentioned here that is fictitious.)

But what should concern you more than their basic *needs* is what they really *want*. They don't need just any old left-handed framazoids. They need framazoids that not only work seven days a week but also bring them the morning paper and shine their shoes.

So your challenge is to match your products to what the government wants. To do that, you first have to know what the government wants. Then see if what you already make fits the bill, or determine if you can make adjustments to existing products to match their wants. Often, your understanding begins with at best a vague idea of that match. Your job is to gain more knowledge about what the government wants to buy and how your specific customer's wants fit with something you already provide to another customer. Or you need to figure out how you can change what you already make and sell to another customer to bring your product into line with government requirements.

In later chapters, and especially Chapter 5, we guide you through the details of homing in on the wants of a specific customer and building a case for why your organization is the one to satisfy those wants. For now, you are at the 50,000-foot level, simply surveying the market to see what is generally in demand and whether there is a market for your products.

Finding Government Opportunities

At the national level, the website of Federal Business Opportunities (www.FedBizOpps.gov) is the best source for identifying impending government solicitations and reporting the award of contracts all through the procurement cycle. (Note: you may also reach the site by www.fbo.gov.)

The Federal Acquisition Regulation (FAR) now designates the Federal Business Opportunities as the single point of universal electronic public access on the Internet to government-wide federal procurement opportunities that exceed $25,000. The General Services Administration (GSA) operates this website.

On FedBizOpps, government buyers announce their needs, wants, and business opportunities, which means you can filter through this mass of data. Having all this on one site enables you to search, monitor, and retrieve opportunities solicited by the entire federal contracting community. About 95 percent of the total government opportunities are listed on this site. The nature of the remaining government business is not for public access, for various reasons, such as national security.

Its ease of use and strict requirements on the agencies who post the opportunities provides an easy and inexpensive way for all businesses, and especially small businesses, to access government opportunities.

Government buyers (usually the KOs—the government Contracting Officers) upload their opportunities directly onto this website. Under the sponsorship and supervision of the General Services Administration (GSA), it creates synopses of current procurements.

In addition, you can find notices of proposed contract actions, contract solicitations, amendments and modifications, and contract awards. Most importantly for small businesses, you can find opportunities for subcontracting.

Government Insider

Although GSA provides the electronic framework for the Federal Business Opportunities website, the individual agencies that post on it are responsible for their own quality control. So don't complain to GSA about wrong dates or information. Take your issue to the relevant agency's KO.

Beltway Buzz

FedBizOpps has a great feature that separates current from old (archived) information. So if you're interested in only current procurement actions, you can limit your searches to current records only. Other features allow you to focus on small subsets of the data and further limit searches by geography, dates, agency, type of procurement, small business set-aside programs (see Chapter 9), and classification of products.

Not surprisingly, the volume on this site is large and growing. Whatever figures appear here will undoubtedly be incorrect by the time you read this book. So let's just say there are easily hundreds of entries each day.

This site has public information; nothing is close-hold, classified, or otherwise restricted. There's no reason for you to avoid just jumping in and using it. We'll even give you a step-by-step walk-through of the process, so you'll want to find a quiet place, with a computer and Internet access, and explore away. If not now, when? If not you, who?

Walking Through FedBizOpps.gov

As with any rich website, you can search for information you need or even information you didn't know you need in so many ways! These four steps will get you started with the basics.

1. Log on and read the guide.

    Go to www.fedbizopps.gov or www.fbo.gov. Read the appropriate "User Guide" at the far right of the home page. You will undoubtedly want the "Vendor" Guide, which provides lots of good descriptions of the site's capability.

Government Insider

Although the User Guide for Vendors shows how to log on to FedBizOpps, you don't need to have a user account to access many of the features of this site. But if you want to post your company's capabilities, you'll need to register in the way described.

2. Search for opportunities.

    You can now do a search for opportunities, using various search criteria— whichever ones are relevant to you. The choices are:

    ◆ keyword

    ◆ opportunity/procurement type

    ◆ posting date

    ◆ response deadline

    ◆ last modified date

- place of performance zip code

- set-aside code ("set aside" solicitations allow only specified business concerns)

- classification code

- NAICS (North American Industry Classification System) code

- agency/office(s)

3. Look at your search results, and decide what refinements you'd like to make.

   Here's an example of results you might get from a relatively simple search. This search was done on NAICS code 236XX, within the Department of Energy. (236XX means any five-digit code beginning with 236. "236" means "Construction of Buildings." The final two digits describe more specific types of buildings.) Looking for only Active Documents (and no restriction on the age of the document), the search got seven hits. Four were for "Sources Sought" and three were for "Pre-Solicitation."

   You may want to stop now and do a real-time search, using www.fbo.gov and an NAICS code relevant to your own company's capabilities to see what results you get. It shouldn't take you long to become at least passably familiar with the way to find opportunities of interest to you and your company.

4. Refine your search to location.

   Continue using the example from Step 3. You may already have a better example, one you developed from that step. If so, then you're off and running, so feel free to continue using your own rather than the example provided here. Try confining your search to a specific place of performance, such as by zip code. The sample search above revealed seven potentials at five different locations around the United States, all of which were for the enhancement of facilities at DoE's national laboratories. So if your interest were only at Brookhaven National Laboratory, you would have seen two "hits": one for Sources Sought and the other for pre-solicitation. However, in early 2009, you would have noticed that, although the pre-solicitation is an "active" document,

   > **Beltway Buzz**
   >
   > In addition to information posted on FedBizOpps.gov, there are pay-for-service organizations offering more convenient and focused analysis of current or upcoming procurements. These businesses are listed in Appendix B.

it bears a date of 2005. Without knowing anything more about the opportunity, that's not exactly a high-priority posting. This construction project appears to be in some sort of limbo.

This short excursion through fbo.gov is only a high-level look. Once you get a feel for the site, you can quickly harness the power of it as a source of leads and dig deeper with more complex search strategies.

Learn About Your Competitors Through Your Customers

The best source of data about your competition is your customer. Remember, we use the term "customer" in this book to mean a prospective customer, the government entity that you're trying to get a contract with. So you might find it odd that you would go to your potential customer to learn about the competitors going after that same customer. Well, here's how it works.

So long as it's not in the context of a specific opportunity, you can and should take the time and effort to meet with your customer at his place of business (see Chapter 5) because this is a chance for you to tell him about your company and your capabilities of providing what he wants. But if you use the session wisely, you can have a goal of getting information about your customer's situation and problems and also getting insight into your competition. You probably already know who the *incumbent* is and what other companies have expressed an interest in solving the customer's problems.

def•i•ni•tion

The contractor currently supplying the government with products or services is the **incumbent**.

Devoting Resources to Your Search

With so much free information online, any business that's serious about getting government contracts should consider designating someone in-house to regularly cruise the local and national websites of agencies you've identified as potentially good marketing targets. Even if carrying this responsibility is only a fraction of an employee's workload, this person can develop an "institutional memory" within your company. Then that individual could be in charge of engaging one of the fee-for-service providers to take the research to the next level. Even in a relatively small company, such a single-point-of-contact can avoid unnecessary fees caused by over-enthusiastic sales and marketing staff asking for results on inappropriate opportunities.

> **Red Flag** _____
>
> You may find that using a fee-for-service provider meets your needs. But you must carefully monitor the use of that service. If you don't control the use, you could be in for an unpleasant surprise, such as unexpectedly large fees caused by, in hindsight, foolish and unnecessary requests.

Your First Bid Decision

Staff work, led by the capture manager, the proposal manager, and the relationship manager, support the bid decision points. Top management (TM) chairs the meetings at those points and makes the decision at the end of the meeting about whether to proceed with the efforts to create a winning proposal or to suspend such activities. Sometimes the decision to continue or to suspend is subject to further developments, such as getting cooperation from a key subcontractor.

The bid decision points described in this book occur at pivotal times in the proposal process. These points are presented at specific times, but the process from identification of opportunity to delivery of the proposal is seldom smooth. Therefore, the decision points may arise at times other than in this nominal schedule. But that's no problem. Things happen, and you need to have a decision point when you see a major change in circumstances.

The format of the decision point activities is the same, but the data supporting the decisions changes. You can reasonably expect to see clear improvements in the accuracy of the information each time you have a decision point.

Of all the functions of top management, participating in and leading the bid decisions is among a small number of responsibilities—perhaps three—that are truly not only important but also high leverage. An incorrect decision—either way—can be not only costly in dollars (wasting money on bidding the wrong competitions) but also costly in lost opportunities (failing to bid in a competition that you could have won).

Some of the considerations in deciding to bid or not to bid are as follows:

♦ Have your company's people had pre-solicitation contact with the customer so as to both give and get the critically important information? If not, that's a strong "no-bid" signal.

♦ Is your best information that the customer either *wants* you to win or at least *doesn't mind* if you win? If you have no knowledge of this, that's a strong "no-bid" signal.

◆ Where do you stack up with the customer in relation to the competition? If you have reason to believe that you're no worse than third in the customer's mind, that's again a strong "no-bid" signal.

◆ Do you know what the customer's view of the "should cost" is? That is, about what cost is the customer expecting to see from the offerors? Can you meet or beat that price and still make a profit? If you either have no clue what the customer expects, or your company can't meet or beat that number (even if it's a difficult proposition), then that's a strong "no-bid" signal.

◆ If you fail to bid and win this job, how large is the stream of business and length of the contract that you will miss out on? Sometimes, you may feel compelled to put forth a super-duper effort to win this contract, because the non-winners are frozen out of a large amount of business for the life of this specific contract. So if this is the case, it's a strong "bid" signal.

◆ Are there clear ways to expand the contract after an award in such a way as to greatly increase the profitability of the contract through Change Orders? So even if you have to bid the initial contract at a very low margin, and even at a loss, are there opportunities to obtain follow-on work, at higher margins, so as to recover from an initial high-risk, low-margin situation, and result in a much better circumstance, in the long run? If so, that's also a strong "bid" signal.

◆ Do you have a program manager-designate who is not only well qualified but also has positive name and face recognition with this customer?

◆ Do you, in combination with any business partners (subcontractors), have the right technical and managerial exposure to the customer?

◆ Is getting this contract consistent with or at least not in conflict with your strategic plan?

◆ Is this program real? That is, is it a part of the customer's budget, *or* is it just someone's dream and will never actually result in a contract for *anyone*? To guard against such a "phantom program," you should do your best to verify, from budget and planning documents within the funding agency, that there really *is* funding earmarked for the program you think is real. This is a difficult task, and sometimes you get a false answer, but checking with independent sources, such as other agency documents, is a necessary step in avoiding these programs.

◆ Can you, in combination with your business partners (subcontractors), offer past performance citations that will be at least as good as those of your competitors?

If not, should you look for additional subcontractors to fill the gaps in your own capabilities? Over and above citations required, can those same subcontractors, or other subcontractors, help to fill the gaps between what your company can do well, and the total task?

◆ What is the "Precipitating Event"? The precipitating event is the reason, or reasons, the customer is conducting this competition at this time, in this way. If you don't understand the precipitating event, your response is very likely to fail to address the customer's real concerns. These concerns may or may not be clear from an analysis of the solicitation.

◆ If this is an existing contract, and there is an incumbent, what information do you find about that contractor's performance on that existing contract as revealed in the public record of that contract (obtained under the Freedom of Information Act)?

◆ What are your hard-core discriminators and win themes that show you are not only different from but also better than your competitors in ways that are important to the customer? Note that many of the important considerations are reflected in "Section M, Evaluation Criteria."

◆ Do you have the right combination of in-house employees and contracted staff supplementation to create a winning proposal at a reasonable cost?

At this early stage, the TM's reasonable expectation is that some of these questions will not be answered completely. Perhaps many are not well covered. The good news is that those not well covered then go onto an action item list for work to close the knowledge gap.

The Least You Need to Know

◆ You must match your products to what the government *wants* to buy.

◆ Your search for relevant data should focus not only on narrow products but also broader markets.

◆ The website www.fbo.gov is a wonderful source of information about past and current government markets; learn to use it effectively.

◆ Bid Decision Point #1 will help you discover whether your top management (TM) supports going forward with the plan to try to get into this market or not.

Understanding the Procurement Process

In This Chapter

♦ Procurement: what it is and how it works

♦ Seven steps of the procurement process

♦ Factors that slow the flow of money

♦ Ways your business's size relates to procurement

♦ Ways to influence procurement

If you're already doing business with governments, it's likely you've been dealing with people relatively far down the procurement food chain. And maybe that's all you really need to know to do your job day-to-day. But if you're curious about how the authority to expend government funds flows through the procurement cycle, then this chapter is for you. And even if you believe you are not affected by all that wrangling and political bickering in Washington, you may benefit from having some insight into why things are the way they are. What you learn here can influence your strategic approach to getting government contracts.

This chapter describes the federal process. But analogous, if far less complex, processes are taking place in all the states and local governments, too. So if you're interested in that market, you can read this chapter to get a basic understanding of the process in general, then adjust the particulars as dictated by your own state or local government customer's processes.

First we explain how the procurement process works. (It *does* work, however imperfectly!) Seven steps explain how money flows from federal budget setting to the agencies that offer contracts, to an award on your company's doorstep. Then you can see how your business's size factors into the process and where you have a chance to influence outcomes, if at all.

What the Procurement Process Looks Like

The procurement process is complex and involves the interests of many parties, which are often dissimilar and even competing. Some may wonder how anything ever gets done, with one powerful interest group wanting one thing and another powerful interest group wanting something entirely different. Witness the controversy over energy policy.

The country's decisions on energy policy have many players: individual companies (Exxon Mobil, Commonwealth Edison, General Electric, to name a few); trade and industry groups and their lobbyists (walk down K Street NW in Washington and you'll find one without any trouble); government agencies (Department of Energy, Department of the Interior, Environmental Protection Agency); academic institutions (University of California, University of New Mexico); and "think tanks" (Brookings Institution, Hoover Institution). The list could go on and on. Each of these has an idea of what the energy policy should be. They can't all be right, and they can't all be wrong. The question is, which forces or combination of forces will prevail? The living, changing answer is to look at the budget process, along with our tax policies, and you can see which of these is winning at any given time.

The current budget process has evolved over time. Until the early 1900s, the government was much smaller in relation to the entire United States economy than it is today. But early in the twentieth century, the government was, basically, out of control. It was hamstrung by archaic processes. Getting anything done well required an Act of Congress! The practices have elements that are constitutional (such as Article I, Section 7, 8, and 9), legislative (The Budget and Accounting Act of 1921, as amended), executive (various regulations set by executive agencies, such as the Federal Acquisition Regulation, and Executive Orders, issued by the President), and judicial (case law).

Seven Steps to Procurement

Let's look at the seven-step path that money takes from being just a wish list of a federal agency, to passing through presidential and congressional gatekeepers, to ending up as real budget money at an agency and eventually getting into your hands through the award of a contract.

Here is an overview of the process:

1. Agencies submit budget requests to the Office of Management and Budget (OMB).

2. The President submits his budget to Congress.

3. Agencies testify to Congress to state the case for their budget requests.

4. Congress takes action on budget approvals (both Authorization and Appropriation bills).

5. Agencies create formal procurement plans for major procurements.

6. Agencies release solicitations.

7. Agencies award contracts and authorizations to proceed.

Step 1: Agency Submissions to the OMB

Agencies submit their budget requests to the OMB with a deadline of September 15 each year. Each agency has its own way of developing its budget requests to OMB. Because agency submissions are due in mid-September, the real work on budgets begins shortly after submission of the President's budget the previous January. The budgeting process is a year-round, never-ending process. No sooner has the President's budget gone to Congress than the agencies begin preparing the *next* September's submission.

Within the agencies, there is always a conflict of priorities. Each sub-part of an agency believes in the work it does, fiercely defends its current budget, and requests an increase in funding. However, the upper echelons of the agencies know that requests for more money will not likely survive a review process. So what the Congress sees is the result of a great deal of negotiations within the agencies. Because the agency heads must conform to the guidance of OMB or appeal directly to the White House for budget relief, the agency position is not the true desires of the agency. Typically, the agencies would like to ask for more funds, but this budget is often the most possible, under the total circumstances. You can be certain subagencies are requesting and justifying much higher funding.

Agency submissions must follow the format prescribed in (the dreaded!) OBM Circular A-11 and be consistent with the planning guidance the OMB gives to the agencies. Why is this dreaded? Well, the Circular A-11 for 2008, for example, (used for formulating the fiscal year 2010 budget) was a tidy little 700 pages and a mere 7 megabytes!

Step 2: President's Budget Submitted to Congress

The President submits his budget to Congress at the beginning of each congressional session, typically in January. From September 15 until mid-October prior to that January, OMB staff members hold hearings with agency heads and high-level staff to more fully understand the details of their budget requests. Each element of OMB has a target budget at the total agency level, and sometimes it has subtotals within those totals. Although somewhere, perhaps in another universe, there is an OMB target number *higher* than the agency request, a careful review of history says that this has not happened yet.

So negotiations take place between the agency and OMB staff and management about what to present to the President as a baseline solution to the gap between the agency request and the OMB solution. The President and his own top management team then make the difficult decision of what to submit as the President's budget. After many hours of hard bargaining and difficult decisions at many levels regarding what to give priority in the budget, a President's budget actually does emerge and is then sent to Congress for Congress to do its thing.

Red Flag

Don't try to get meetings with individuals at OMB without clearance from the appropriate authorities within OMB and without consulting your legal counsel.

Between September 15 and the formal transmission of the President's budget early in the next calendar year, individual companies have only limited opportunity to influence the negotiations that invariably take place. In fact, OMB staff have strict prohibitions on communicating with outsiders during this time. On the other hand, there is less sensitivity to accepting inputs from individual companies in the March to June period. Because there is no active, specific consideration of programs, the staff has a chance to hear from the private sector. So this is the time to carefully provide white papers and other technical and programmatic inputs to OMB staff as well as to agency personnel.

Step 3: Agency Testimony Before Congress

Agency heads or their designees have the duty and the right to testify before (typically) both the House and Senate committees. There are two separate, but related, tracks: before the Authorizing Committees of each body and before the Appropriations Committees. Authorizing Committees give the general authority to agencies to proceed with programs, and Appropriations Committees give permission to actually draw down funds from the public treasury. This gives the testifiers four chances to present justification for their budget requests as approved by the President. The amended Budget and Accounting Act of 1921 requires that agency personnel support the President's budget. This can be tricky because sometimes the agency testifiers would rather ask for a different amount, either higher or lower, but the act requires each individual to support the President's budget.

Step 4: Budget Approval from Congress

The term "approval" says that is the resultant state. Between the receipt of the President's budget and the passing of legislation for the President's signature, a flurry of activity takes place on both the Authorization and Appropriations Committees and on both sides of Capitol Hill—the House of Representatives and the Senate.

Once the President's budget has gone to Congress and depending on the specific agencies, you can talk to the agency people about alternative funding streams. However, you must realize that the agency people can do little about this until the next budget cycle. There are exceptions, for emergency situations, but it's a good rule that once the President's budget goes to Congress, nothing else can happen until the next fiscal year. It is possible, although rare, to submit materials to an agency, which can then become part of the supporting materials for the agencies' testimony to Congress.

The Congress—whether Republicans or Democrats are in power—has an unenviable record of being late to the September 30 deadline for approving funds for the new fiscal year beginning the next day. But *eventually*, the budget bill moves through the authorization process, which means "it's okay in principle to spend the money." Then it goes through the appropriation process which is government speak for "upon the President's signature into law, the funds may now be provided by the Treasury." After all this is complete, the agencies may actually spend the funds.

Beltway Buzz

With experts predicting an unusually high degree of stress on the budget process in the coming years, poor economic conditions for the foreseeable future are creating the perfect storm of falling revenues (unemployed people don't pay withholding taxes) and rising demands for the safety net of entitlement programs. This puts a squeeze on the "controllable" parts of the budget, which exclude entitlement programs, interest on the national debt, and others. So for funding programs such as long-term "nice to haves," well, who knows how much of that there will be.

Step 5: Agency Creation of Formal Procurement Plans

Often in anticipation of the release of funds, agencies begin to build formal plans for spending the money. It is illegal, under the amended Budget and Accounting Act of 1921, to actually commit funding until the President signs the Authorization and Appropriations bills into law. But some agencies (very appropriately) go ahead with detailed plans, contingent upon release of the funds.

Step 6: Release of Solicitations

Based on the high-level procurement plans, the procuring agencies then release detailed solicitations. These may be in the form of a Request for Proposal (RFP)—typically the most competitive procurements—or a Request for Quotation (RFQ). A major difference between these is that agencies use an RFQ when they know, rather exactly, what they want; for example, a Model 455 solar-powered thingamabob. Typically, RFPs are awarded on the basis of so-called "best value," where the agency states in the solicitation that it reserves the right to choose a winner on the basis other than lowest offered price, among acceptable offers. RFQs are awarded to the qualifying offeror with the lowest offered price.

Step 7: Contract Award and Authorization to Proceed

So now the process gets interesting and more relevant to you as someone seeking government contracts. Now that the money is available, the agency—your customer—is ready to go through the selection process. This selection process focuses on creating and releasing clear and relevant solicitations. The focus then shifts to proposal evaluation.

The customer does the magic in the selection of a winner or winners in a multiple-award solicitation. Then comes the wonderful day of the contract award!

Red Flag

You've been awarded a contract. But wait! There's more! Sometimes there is a significant gap between contract award and Authorization to Proceed as the winner and customer negotiate the fine details of the contract.

There's also always the threat that a loser in the competition may lodge a protest, claiming the contract was awarded using flawed processes. Protests normally then result in the delay in the Authorization to Proceed, effectively blocking the beginning of the contract (or in worse cases, the suspension of an ongoing contract!) pending resolution of the protest.

The Size of Your Business and Procurement

There are three levels of understanding and involvement for complex processes such as the flow of money for government contracts:

+ Level 1: *What* happens?

+ Level 2: *Why* does it happen that way?

+ Level 3: *How* do you influence outcomes?

If you are a small business dealing as a prime contractor on small contracts, a subcontractor working mostly if not exclusively through large contractors, or a supplier selling commodity products to the government or near-commodity products to prime contractors, your interest in this chapter is probably minimal. You may have only a little interest in Level 1. However, as you move up the scale to larger and larger contracts and take on the role as a prime contractor, you may need to know Level 2, *why* things happen that way.

The ultimate Level 3 applies to large contractors, for example, Boeing, Computer Science Corporation, SAIC, Northrop Grumman, or General Dynamics. These companies surely do need to understand the process through Level 3 so that they have the ability to influence outcomes; Boeing, for example, needs to know in great detail the Level 1 and 2 facts and be able to go on to Level 3 for the USAF Tanker Replacement contract.

What we can accurately say is that each stage offers opportunities for your company to provide data and analysis (white papers) that are consistent with your own company's technical and/or management approach or solution. For example, industry groups create those white papers with the intent of influencing the decision-makers.

Even if you're a small company, the industry groups that represent small companies actually have influence through those papers. You may want to figure out which of these many groups best represent your interests. Then join the group, and support it through your contribution to those papers. More specifically, you should:

- Strive to become involved as soon as possible, which means at Level 2 and then Level 3.

- Adopt the stance that you are providing your input in the role of a solid citizen as much as an advocate for your approach or solution.

- Act as a helpful and careful reader of government documents, being quick to identify mistakes (in the most positive and helpful way) and, as appropriate, suggest fixes for those mistakes.

- Keep all your actions inside both the law and ethics. Consult your company attorney or outside counsel on the legalities. Typically, your Contracts Manager is knowledgeable about the legalities, but the company attorney or outside counsel is your most reliable source. Your Ethics Department (in larger companies) or your Human Resources Department (in smaller companies) may have sources as well. See also the discussion of legal and ethical issues in Chapter 3.

The Least You Need to Know

- There *are* points where large businesses can and do influence what the government buys.

- If you're a small business or subcontractor, you can do little to influence outcomes of the process, except as noted in the key points of influence.

- Government procurement provides a great deal of transparency that is not present in commercial contracting, so it's possible to know well in advance the types of needs the government will have.

Chapter 6

Building a Winning Team

In This Chapter

- ◆ Assigning the right people to the right roles
- ◆ Getting good leadership in place
- ◆ Team members and their duties
- ◆ Three especially important team members

You've reached the point where you're seriously considering going for it; you're committed to finding a government market for your products or services, or maybe you already know of a government opportunity. Now it's time to begin building your proposal team, something you need to do even if you've not yet identified a specific opportunity.

This chapter describes the three key questions a team must work together to address and the 13 roles the team members must fulfill.

Why the Team in Teamwork Makes a Difference

Customers' solicitations vary in nature, so responses vary as well. But there is a lot of commonality in the form most responses need to take. No matter what a particular opportunity's unique features are, the team must work together to answer three questions the customer usually has:

♦ What will you do technically to achieve the customer's purpose?

♦ How will you manage the program?

♦ What is your cost or price to the customer for this program?

In Chapters 16, 17, and 18, you learn how to respond to an opportunity with a proposal that addresses these three questions. For now, you only need to know that your response will have a technical part, a management part, and a cost/price part. These parts are often called "volumes" or "approaches," as in management approach. This is basically like saying "Here's how our organization would approach this project from a management perspective." But don't worry about the terminology; whichever word is used, volume, part, approach, or a comparable term, it's all the same.

For now, as you assemble your team, the thing to know is that some members of your team might work only on a particular part, while others might touch on multiple parts. But no matter how you divide the work, no one team member—or subset of people within the team—should bear the burden of creating a winning proposal. For example, there's no such thing as a proposal team creating a winning technical part but a losing price/cost part. Nor does a team win on the technical part and lose on the management part. You either *win* as a team or *lose* as a team. Keep this in mind as you select team members; each person must be in it to win as a group and not as an individual.

The Roles on a Proposal Team

When it comes to putting together teams to go after government contracts, 13 is a lucky number, as typically 13 roles need to be filled. This doesn't necessarily mean your team will have exactly 13 people, however. Depending on the size of your organization and the complexity of the opportunity you're vying for, you may need fewer or more people.

def•i•ni•tion

Head is government jargon for an individual person. A head may carry out only one or multiple roles.

In large organizations, such as major federal government contractors, each role may have many individuals, or *heads*, covering that role. For example, in a large company, a half-dozen senior officials may carry the role of Top Management (TM), while in a small company, TM may be a single individual who plays one or more additional roles.

Just as the final number of people on your team may vary, so does the timing for bringing them on board. You won't need to fill all roles at once. For example, you won't need a proposal coordinator until the proposal effort is under full sail, but you do need a proposal manager and a capture manager from the get-go.

If yours is a small company, you undoubtedly have limited resources within the organization. So to cover all these roles, you can ask some individuals in your company to fill multiple roles. When you've exhausted your own resources, you can use temporary people with particular skills to fill any roles you cannot cover internally.

The roles you ultimately need to fill are:

Top Management	Proposal Coordinator
Relationship Manager	Evaluation Team Member(s)
Capture Manager	Orals Coach
Proposal Manager	Contracts Manager
Pricing Manager	Legal Counsel
Program Manager-Designate	Subject Matter Experts
Technical Champion	

The following sections describe the duties these roles entail and the types of qualifications needed for each.

Team Roles with Full-Time (or Near Full-Time) Intensity

Some roles on the team require such intensity of effort that a full-time or close to full-time commitment is necessary. Your situation may vary depending on the size of your organization and the contract you're seeking, so don't worry if some of the people in these roles can't leave their other responsibilities to make a full-time commitment. But in an ideal world, the roles of relationship manager, capture manager, proposal manager, and pricing manager would be carried out with a singular, full-time focus.

Relationship Manager

The relationship manager interacts directly with the customer. The best person for the relationship manager role is someone who already has or can easily cultivate ongoing relationships with the important people in the customer organization. They might attend professional meetings with the customer's people or social events such as golf outings, holiday parties, and informal gatherings. These are the people, for example, who get invited to going-away parties for important people at the customer organization.

Red Flag

Be aware of limits on the types and frequency of interactions allowable with the potential customer. Whether by law or simply custom, you must stay within the accepted boundaries. See Chapter 3 for ethical and legal issues.

Relationship managers are often recent retirees from the customer organization or someone who is not yet at retirement age but has worked in the recent past for that customer. Or they may have been a relationship manager for another company that did business with that customer. This familiarity can be both good news and bad news. If you don't know this person well, you might be deceived. The candidate for the role might claim to have lots of connections and good relationships in the customer community, but be sure to vet that claim against at least two independent sources. The wrong person could do more harm than good.

Also, many likely prospects for relationship manager lack training in how to do the job, especially around the issue of ethics rules. You must insist that everyone with responsibility for customer contact and, therefore, most affected by the ethics rules and regulations that apply to contractor–government relationships be thoroughly trained and monitored through periodic reporting of activities, as well as receive periodic refresher training in ethics.

Capture Manager

The capture manager is the pipeline through which the proposal manager or other team members speak to TM. For example, if the team discovers that it needs a critical technical resource, the capture manager goes to TM and makes the case for that resource. If the team believes the price being contemplated is too high (or too low), then the capture manager carries that message to TM for resolution and response.

Also, this person is a full member of the proposal team. The capture manager must be in the boat rowing and not on the bank watching the other proposal team members row. Capture managers attend daily meetings and fully participate in all aspects of the effort.

In many cases, the Capture Manager works with the Relationship Manager to gain customer intelligence, identifying the customer hot buttons, and serious customer concerns. All these are important to know as the proposal team develops a winning solution.

Proposal Manager

The proposal manager has two main responsibilities: discovering the best *case* for your company to make in this competition and communicating that case.

This means the proposal manager is not just a traffic cop, refereeing the activities of the team members. Although chairing meetings and ensuring version control of various outlines, graphics, and texts are each important subtasks, the real tasks are centered around building and communicating the case. Therefore, the proposal manager should have a high standing among the team members and not be just a glorified clerk.

def•i•ni•tion

Your **case** includes all the positive aspects of the solution that you present in your proposal, much like the case attorneys build for their clients.

Well-qualified, good proposal managers are difficult to find and just as hard to keep. A good source of candidates is the Association of Proposal Management Professionals (APMP). This organization is listed, along with other professional nonprofit organizations, in Appendix B.

Government Insider

Use the APMP job board at www.apmp.org as a relatively inexpensive way to list a proposal manager opening. You're likely to get responses from well-qualified candidates without paying a large placement or finder's fee.

Proposal Managers Discovering the Case

The task of discovering or building the case for why your organization's solution is the winning one can be challenging because it cuts across organization lines within your company and often includes dealing with a variety of individuals from your subcontractors. The best approach is to believe that there *is* a good case and employ a variety of techniques and processes to discover that case. It's a lot easier to discover a case when you believe it really exists!

At the same time, though, the proposal manager must understand the limitations of the role. For example, he cannot create a wonderful technical or management solution for your company if none exists. The best he can do is strive to find the best case possible. So an important part of the proposal manager's job is to challenge—in the most positive way—not only the technical solutions being offered but also the management solutions being offered.

Beltway Buzz

In a well-run proposal effort, the first casualty is everyone's ego. Each team member is likely to be a highly qualified professional who has earned the right to have a healthy ego, but no team member has the right to display that ego to the detriment of the team. Everyone must be willing to accept constructive criticism.

Proposal Managers Communicating the Case

Communicating the best case can be a daunting task. It involves at least these three subtasks:

- **Creating Visuals**—Visuals are an important element of winning proposals and require much effort by the team. Usually, many proposal team members create candidates for inclusion as visuals. Some members are very skilled at creating visuals; others, not so skilled. So the visuals arrive at the proposal manager's desk or e-mail inbox with a wide range in quality. Some are rough hand-drawn hard copies, while others are clean copies in electronic form. The proposal manager is often tasked with assisting individual authors or subject matter experts in creating usable versions of the visuals. He must be able to roll up his sleeves and get involved in creating what often turns out to be a half-dozen visuals that say not only how your solution is *different* but also why it is *better* than that of your competitors.

- **Version Control**—*Version control* is the task of keeping track of which version incorporates the most recent and best thinking of the author or subject matter expert. In theory, you might think an individual of lesser skill and lower cost could do this task, but that's not the case. Unless the proposal manager has a proposal coordinator or someone in the proposal production function with the right amount of authority and responsibility, bad things happen when there is a lack of strict version control.

Red Flag

Your proposal documents undergo many changes as you create your proposal, so you must be sure each person has the latest-and-greatest version of a document. Losing **version control** means wasted time and money because it leads to redundant or unnecessary work.

◆ **Ongoing Communication**—Over and above the relatively mundane preceding subtasks, the proposal manager has a higher responsibility and authority, which is to ensure effective communication with the customer, particularly after submission of the proposal. Remember that all communication with the customer, at any time, must be with the full knowledge of, and approval of, your Contracts Manager. The post-submission activities, especially the oral presentation if required, are so important that they are often the deciding factor in the mind of the customer.

Riding Herd on the Proposal Team Members

The proposal manager typically conducts two daily meetings. Through these meetings and also by constantly changing the "03 Proposal Development Schedule" and the "01 Contact List," (see Chapter 12), the proposal manager is in a uniquely good position to observe the activities—or lack thereof—of all proposal team members. The proposal manager, therefore, can keep the members on task and on track toward a winning proposal.

Pricing Manager

This role is often the most abused and least valued function on the proposal team. Too often, the proposal team leadership hurries to create a proposal and doesn't think to bring along someone to handle the pricing function. Then three days before the due date for the proposal, the authors of all the other parts of the proposal call in the pricing manager, hand over a matrix of bid hours, materials, and other elements of the price volume, and expect the pricing manager to create a responsive, winning solution. This is all the more unfortunate, because for many competitions, the offered price is, in the final analysis, either *the* determining factor in the award or at least one of only a few determining factors.

The best use of the pricing manager's skills and knowledge is to weave the role into the fabric of the proposal.

Team Roles with Part-Time Intensity

Depending on the size and scope of the proposal, you will need additional roles carried out on a less than full-time or even just as-needed basis. These roles are: TM, program manager-designate, technical champion, proposal coordinator, evaluation team members, orals coach, contracts manager, legal counsel, and subject matter experts.

You may not need different people to handle all these roles; some people can do double duty, and some roles might not be needed at all. For small proposals, for example, the proposal manager will likely double as the proposal coordinator. And if there's no requirement for orals, you won't need an orals coach at all.

Securing Top Management

In the world of government contracts and in business, the TM holds an important role. With the resources and authority to lead the team in creating a winning proposal, TM people generally know what they're doing. Their sphere of influence is greater than that of other team members, and typically, they have more to lose by losing and more to gain by winning than other members of the team.

> **Beltway Buzz**
>
> The number-one reason for losing out on government contracts is the lack of TM involvement in the process. TM must be more than a figurehead lending an impressive name or title to a proposal. TM must pitch in and help make a win happen!

Program Manager-Designate

The program manager-*designate* helps the proposal team describe to the customer how they will manage the program if they win the contract. This program manager-designate *must* be a full member of the team. Unfortunately and typically, if this person is qualified to be the program manager of the new program, then she's probably already fulfilling that role for another current program. The current job, her "day job," probably has been taking all her time. So if the program manager-designate needs relief from some duties of that current job, the capture manager makes

> **def•i•ni•tion**
>
> **Designate** means that the program manager is not yet in charge of the program but will be upon receiving the contract award.

that request to TM. TM should understand that to grow the business, it is sometimes necessary to sacrifice short-term revenues (for example, the program manager-designate must give up billing the current customer) for the long-term gains represented by winning this new government contract.

Technical Champion

This individual has the technical skills to carry out the program. This person also has the most to gain when your company is awarded the contract. Typically upon award, the technical champion takes on the role within the program team of chief engineer, chief scientist, or engineering manager. He also often guides the critical sections of the technical part of your solution.

Proposal Coordinator

This person serves as the right hand of the proposal manager; he keeps records, fills in during the proposal manager's absence, may handle the maintenance of the proposal management documents, and generally coordinates the activities of the team members. This position is one level of responsibility below the proposal manager.

Evaluation Team Members

Evaluation teams assist the proposal team by evaluating the current state of the proposal documents. What's important here is that evaluation team members be both qualified and motivated, qualified meaning the person has skills relevant to the proposal under development and motivated meaning the person has some interest in improving the proposal.

Typically, the evaluation team members are experienced in creating winning proposals. In some companies, reviews are tagged as "greybeard reviews." This is not a derogatory term but simply a descriptive one as the reviewers tend to be highly experienced and are often significantly older than the average proposal team member.

Orals Coach

Not all proposals, but an increasing number of them, require the candidate team to present an oral briefing to a customer panel, before an award decision. This session gives an opportunity for your company's team to supplement and perhaps clarify the written proposal. In addition, it allows you to demonstrate the strengths of your team and especially the strength and suitability of your choice for program manager. For large teams, oral presentations offer you a chance to see how the team, led by your company as the prime, works with your subcontractors.

Orals coaches help your team with this important review by sharing their experience in leading other teams to successes in this type of examination. These individuals have usually acquired their skills from many years of concentrating on this specific niche market of business development.

One of the customer's implicit evaluation criteria is how well you and your team members—whether it's just a small company or a large company with many subcontractors on the team—appear to be working as a team and not simply as a jumble of individuals trying to get a contract. It's not easy to hide dissonance among members of the team when giving an oral presentation. Therefore, your team should practice, take dry runs, do whatever it takes to prepare for not only the stated agenda but also those extra difficult questions the customer invariably asks to test the team for cohesiveness.

Red Flag

If you take your program manager-designate along with the proposal team to an oral presentation (as you should), make sure that person is fully up to speed on the project. If the program manager reveals ignorance of what's in the proposal or stumbles badly on questions not on the agenda, then the customer may legitimately question whether you are really serious about this work.

While it's a stretch to say that oral sessions are *the* deciding factor, it's fair to say that a poor oral presentation can mean a loss, and a superior presentation can bring a team across the finish line if the competition is close on all other evaluation factors.

Government Insider

If you don't have someone in your organization qualified to coach your team for the oral presentation, consider hiring an oral coach on a fee-for-service basis. Coaches are listed in Appendix B.

Contracts Manager

In virtually all solicitations, the customer directs you to contact them through their contracting officer and only through the contracting officer (KO). Failure to adhere to that request is a serious matter. Many solicitations contain a clause stating that communicating with (in *any* way) anyone other than the KO (or the KO's designee) can be cause for disqualification. Even in absence of that clause, best practices and convention dictate that your company's people—anyone representing your company in any way—correspond with the KO only. To simplify and control message traffic, your own contracts manager (CM) should be the single point of contact to speak for your company.

But the role of CM isn't just as a conduit. Experienced CMs can be of huge value to your proposal team and, hence, to your company. Your contracts manager adds value to the team by:

- ◆ Reviewing the parts of the solicitation affecting the resulting contract.

- ◆ Assisting the proposal manager in achieving compliance with the solicitation.

- ◆ Acting as the single point of contact with the customer, through the customer's KO.

- ◆ Coordinating with the company's legal counsel regarding any risk (technical, schedule, or cost) your company way be taking on by winning this contract.

As with proposal managers, really good CMs are difficult to find and difficult to keep, but it's worth the effort to find and retain a good one.

Government Insider

To fill a contracts manager opening, contact the National Contracts Management Association (NCMA) and post your opening at their website: www.ncmahq.org.

Legal Counsel

It is typical to see a requirement that you submit to the customer an offer ready for signature. In effect, this is the submission of a binding offer and must be viewed as a serious matter because the majority of offers could be converted into a contract simply when the buyer (through an authorized CO) affixes a signature to the completed submission. Therefore, such a document going outside the company surely requires an attorney's review. If you're in a small

Red Flag

Expecting a general corporate attorney to deal with the intricacies of government contracting is unfair to the attorney and potentially dangerous to you. The cost of an attorney experienced in government contracting law is low relative to the potential value.

company, you probably already have an attorney you use for most corporate matters. This individual or firm may have been fine for your purposes so far but might not be experienced and skilled in government contracts. Government contracting is a niche market in law with its own specialized practices and conventions, which makes it difficult for an attorney inexperienced in this niche to handle.

Subject Matter Experts

All proposals depend on focused subject matter expertise to create a winning solution. The good news is that your company probably has a number of *subject matter experts* (SMEs); the bad news is that proposal creation is probably not the strong suit of these SMEs. In fact, it's fair to say that most SMEs very much enjoy doing the work under a government contract but typically have little or no interest in helping with a specific proposal to *get* a government contract. In fact, many have a real dislike for the proposal process.

def•i•ni•tion

SME, the acronym for **subject matter expert,** is someone who has an in-depth understanding of a specific subject, such as telecommunications systems or military logistics.

I have seen many—too many by any measure—super-qualified technical people who disdain anything that appears to be "sales." This is truly unfortunate, because no work can be done until someone *sells* something. They often forget that the work they are doing today has resulted directly or indirectly from the efforts of someone who sold something a while back.

SMEs are often among the most important contributors to creating a winning proposal, so it's vital that all team members and especially the proposal manager and capture manager find a way to motivate these experts and recognize their contributions, to exploit their strengths and work around their weaknesses.

The Special Importance of Three Team Members

Three team members have special importance to proposal teams: the program manager-designate, the capture manager, and the proposal manager. These people often make up a sort of core team within the team, so let's look at why their roles are so special.

The Program Manager-Designate's Core Role

Every winning bid has a small handful of important individuals. Whoever is in this small circle, the program manager-designate is always included. The importance of this role cannot be overestimated. Why is that?

Customers buy not only an *organization* (say, Lockheed Martin) but also the *people*. The single most important "people" the customer has an opportunity to "buy" is the program manager. This is the individual with first-line responsibility—and corresponding authority—to ensure successful execution of the program. Therefore, if the customer either doesn't know the program manager or knows and doesn't like that individual, then the entire organization and the entire proposal is swimming upstream in that competition.

The proposal team needs a countervailing force to the capture manager and the relationship manager. These two team members' primary concern is winning the competition, and they are typically not nearly so concerned about how to execute the program or how to make money on the program at the offered price. The relationship manager may be interested in earning a sales commission, which would only kick in if the contract is won. The program manager, on the other hand, knows (or should know) the implications the proposal has for program execution. So the program manager brings to the proposal team a steady hand that prevents over-promising or under-bidding.

Why Program Manager-Designates Can Be Hard to Get and Keep

There are often problems in achieving the full participation of the program manager-designate. Truly qualified program managers are indeed scarce, and difficult to identify. The normal situation is that good program managers are already the program manager on another, existing program. The following two responses are not really reasons, but excuses, for not having a program manager-designate fully engaged on the proposal team:

- ◆ "We don't have anybody." Even in large organizations, the perceived field of talented, skilled program managers is narrow. Limiting the choice to those with name and face recognition with the customer even further narrows the field. Therefore, the inventory of program managers meeting the criteria is thin or nonexistent. Then either find someone, within the company or outside, who does meet these qualifications, or seriously consider a no-bid.

- ◆ "We have somebody, but he/she is already tied up with another program and can't be spared." That's another way of saying, "We want to win, but not badly enough to get really qualified people on the proposal effort." Then this is a signal that TM is not *really* committed to winning and again is a no-bid signal. Remember, "commitment" is without meaning unless that commitment is backed by willingness to spend money to achieve a win.

Placing the right program manager-designate on the proposal team has two benefits. It sends the right message to the customer and improves the probability that the proposal, as submitted, can be executed at a profit.

The Capture Manager

As the proposal team's representative to TM, this function plays a pivotal role in not only keeping TM informed of the proposal team's progress and needs but also keeping the proposal team advised of TM's own thinking. Therefore, the capture manager must set aside competing responsibilities to strive for excellence in this role.

The Proposal Manager

The proposal manager's importance derives from the role of the "Doer of Last Resort." This means that if and when other members of the team fail to provide contributions to the proposal creation, the manager fills the gap between what *has been* accomplished and what *must be* accomplished. Typically, proposal managers have come to that role after having filled many different roles on proposal teams. Therefore, this person is often the best one to turn to when gaps need to be filled.

The Least You Need to Know

- What ensures a winning team is not what any one individual does but how all the individuals work as a team.
- Engaging TM in the process is a key to success.
- You improve your chances of winning with strong people as program manager-designate, capture manager, and proposal manager.
- For small companies and for small proposals, only a handful of people may be involved, but each of the 13 roles must be filled.
- Don't be afraid to engage temporary help from outside your company to fill any roles you don't have covered.

Part 3

Choosing Your Targets

The trick to finding a government contract is to zero in on just which government entity and which exact opportunity is the right match for precisely which products or services you can offer. Targeting a specific customer (an area of federal, state, or local government) and a specific opportunity (the contract being offered) are covered here. Never fear, even if you're not with Boeing or Lockheed or any of the big guys. We take a special look at small businesses and how they can make it big in government contracting, including a whole chapter devoted to the General Services Administration (GSA) Schedule Contracts, which are one of the best ways for small businesses to break in.

Chapter 7

Targeting a Specific Customer

In This Chapter

♦ Finding potential customers right for your business

♦ Focusing on teaming arrangements

♦ Gaining knowledge of the customer

♦ Using the competition to learn about the customer

You've gone this far. You have a good feeling about the match between your company's capabilities and the government needs. You either have a product you think you can sell to the government, or you've already found a customer needing a product you can provide. Your next steps are to fully assess how this customer contracts for these needs and to concurrently learn which other companies are providing products to that customer. It would be a shame to find out that there's already a competitor who is in firm control of the market for the customer you're targeting. So getting both knowledge of the customer and knowledge of the competition (if any) are important. It's also time to start considering teaming arrangements—individuals or companies you can partner with in some fashion to bring the strongest team to the customer.

Analyzing the Competition to Find Potential Customers

In Chapter 4 you learned that the best source of knowledge about your competition is your customer. But that knowledge is not enough; you should know more, and here is how you can learn more:

♦ Attend professional meetings, and mingle with your competition.

♦ Don't ignore the possibilities brought by the electronic age. Informal Internet-based networking groups are springing up like weeds. This is "neutral ground" and may therefore be helpful in establishing the type of one-on-one and many-on-many relationships that provide a basis for fruitful discussions. Be careful, of course, to obey the rules of contact with individuals in the customer community during certain periods. (See more about these rules in Chapter 3.)

♦ If you're a subcontractor looking for your piece of large contracts coming up for bid shortly, approach the larger companies, not only with the idea of getting a spot on a team but secondarily to learn, from the large companies, about your competition for the same piece of business you're interested in capturing.

♦ Pay attention to ads in newspapers and on job boards to see which competitors are recruiting for the kinds of skills you and your people have.

This competition analysis has four uses:

♦ Bidding decisions

♦ Pricing decisions

♦ Anti-competition themes

♦ Teaming arrangements

Bid Decisions

The first and perhaps the most important use of competition information is in bid decisions. This book shows four different times in the proposal creation cycle when you reach bid decision points, which is only a minimum number. You may well want to conduct formal bid decisions more often. The trigger for additional discussions can be any new, startlingly significant, information you get. What is "startlingly significant?" It's a loosely defined term, but with a little experience, "You'll know it when you see it."

Consider the single-award scenario. Refrain from bidding when the competition clearly has the inside track to victory *and* you cannot convince the contract officer (KO) that no other company, including yours, has a reasonable chance of winning. Don't spend a lot of money to come from fourth to second place in the customer's eyes on a single-award opportunity.

Pricing Decisions

The price volume you submit must reflect not only what the customer wants to buy and approximately expects to pay, but also what prices your competitors are likely to offer. You must know where your price is likely to stand, in relation to those of other offerors.

There is no one right answer to the question, "What is the winning price?" because the answer is highly dependent on the total circumstances. Here are some considerations:

- How sensitive is your customer to awarding on price? Is this a customer who almost always awards to the very lowest price offered, among the technically qualified offerors? (This is also known as the "pass/fail technical, lowest offered price" award criteria). If so, make sure you can meet the competition's best price offer.

- Are there any major, deal-breaking past performances for either your company or a competitor relating to price? If so, you should be able to exploit any negative characteristics of your competitors' history through anti-competition themes (see above). If you have deal-breaking negatives, seriously consider not bidding.

- Does the competitor have a reputation for offering a minimally acceptable technical solution and then offering a very low price? This strategy can work, if the winner can make a high margin on any of the resulting contract changes that typically accompany such offers.

Offered price may be the most important evaluation criterion. If this is true, it is typically stated as such in Section M of the solicitation. Even more importantly, your price may be given additional weight if the technical and management solutions are more similar. This leaves price as *the* determining factor. So your attention to your own price, in relation to your estimates of what your competition is likely to offer, is an important consideration in your own proposal.

Anti-Competition Themes

Chapter 12 gives examples of winning themes, including anti-competition themes. Anti-competition themes are those positive things you can say about your own solution that are not only different from but also better than those offered by your competition.

You can't create good anti-competition themes unless you know what the competition is likely to submit as their solutions. The most important consideration about anti-competition themes is this: an anti-competition theme works well for you if and only if the theme hits the mark. Unfortunately, themes that miss the mark are double trouble.

Here's an example, oversimplified to make a point. Let's say you are submitting a Mac solution, and you're sure the competition is submitting a Windows-based solution. You put in anti-competition themes showing how much better a Mac solution is than a Windows-based one. But the competition does not submit a Windows-based solution; they submit instead a Mac one or a Unix-based solution. Not only did your theme miss the mark, but also missing the mark makes you look foolish for making wrong assumptions about the competition's solution.

Now you're in a hole. The first rule of holes is: when you see you're in a hole, stop digging. But you don't have a chance to stop digging because your proposal now contains a glaring error. What effect does this error have on the evaluation team? This error now casts doubt on your entire proposal. Having found a glaring error, the evaluators now ask themselves, "How many *more* errors are in here?" This is definitely *not* what you want.

Teaming Arrangements

The fourth use of competition analysis is teaming and teaming arrangements. Knowing the other potential players' strengths and weaknesses, as well as your own, can sometimes suggest a teaming arrangement. If your company and Company X have strengths in all important criteria, there's a chance to build a team with all the required strengths. So let's take a look at teaming arrangements in detail.

Arrange Your Team to Achieve Your Goals

On a large procurement, achieving your goal of creating the winning proposal that results in a profitable contract execution is a multi-faceted activity, stretching over at least months if not years. Building a winning team includes having the right prime contractor and the right set of subcontractors.

You have many ways of accomplishing the goal and many considerations about who, what, when, where, and how to go about teaming. This section gives structure to the decision-making process, and your analysis should focus on the right questions in search of the right answers. This analysis assumes you are playing the role of subcontractor and not the prime contractor. It's an example of how you, as a small business, can play a role on large contracts.

First Principle of Teaming

Before the solicitation comes out in final form, you must strive to create the winning team. Note that it's not "Get on the winning team," because usually the winning team does not actually exist in the abstract. Your job is to create that winning team.

Assumptions

Teaming arrangements involve the prime contractor on the one hand and subcontractors on the other. We can describe how to build those arrangements from either perspective: you as the prime or you as the subcontractor. So let's consider how to accomplish teaming arrangements from the point of view of the subcontractor. If you're the prime, you need to understand how this can work from the subcontractors' viewpoint.

Let's look at some assumptions or beliefs:

- ◆ You are not capable of bidding this opportunity as a prime contractor. You're not big enough, and you lack capacity.

- ◆ You are a small business, XYZ, but with a significant position in a market niche, which is specialized hardware of the type the customer wants to buy.

- ◆ Your company now enjoys a position in the marketplace that is so strong that your presence on a team *could* (not *will* or *must*) make the difference to a prime between winning and losing. You're looking for the right team to support through your subcontractor role.

- ◆ Of the four deliverables (hardware, facilities management, software conversion, training), ABC, a good candidate for the prime contractor on the winning team, has demonstrated capability to deliver three (labeled from here forward the "three ABC deliverables": facilities management, software conversion, and training), on time and within budget. Your specific relationship with the customer (which may grow significantly as you win the *Wingnut Program* and others through your ongoing marketing efforts) adds credibility to any team you choose to join.

♦ Because cost/price is an issue, you've decided to use the part of your company that can offer the lowest possible labor rates as an incentive to any prime contractor to have you on their team.

What Is the Customer Looking For?

This is another way of phrasing "Who will make the procurement decision? What criteria will they use?" You must know the answer to these questions as it's a part of your preliminary analysis, the one that led to your interest in this opportunity. Let's say your best information says this is what the customer is looking for:

♦ Low price offer (This particular customer is famous—or notorious—for awarding contracts to the team offering the lowest believable price.)

♦ Low technical risk (unlike some parts of DOD or DoE, this customer can't take a chance on gee-whiz, risky technology to solve its problems.)

♦ Low schedule risk (This customer absolutely *must* have its systems delivered on time.)

In addition, this customer may respond to another cost/price consideration: low price risk. For cost-type contracts, there's a great difference between *offering* a low price and *delivering* a low price. The superior, winning claim, as substantiated in your team's proposal, can be that "The ABC/XYZ Team offers not only low price but also low *uncertainty* about the ultimate price the customer will pay."

Three-Step Action Plan for Teaming

Use the following three-step action plan to help you decide which team to join.

Action Step 1

Reach a tentative judgment about the four primes with the greatest probability of winning the competition in the absence of your own company on any team. Using the criteria you believe the customer plans to use, do a "Strengths and Weaknesses Analysis" of each prime, for each of the deliverables (the number of deliverables is usually a small number, such as five). Let's say, for the sake of example, that you have identified exactly four possible competitors, and that there are five deliverables. So you have a chart that is four (primes) by five (deliverables).

Action Step 2

For each of the top four potential prime contractors, your company makes a presentation of your own view of the customer's decision criteria and your own capabilities. In exchange, you solicit presentations (say, the next week) by each of the primes as to why your company should choose that particular team. By your own criteria, you tell each prime you're looking to create the winner. You're not making legally-binding offers to join their team; you're soliciting offers from the *primes* to have your company join their team. If you do a good job, you set up a *"you-gotta-do-better-than-that"* situation, in which you're in a position to choose from between/among competing offers to team, but only your company has information about the offers of the competing parties. The crunch is in the form of "You've-gotta-do-better-than-that."

def•i•ni•tion

You-gotta-do-better-than-that is a negotiation technique wherein one party places the parties on the opposite side of the negotiations against each other in an effort to extract the absolutely most favorable terms from the eventual winner.

You explain to all primes that your commitment is to create the winning team or to no-bid and, therefore, not participate in the opportunity. As a desired fortunate consequence, it may be that if the primes are persuaded by your arguments, the nonchosen may themselves opt to no-bid and thereby narrow the total field of bidders.

Action Step 3

On the basis of the presentations by the primes, create not only the winning team but also the team that maximizes your own participation in the total work effort. Mechanically, revisit your analysis from Step 1 to display the influence of the addition of your own capability to each prime's capability and show how that reshuffles the win probabilities. You're likely to find that one prime can win only if they have your company on their team. Usually, that team looks most like a winner. For example, company Big Orange may have an inherent cost/price advantage (lower conversion costs from existing systems to new hardware systems) but is weak in two of the other three deliverables. Adding your company, XYZ, to that team means the Big Orange/ XYZ Team offers the winning approach in all the customer's criteria, including low price and, incidentally, low price uncertainty.

All the above plan requires concentrated efforts and is not for the faint-hearted. However, the payoff can be large, including having built the winning team on a large opportunity.

No Guts, No Glory?

This process is surely gutsy. It may well differ from the recommendations made by more conventional, risk-averse members of your company. The best outcome is that through your briefing to the primes, you'll be able to demonstrate to your own satisfaction that XYZ is creating the winning team. It is also true that, by creating circumstances in which the primes come to you with offers to join their team, you could also maximize your own share of the winning contract. And you can help control important parts of the proposal creation process, including the all-important price issues.

Importance of Price

Because price is so important, you should launch an immediate task force to explore the relationships between alternative technical and management approaches and cost/ price. This will get complicated but is bounded by the four classes of deliverables. Presenting the methodology (but not the numbers, of course) to the four primes helps convince them that your company is serious about winning and that an important part of your contribution to the team is both low price and low price uncertainty. Your theme is "The Big Orange/XYZ team's (experience and success with similar programs), (position in the marketplace yields economies of scale), (proprietary products), (cadre of experienced programmers) allows you to offer training, facilities management, and software conversion at lower prices and with less uncertainty about prices."

If you're really gutsy, you can try to influence the customer to solicit proposals or, alternatively, allow alternate proposals that switch some deliverables where you have an advantage from cost-type to fixed price!

What the Competition May Know About the Customer

Because today's partner is tomorrow's competitor, you must be careful to guard your own proprietary data and insist on *nondisclosure agreements* (NDAs) with anyone on your team. Of course, these agreements must be reciprocal. Such nondisclosure agreements are common among government contractors.

Nondisclosure agreements protect each company against the inappropriate leakage of proprietary information about the other company. The importance of these agreements means that both your legal staff and your contracts staff must assist in obtaining an appropriate agreement.

def•i•ni•tion

A **nondisclosure agreement** is an agreement between two companies to refrain from disclosing to other parties the proprietary data they may acquire as a result of working together on a specific opportunity.

Your competition may know a great deal about your customer, and under selected circumstances, that competitor may be willing to share its knowledge with you in exchange for your knowledge about that customer or another customer. Although you must guard any proprietary data you've obtained under an NDA, nothing prevents you from sharing nonproprietary data with other companies.

Your Knowledge of the Customer

There's no better way of finding out about the customer than meeting with that customer at his place of business (see Chapter 4 for a baseline scenario for such a meeting). And you've done that while building your team. While that scenario was a good example, it's not the only or final step in getting to know your customer. Here are two more ways of gaining that knowledge.

First, invite the customer to meet with you and your company's people at *your* place of business. This is your chance to show the customer your facilities, and particularly those facilities that match that customer's interests. While you're on your own turf, you should be more comfortable in discussing sensitive issues there than at the customer site, or at neutral sites. At the other locations, "the walls have ears," and proprietary or sensitive discussions could be inappropriately leaked to your competition.

If the customer comes to your place of business, remember to observe the restrictions about providing anything of value over a certain dollar amount. For example, you can't pick up the tab for a lavish dinner at a fancy restaurant. For meals served to employees at your facility, you must recover the fair value of that meal. 5 CFR paragraph 2635.204(a) states that "a (government) employee may accept unsolicited gifts having an aggregate market value of $20 or less per source per occasion, provided that the aggregate market value of individual gifts received from any one person under the authority of this paragraph shall not exceed $50 in a calendar year."

Second, join and participate in professional societies and/or trade associations where you might have an opportunity to converse with your customer personnel. There again, you must take care to avoid undue familiarity and not cross the line into influencing or attempting to influence the customer's decisions regarding an opportunity under competition.

Seriously consider acquiring information about your customer through the fee-for-service providers shown in Appendix B. After you've exhausted your other, lower-cost sources, at least try these other sources to see if you get important new information from them.

Other Good Sources

In addition to the preferred ways listed above, some very good sources are available to you, largely from public postings on the Internet. Government customers have websites and typically post much very good information. They list their vision, mission, strategies, core values, organization, and phone lists showing personnel (except for classified agencies; they don't do so, for obvious reasons). If you're new to this business, you have no realization of how helpful and accessible this type of information has become. Those who have been doing this for a while used to have to work very hard for this type of information, and now, here it is in plain view. Take advantage of it before you take the next step, which is to fill in your knowledge gaps.

Fill the Gaps in Your Knowledge

Your next step is to see what holes you have in your knowledge and figure out how to plug those holes. First, go the relatively inexpensive way, which is to do the digging yourself. This is particularly true if you're working with a customer in your own geographic area *or* if you have an agent (typically a part-timer not looking for steady work) in the customer's area. The next best way is probably to engage a fee-for-service provider of information about that specific customer. Appendix B has a list of selected sources. Every source has a slightly different method of providing information. Fee structures are different. As a prudent buyer, you should solicit more than one before parting with your money. Typically, these sources have been around a long time and have demonstrated their value to their users. Nonetheless, choosing which one or ones and when is still a business decision requiring your closest attention.

The Door Slams Shut

Whenever you're getting information about the customer, you must remember you're always holding a ticking bomb. Your time is limited, at least with regard to a specific opportunity. The FAR and the Competition in Contracting Act (1966) severely limit contact between prospective offerors such as yourself and the government employees. You must gather anything you want to know or need to know before the solicitation is released. Depending on the interpretation of each agency, this restriction may be imposed even before the final solicitation is released. For example, some KOs insist that they be the single point of contact after the release of a Request for Information (RFI). Whether this is or is not the intent of the FAR and the Competition in Contracting Act is a moot point. The government may make up its own more restrictive rules as it goes along, and it's up to you to be aware of local practice, another reason to become very familiar with your customer.

The Least You Need to Know

- You can get useful information on your competition from your customer.

- You can get useful information on your customers from your competition.

- Start with relatively inexpensive sources (Internet, libraries, FOIA documents), but be prepared to use fee-for-service sources to find out more about critical opportunities and customers.

- Even as a subcontractor, you may have significant power to create the winning team.

- Your positive contributions to any team can give you significant bargaining power.

- This action plan requires some risk-taking on your part.

Chapter 8

Targeting a Specific Opportunity

In This Chapter

- Discovering opportunities
- Dealing with surprise solicitations
- The four proposal drivers
- Bid only to win
- Bid decision point #2

At this point, you've at least tentatively decided to make a bid on an opportunity. From the discussion in Chapter 7, you know more about the customer you've targeted—or at least know how to learn more. You also know something about the competitors going after the same customer or already doing work for that customer. So now it's time to move ahead and conduct the final analysis of a specific opportunity before you begin spending real money on it. The steps you take to do this analysis will not only help you build a strong case for a winning bid but also help you make the decision to bid or not bid in the first place.

How and Where to Find Out About Opportunities

So you've identified a customer who is a good prospect for your company. This customer usually buys products your company either already produces or could produce if you were to make relatively minor changes to your existing products. But nothing can happen until you identify a promising specific opportunity, one you know is going to be released soon and one you believe you can offer a good product for, at a competitive price. So let's look at the criteria for homing in on a contract you can win.

Get an Early Start

The *Commerce Business Daily* (*CBD*) was a daily multi-page publication that served the government business development community well for many years until it folded in January 2002. The *CBD* contained many detailed announcements about the planned release of solicitations, the actual release of solicitations, notices of awards, and other notices of interest to those in the federal marketplace. But gradually, agencies began to use various new methods of solicitation publication, mostly featuring electronic means. The initial use of electronic ways of announcing opportunities resulted in a proliferation of electronic bulletin boards. These decentralized boards made finding opportunities difficult for the general public. Which ones were relevant to which opportunities? The variety contributed to confusion and spotty results. By the time the *CBD* ceased publication, it had lost all relevance, so the *CBD* joined Braniff Airlines, Montgomery Ward, and nickel phone calls in our book of golden memories. Today all solicitations are posted on the Internet, and the Federal Business Opportunities web site (www. FedBizOpps.gov) releases government notices.

> **Beltway Buzz**
>
> Even a small company can afford to have someone watch postings on FebBizOpps.gov each day. This task takes no more than an hour a day, and an entry-level person or someone with perhaps only a few years of experience can do it.

So whether it was the former *CBD* notice or today's electronic posting on the Internet, the point remains the same: the posting is not the *beginning* of the competition; it's the *beginning* of the *end* of the competition. That's important because if this release of the solicitation is a surprise, that's a strong red flag that you don't have a reasonable chance to win.

Responding to solicitations when your first knowledge of the opportunity is a posting on Input, Federal Sources, or FedBizOpps is probably responding too late. If you don't know anything about a solicitation until it is formally announced and posted, then you might fail to understand the true essence of the solicitation. You are likely to respond to the solicitation, not the procurement. Responding to the solicitation means you know nothing about the underlying reasons for why the solicitation is the way it is. Responding to the procurement means you know such important things as the customer hot buttons (for example, how has this customer been disappointed recently in results from other contracts and contractors and who is really in charge of the evaluation team?).

Government Insider _____

Input, Federal Sources, and FedBizOpps are all sources of solicitation schedules. See Appendix B for these website listings and other sources.

Government needs begin with agency budget requests as described in Chapter 5. For major contracts, the budget requests and the trail through the various budget reviews, through the Congress, and into law, leave a (mostly public) trail of actions. These can all be part of your understanding of the procurement. In contrast, the solicitation is only a small window into what the government wants to buy; it doesn't give the entire story. The solicitation is like a porthole on a ship while the procurement is like a picture window that offers a more expansive view.

Responding without prior knowledge of the procurement means that your company has no influence on the details of how the government will conduct the selection of the winner, and therefore you have no chance of influencing the process to favor your approach. Also, if your company is looking to be a subcontractor rather than the prime, you have a greatly reduced chance of getting on a winning team because only the less-desirable relationships may be available. And, finally, your company has probably not properly planned for a winning proposal effort, either in terms of funds or the commitment of the important internal and external personnel.

Understanding the Precipitating Event

The solicitation will tell you nothing about what is called the precipitating event. The precipitating event is the reason the government is procuring this product or service at this time and in this way. Sometimes the precipitating event is simply the expiration of existing contracts, such as when a five-year support contract is about to enter its fifth year, the government must put the job out for recompetition. Or it can be a need that a government agency has for a new or better product or service to meet an old or new need at a better price. Through a prior relationship with the customer or by having taken time to do your research on the customer, you can build the better case for why you are the best choice to meet the customer's needs.

Getting a Grip on a Precipitating Event: Lesson Learned

The precipitating event for an opportunity might be like that of a competition I led for a complete, integrated set of encrypted radios for the United States Air Force (USAF). The precipitating event was a training exercise involving deployment of large numbers of USAF units to Western Europe. The encrypted radios would not "talk" to each other. The handhelds, mobile units, and base stations did not operate across the unit boundaries.

It turned out that three different systems had been approved for use, and each base commander could choose from among these approved technologies to satisfy his local needs. As long as the users were on that base or communicating with others using that technology, things went well. But when challenged to communicate in a near-real circumstance, the results were disastrous. As a real-time work-around, some troops were using their AT&T calling cards to reach other units! This was a highly inappropriate use of nonsecure commercial networks to pass what should have been highly classified communications.

So the USAF sent out a high-priority requirement for a single system to replace the three existing, incompatible ones. Potential bidders for those radios looking only at the specifications in the solicitation without knowledge of the history of why the government wished to procure the system of encrypted radios at this time failed to understand the total circumstances, failed to understand the procurement, and didn't win the contract.

Get the Current Contract Through FOIA

If a competitor is now providing this product or service under an existing contract, then the first things you need to know are the details of that current contract and the corresponding winning proposal. Thankfully, for government contracts (this is not true in the commercial world), you have the advantage of the Freedom of Information Act (FOIA) of 1966 as amended through 2007.

This act, now over 40 years old, has gone through many changes and interpretations. Most of the changes (both amendments to the act and case law) have resulted in an increase in the public's access to public documents. Early in the act's implementation, many agencies actively resisted granting almost any requests for information, citing various reasons that included national security, personal privacy, the cost to the agencies of compliance, and sensitivity of ongoing activities. In fact, some resisted entirely and gave up almost nothing. Thankfully for you as a challenger, much of the information you would like about most existing contracts and winning proposals should be available and forthcoming. That said, the time lag between your request for information and actual receipt is sometimes frustratingly long, so try to submit your request well in advance of your need.

> **Beltway Buzz**
>
> You can read about the Freedom of Information Act at the U.S. Department of Justice website (www.usdoj.gov). Just click on the FOIA page.

Get Other Information Through FOIA

You can also use FOIA to get many other types of information, including other solicitations and winning proposals. Here's what you might get, and why it's helpful to you:

- ◆ Solicitations and winning proposals from similar procurements from the same contracting office planning to issue the opportunity of your interest can be useful in many ways. The cost/price volumes are of particular interest to you because they reveal the competition's prices and pricing methodology. Some figures may be redacted and therefore not available to you.

- ◆ Solicitations and proposals won by your competition in other venues (other customers, other products) tell you more about your competition and may give you ideas for some winning strategies you can employ in your own responses.

- ◆ Attendance lists at public meetings held by your customer reveal the names and contacts of your competition. An example of such meeting is "Industry Day" meetings, which attract you and your competitors.

The point is to take full advantage of FOIA by getting creative and resourceful, accessing any and all information that could enhance your chances of winning.

Red Flag

Be aware that the requests you make for information under FOIA are also subject to FOIA. So for example, if you ask for a winning proposal submitted in the past by your competition, then your competition will know you're "spying" on them. You may want to use a blind, third-party source to avoid being identified.

Accomplish a Meeting with the Customer

As described in Chapter 5, meeting with your customer is an essential step in achieving your goal: a contract. People buy from people, and people buy more from people they know. Familiarity yields many benefits, providing you achieve that familiarity in the right way.

Surprise Solicitations

A surprise solicitation is one that appears as a final solicitation without your foreknowledge. If this solicitation is for a product your company could have supplied and your company didn't know about it before the solicitation arrived full blown in your "in basket," that's particularly bad. Its appearance could well cause you to find out how this happened. And you must then take steps to prevent this happening again.

Why not bid surprise solicitations? There are many reasons. Here are three big ones:

♦ Some other company, and probably companies, know of this solicitation, and are fully prepared to respond.

♦ You are starting from a "cold start," and others from a rolling start.

♦ If teaming is required, or helpful, all the good subcontractors or all the good primes are already teamed up with teammates, and your company is a late-comer to this party, and must settle for the leftovers at the banquet table of teammates.

The Four Proposal Drivers—Top Level View

Preparatory to the Bid Decision Point #2 is a short, to the point, staff paper called "Proposal Drivers" and is attachment 04 of the proposal plan. This template has four parts, each a question that requires an answer. These questions are so simple they seem deceptive, but you should be able to satisfactorily answer each of these four before reaching a "bid" decision.

The four questions are:

♦ What are the major (about four to seven) selling themes? These answer the customer's implicit question, "Why should I choose your team?"

♦ To demonstrate that your past performance satisfies the customer's evaluation criteria, what are the candidate citations, and how does each relate to the SOW (C), the Instructions to Offerors (L), or and Evaluation Criteria (M)?

- In brief, what is your technical approach or perhaps management approach, if that is more relevant, that is not only *different from* but also *better than* the approach offered by your competitors?

- What is your staffing plan, including most importantly your choice for your team's program manager? In the best case, this individual has positive name and face recognition with the customer.

This list is an overview of the four parts of the Proposal Drivers staff paper, and the next section gives a description of what each part is about and how it fits into the total picture of the opportunity.

Now let's assume you're satisfied with your answers to these four questions and go forward with a "bid" decision. Very likely, at least one of your four answers will change as you get smarter about the details of the opportunity. Therefore, best practice dictates that you and your staff revisit these proposal drivers at least twice a month, to verify that these are still the best answers or to change or correct the answers.

This is dependent, of course, on how much time you have before the response to the solicitation is due.

Red Flag

Let's say you've already submitted a bid. After submission, for whatever reason, you change your mind and really don't want to get an award. You must be careful about how you withdraw a bid. Typically, the cover sheet of the solicitation (Section A) requires that an offer (your bid or proposal) be valid for a minimum number of days. You may not be able to withdraw the offer without penalty. Check with your legal counsel for advice.

The Four Proposal Drivers—Detailed View

Let's take a look at each of the four questions in the proposal drivers:

1. What are the major (about four to seven) selling themes? These answer the customer's implicit question, "Why should I choose your team?"

   Themes come in three types: garden variety, discriminating, and anticompetition.

   a. Garden-variety themes are positive things we say about ourselves, in the almost certain knowledge that the competitors will say the same things or similar things about their own company, hence the label garden variety. All gardens have the same or similar sweet-smelling flowers. All competitors are technically competent and have done similar work for other customers. All competitors have qualified technical people with many years of experience in this field. Ho-Hum. So why do you say things that are garden variety? In short, because if you don't say these things, the reader may (incorrectly) believe you don't have all those characteristics. Silence casts doubt on your qualifications. You include garden-variety themes to make yourself at least equal to your competitors, but that's all they do. That's not enough to win unless you're planning on winning on cost/price alone, but don't count on that.

Here are some examples of garden-variety selling themes, with short comments about each:

◆ "Our worldwide network of support services ensures rapid, inexpensive support of the product in the field."

Well, because this is a requirement of the solicitation, all the competitors can and undoubtedly will say the same thing.

◆ "Our proposal is responsive to all requirements of the solicitation."

Well, duh, all the other offerors will be saying the same thing. Submitting a noncompliant response is not something the competitors are likely to do, at least not on purpose. Also notice this has no stated benefit to the customer. If you must say this, okay, but it's weak.

b. Discriminating themes are also positive things you say about your company and your offer. But these say how you are not only *different from* but also *better than* the technical, the management, and/or the cost and price solutions provided by the competitors.

Here are some examples of discriminating selling themes, with short comments about each:

◆ "As presented, our proposal shows a plan meeting your schedule. As an option, we have provided an *alternate* approach, which delivers all your desired products four months earlier than our baseline schedule, at a cost premium of only 12.5 percent."

Surely, this could represent a major difference between your bid and the others, especially if you already have a rolling start on this program and can more easily attain the customer's schedule than the competitors can.

♦ "Under separate cover (and therefore outside the page limitation of the proposal), we have provided copies of our research studies, which support our manufacturing approach and the accuracy of our cost estimate."

This is really good. You've figured out a way to present material outside the page count that the customer can easily evaluate. And you have given increased credibility to your offer in this way. All customers are risk-averse. That goes for all three types of risk: technical risk (will this really work?), schedule risk (can you do this on the desired schedule?), and cost risk (can you meet the cost/price target?).

♦ "Our personnel turnover rate is two thirds of the industry standard and ensures continuity in management and technical approaches. Our key personnel average 17 years of company service. Continuity of our personnel reduces all customer risks."

Assuming this is true, these figures show a real, important difference between your bid and that of others. See that this one shows a feature and then the benefit to the customer. It plays to every customer's favorite radio station: WII-FM—What's In It, For Me?

♦ "Our computer-based cost model is available to you for cost sensitivity analysis."

This is okay. It is probably different from the competition. And the benefit is implied, which is that your customer now has the ability to verify the correctness and accuracy of your cost/price estimates.

♦ "Our physical plant is now operating at 45 percent of rated capacity and will be operating at only 76 percent of capacity during the peak of this program. Our requirements for facilities are therefore among the lowest possible. And there is virtually no risk of exceeding our capacity, which means schedule risks are virtually nonexistent."

Notice how specific these figures are. Specificity trumps generalities, and you state the benefit to the customer.

> **Beltway Buzz**
>
> Submitting an Alternate Proposal is almost never a good idea. Some solicitations allow them, and some prohibit them. However, if you believe your company can do something significantly better than the competition, and remain within what you believe is the customer's expected cost, you may be able to submit an alternate proposal, and actually win.

Red Flag _____

Be careful here. You've now offered material outside the page count. Some KOs and their evaluators get really excited—in a negative way—about attempts to circumvent the page limitations. More pages mean more work for the evaluators, including the KO. Be careful, and know your customer well before you try this.

c. Anticompetition themes are those that target very specific characteristics you contend are weaknesses in the approach or solutions being offered by your competitors. These could be against a single competitor or against all competitors.

Red Flag _____

Using anticompetition themes are great and appropriate. While we don't usually strive to make ourselves look taller by making our competitors look smaller, it *is* fair to show relevant differences. But be careful; if your anticompetition theme misses the mark and presupposes a competitor's approach that is not in his proposal, you can do a great deal of harm to your own credibility, and the theme backfires on you.

Note that these themes are similar to, yet different from, the discriminating themes in important ways. Discriminating themes are not directly addressing your competitors' weaknesses, whereas anticompetition themes do. When you use these effectively, such themes can cast doubt on the entire competition's case.

Here are some examples of anticompetitor themes, with short comments about each:

◆ "Our confidence in our ability to meet the cost estimates is demonstrated by the fixed-price nature of our offer."

Now this could be a big anticompetition theme. The customer has asked for a cost-type contract with an incentive to the contractor to come in under the estimated cost. This offer is to aggressively replace the cost-type contract, with the risks to the customer, with a fixed-price contract, which puts all the risk on the contractor. This could be very attractive to the customer or not, depending upon the degree of risk the customer is willing to take. This offer will be most important and most effective if you know the customer well, and that having your company take on the risk, at the stated price, is very attractive to this particular customer on this contract.

◆ "The commitment of our Corporate Office to this program is evidenced by the allocation of $2.7 million in capital improvements. These improvements will not be charged to the contract but are funded out of the corporate pool of funds for such purposes."

This type of aggressive commitment—and it's very specific—is certain to get the attention of the evaluators. It then raises just the right questions in their minds: "Well, if this company is willing to do this for us, the customer, why didn't the competition pledge to do this? Are they too cheap to help us out? What is their level of commitment? Let's go back and put pressure on the other folks to do the same or a similar thing." Or, "Hey, this is a real advantage of this bid over all the others."

2. To demonstrate that your past performance satisfies the customer's evaluation criteria, what are the candidate citations, and how does each relate to the SOW (C), the Instructions to Offerors (L), or and Evaluation Criteria (M)?

Virtually all major government opportunities require you to prove to the customer's satisfaction that your company has had successes in other, similar programs. The customer usually asks for at least three, and perhaps many more, citations of your company's work. The label for these is "Past Performance."

Typically, the customer plans to take your citations and then get an evaluation of your work from the KO and/or the government program manager. The complexity and depth of evaluation requested of your other customer's KO and program manager can be anything from "check a box" at one end of the spectrum to the other end, a very extensive set of questions (some of which are designed to elicit what happened during the cited program that was not in accordance with the customer's desires and expectations. A common question is something like, "How did this contractor identify problems with the cited program, and how did the contractor's management recover from those problems?"). Sometimes (and you need to be prepared for this) the soliciting customer requires *you* to obtain those evaluations from your current or past customers and have those evaluators send the results directly to the soliciting customer.

So the choice of those citations is perhaps your second or no greater than third crucial decision (after deciding to bid and deciding on the program manager-designate) about this opportunity. Unfortunately, too often bidders assign this selection process an inappropriately low priority. Consequently, too often the decisions are postponed until it's too late to achieve an acceptable score, using the following criteria for selection.

Over and above the criteria given in the solicitation (such as dollar value, time frame of work performed, type of contract, even customer), here are five good rules for choosing citations:

◆ Make absolutely certain that your cited customers will speak very highly of your work. A less-than-sterling evaluation is a major roadblock in your efforts to get this new contract. You do *not* want to be in the sad position of writing a great proposal only to be eliminated by a single poor rating.

◆ Double-check that the phone numbers and e-mail addresses listed for the KO and program manager are correct and that the same person who monitored your work is still in place. Government personnel, particularly junior military officers, move quickly from assignment to assignment, so for work you did ending two years ago, that junior officer has probably moved on.

◆ Strange things happen to ongoing contracts. Let's say you have the XYZ contract, which you have held for more than four years with high commendations from the customer. You are convinced that things are going smoothly and there's no way you'll get anything other than a great reference on that contract. Enter Murphy's Law: "If anything can go wrong, it will." So in March, you use the citation, and you're good with it. But the third week in September, a week before the proposal is due to the customer, the KO and the customer program manager have a problem with your program manager. Products are being delivered a day or two late, and you're uncharacteristically 8 percent over budget for the quarter. These two things are on the mind of both the KO and the customer program manager when the evaluation form comes in. This is extra work, and they're both out of shape at your company, temporarily, but still out of shape. So what happens? Nothing good—an "acceptable," not stellar, evaluation.

To prevent this situation, you must do two things: first, inform the KO and the customer program manager that the evaluation is coming on this very important opportunity and you would sincerely appreciate their giving your company an impartial, but very good, evaluation. Second, have your own current (or past if that's the case) program manager *hand carry* the evaluation form to the customer evaluators and ask them kindly to fill it out and return directly to the KO of the soliciting customer. E-mail and phone calls will not do for this important step.

◆ You are sometimes presented with this dilemma: should you cite one of your programs closely matching the work of the opportunity but with so-so performance, or should you cite one of your programs with excellent ratings but matching the work of the opportunity only 60 to 70 percent. The answer is: go for the excellent performance rating every time.

3. In brief, what is your technical approach or perhaps management approach,
   if that is more relevant, that is not only *different from* but also *better than* the
   approach offered by your competitors?

So how do you distinguish yourself
from those other guys? The best of
worlds has you saying, with truthful-
ness, that you are different from the
others in *something the customer consid-
ers valuable.* And that's fine. But what
are those things the customer consid-
ers valuable? Two sources: the evaluation criteria (our old friend by now,
Section M) and very importantly your
knowledge of the difference between
the solicitation and the procurement
(see also Chapter 5), the customer's
hot buttons.

 Red Flag

Unfortunately, the government sometimes confuses
the terms "past performance" and
"experience." Past performance
is how well you did something.
Experience is only what you did.
If you're unclear about what the
customer wants, it pays both you
and your customer to clear up
any uncertainties.

4. What is your staffing plan, including most importantly your choice for your
   team's program manager? In the best case, this individual has positive name and
   face recognition with the customer.

Remember the importance of not only *having* a program manager-designate but
also having that person acquire positive name and face recognition with the customer (see Chapter 6). You cannot achieve this unless you plan for your major
opportunities. You must not only designate someone but also see to it that the
customer is aware of your choice. Face to face is best. Pump up the customer
with your choice's qualifications in such a way that the customer will be very
pleased to see this person named as the program manager. Tell the customer,
and mean it, that (using some criteria) your choice would also be the customer's
choice. Submitting a major proposal for a great opportunity and featuring an
individual with a name and face causing the customer to say, "Joe Who??" means
that on page one, you're shoveling sand against the tide.

The staffing plan is also very important. As a part of your transition plan (see
Chapter 21), you'll be showing the ramp-up from your own "rolling start"
through the first 45 to 60 days of the program. These days are easily the highest-
risk times for the program and must be done correctly.

There's a myth abroad that your organization chart has one, and only one, version, which covers the entire program life from start-up to phase-down. This myth is just that—a myth. Many, if not most, programs should have actual differences between the first few days and weeks of a program (start-up) and a steady state (usual). The best presentation of your organization recognizes at least that difference. Particularly on a cost-type contract where the customer is paying all your costs, you should show a ramp-up from perhaps a small core of individuals. Then you add people at an appropriate pace, building to the steady-state organization. This demonstrates to the evaluators your cost-consciousness, a real benefit to the customer.

> **Beltway Buzz**
>
> Your initial complement of personnel may well include some brought onto your team for the transition only. Transition is high in all three types of risk: technical, schedule, and cost. Therefore, any steps you can show to mitigate those risks will yield favorable evaluations.

The results of a review of the 02 Proposal Drivers is an important element in the Bid Decision Point #2.

Your Second Bid Decision

You and your team are deep into consideration of a specific opportunity. As with the other bid decision points, the proposal team reviews the then-current state of the procurement. You should now have more and better information than you had at Decision Point #1.

This Bid Decision Point #2 is very similar to Decision Point #1 (see Chapter 4). Your goal should be to either re-verify that you have an excellent chance to get this contract or that you now realize circumstances have changed, or at least your understanding of them, and therefore you do *not* have an excellent chance to win and should seriously consider dropping out of the competition.

The Least You Need to Know

- Begin to identify specific opportunities well before the customer releases the official solicitation.

- Create and constantly revise the "02 Proposal Drivers."

- Develop and track the half-dozen or so of your really powerful win themes.

Chapter 9

Spotlight on Small Businesses

In This Chapter

- ◆ The basics of small business
- ◆ Opportunities for small business
- ◆ Understanding multiple-award contracts
- ◆ Ways to submit unsolicited proposals

The federal government is the largest purchaser of goods and services in the world—hands down. Add state and local governments (S&Ls), and Uncle Sam has even larger purchasing power. Small businesses aren't exactly peanuts, either. Small business activity is the driving force behind the United States economy. Ninety-nine percent of employers in the United States are small businesses, and small businesses employ about half of the private (nongovernment) workforce. Yet, of the approximately 23 million small businesses in the United States, only a tiny percentage actually sells to the government. So it's worthwhile at least to consider going after government contracts, no matter how small your business is.

This chapter describes the various types of opportunities you can seek within the large and growing government market for small businesses. You also learn about the advantages of multiple-award contracts, including the very important GSA Schedule Contracts, and about unsolicited proposals—what to include in them and how to use them. The chapter concludes with a look at 13 common mistakes small businesses make regarding government contracts. Before getting into all that, though, let's first look more closely at what exactly a small business is.

Defining Small Business

Is your business a small business? What exactly is a small business, anyway? Precisely what we can classify as a small business is an important matter when it comes to government contracting. You might think of a small business as a business that just hasn't grown up yet, and you'd be right. You might consider yourself a small business because you have very few employees or small revenues. But only the Small Business Administration (SBA) has the official authority to determine what constitutes a small business. Founded in 1953, the SBA is an independent agency of the federal government that assists and protects the interests of small businesses. The SBA's mission is to help Americans start, build, and grow businesses.

> **Beltway Buzz**
>
> Small businesses provide about three in four new jobs in the United States.

Small Business Basics

The first part of the SBA's classification of a business as small is that it is a business organized for profit. (No wisecracks about how you're not actually profitable yet!) The business can be a sole proprietorship, partnership, Subchapter S Corporation, Limited Liability Company (LLC), or some other form of legal entity. Second, it pays taxes and uses American factors of production, such as labor, products, and materials. Third, it operates in the United States. And fourth, it does not exceed the size limitations for its specific industry. A small business in one industry may not be a small business in another.

Small Business Classification

Always consult the SBA website (www.sba.gov) for the most accurate information, but here are recent general standards. If a business comes in at or below these levels, it is considered a small business.

❏ 500 employees for most manufacturing and mining industries

❏ 100 employees for all wholesale trade industries

❏ $6.5 million for most retail and service industries

❏ $31 million for most general and heavy construction industries

❏ $13 million for all special trade contractors

❏ $750,000 for most agricultural industries

Government Insider _____

Visit the SBA website (www.sba.gov), and look for size standards information to verify that your company is, in fact, a small business. Even if you've been on the site in the past, it's a good idea to check again because SBA size standard guidelines change or your business may have outgrown the designation.

Small Business Certification

If you do qualify as the special classification of small business according to the SBA guidelines, you may now declare the SBA your new best friend—a very helpful friend. Before you can take advantage of that help, though, be aware that the opportunities for selected categories of small businesses require that you first get a certification from the SBA to confirm that you are, in fact, a small business. In other words, just reading the guidelines on the SBA site is sometimes not enough. Some opportunities require that you be officially certified.

This situation applies only to two classifications of businesses: Small Disadvantaged Business (referred to as the 8(a) Program) and Small Business Disabled Veteran-Owned Business. If you wish to be classified as either of these types of small business, you must submit data to prove you are such a business. You must meet strict criteria for certification, but the effort is worth it as the certification gives you access to contracts not available to other businesses. (Consult the SBA website for more details on the criteria for these designations.)

Where the Opportunities Are for Small Business

Due to federal government regulations, large contractors are required to show that a major percentage of their subcontractors are small businesses. So there is an open invitation to qualified small businesses to get and retain a large number of contracts to supply government needs, and the total value of these contracts is very large.

Increasingly, S&L governments follow the federal lead by encouraging small business participation, both as subcontractors and prime contractors. So the market is ripe for small business participation *if* you know how to participate. There are four basic categories of contract opportunities for small businesses:

- Serving as a subcontractor or *supplier*
- Participating in SBA set-aside programs
- Capitalizing on recompetitions
- Seeking sole-source awards

Don't worry if you don't know exactly what these categories are. I'll explain all of them in the sections that follow.

def•i•ni•tion

A **supplier (or vendor)** may have a subcontract with the prime contractor but doesn't contribute entrepreneurial skills to the proposal team and may be on more than one bidding team. They supply only price and availability information but no help in selling that team's solution.

Subcontractor or Supplier Opportunities

The first specific class of opportunities for your small business is as a subcontractor or a supplier to a larger company already under contract to the government. That company is the *prime contractor*. If it's an existing contract, you'll most likely be coming in as a supplier because the opportunity to be a *subcontractor* in the way used in this book has now passed. But don't be confused by that label. The arrangement you'll be making with the prime could be termed, legally (in the view of the government), as a subcontract. Or it could be under a blanket order or some other arrangement that works for all parties. The important thing is that your participation benefits the prime contractor, and you, too, of course.

def•i•ni•tion

The **prime contractor** is the company with a contract directly with the funding agency. This company is the "captain of the ship" in any teaming arrangement and runs the show.

Companies serving as **subcontractors** (on a large contract, there are many) work through the prime contractor, who in turn works for and reports contractually to the government contract officer (KO). The subcontractors are paid by and report to the prime.

The prime might be very interested in using you as a supplier because you might be able to improve the prime's performance or profitability. And your status as a small business helps fulfill the requirement for small businesses participation under the prime contract. If you meet these criteria, then you should seriously consider launching a business development effort to find these opportunities. See Chapter 4 for tips for doing this.

Government Insider

As a small business serving as a part of a bid on a large opportunity, here are some strategies for success:

- ◆ Show up and provide lots of help.
- ◆ Be "at the table" to assure your current position (the content of the work you'll do and the amount of work).
- ◆ Pick up the table scraps (work that has not been claimed by the prime contractor or other subcontractors).
- ◆ Pick up the pieces from other teaming partners who have defaulted or disappointed.
- ◆ Assure yourself at least the same position or a better one for the next competition with that prime.

Small Business Set-Asides

The second class of opportunities is set-asides. Under the general program the SBA supervises, there are many competitions in which the bidders, and therefore the contract awardees, must be from that special classification of businesses. There is a wide spectrum of such arrangements. The HUBZone and 8(a) small businesses are two.

This list of the SBA Set-Aside Programs gives a basic description of which businesses qualify for each designation.

- Small Business Concern (just a small business, not qualified for any of the categories below)

- Very Small Business Concern (average of no more than 15 full-time employees during the last three years and average annual receipts not to exceed $1 million)

- Woman-Owned Business Concern (at least 51 percent owned by a woman who *also* works in that business full-time)

> **Beltway Buzz**
>
> Individual agencies decide which contracts will be set aside for small business. Sometimes legislation or regulations establish specific goals for small business participation.

- Small Disadvantaged 8(a) Businesses

- Minority-Owned and Small Minority-Owned Businesses (not necessarily a small business, but at least 51 percent owned and operated by a minority)

- HUBZone Business

- Veteran-Owned and Service-Disabled Veteran-Owned Businesses

The above business classifications are easily understood, except for HUBZone Businesses. A HUBZone is government language for a Historically Underutilized Business Zone. Typically, these are cities or rural areas, characterized by high unemployment, low wages, and limited economic opportunities, over a long period of time.

Each of these previous categories has a set of specific criteria a candidate business must satisfy before it is officially classified as being in that category. Some categories have restrictions on the length of time a business may be classified in that way. For example, the 8(a) Program is usually limited to eight years. In addition, the number of employees and gross revenues averaged over the past three years have size limits. These limitations vary by the industry classification, designated by an NAICS Code, which we explain later in this chapter. When the eligibility for 8(a) contracts ends, the term you'll hear is that the business has "graduated" from the 8(a) Program.

> **Beltway Buzz**
>
> Certain subcategories of businesses within the 8(a) program are exempt from the eight-year time limit and size restrictions. Native American businesses, for example, are not subject to those "graduation" rules and remain eligible as an 8(a) in perpetuity.

The 8(a) Program is among the most valuable of the SBA programs. Therefore, it is to your advantage as a small business contracting with the government to get your 8(a) certification.

Recompetitions

A third category of opportunities is when an existing contract is expiring or is being terminated for some reason. If the contract is now held by a large business or a small business that is no longer eligible for special consideration, then you may, as a small business, have a good opportunity to get in on the action. The industry term for this is *recompetition*.

For example, Northrop Grumman may have had a support contract at the Army's Fort Dizzy for the last 20 years, under a total of six different contracts. (Fort Dizzy is fictional.) The current contract is ending in 12 months, and all possible extensions of that contract have already been exercised, so the Army is legally required to conduct a recompetition. The Small Business Advocate within the Army notes the Army is now below its legislated goal for small business participation (the actual level is 8 percent, while the goal is 10 percent—these are fictional numbers for the sake of illustration). So in surveying the field of planned new contracts, the Small Business Advocate has decided a small business could handle the opportunity. When the (draft) solicitation becomes available, the competition is limited to small business, sometimes all small business and sometimes a subset. This represents a golden opportunity for *some* small business to get a rather large contract and replace the large business now doing the work.

def•i•ni•tion

All contracts have a termination date. If the customer still needs that type of product, law requires that the customer hold another competition or a **recompetition** for that product to open the opportunity up to bids from other contractors.

Beltway Buzz

The decision to make an opportunity a set-aside is not easy. Many reviews and approvals are required before a specific opportunity is designated as a set-aside.

So far, so good. But there's a stumbling block you may not know about. When you become registered as a small business, you may register as a small business in certain NAICS Codes. NAICS stands for North American Industry Classification System. The United States Census Bureau maintains NAICS Codes—about 2000 of them, in fact. The six-digit NAICS Code shows the type of work a business does. You can win contracts for any NAICS Code for which you're registered. So the lesson here is that you want to be not only registered but also registered in as many NAICS Codes as you can reasonably perform. You can find a complete list of the NAICS Codes in the NAICS section of the United States Census Bureau site, www.census.gov.

> ### Red Flag
>
> Immediately check the NAICS Code, typically on the first page of the solicitation, to verify that your company is eligible to bid and win this job. You must have that NIACS Code for your business to win. If you don't have it already, consider changing your registration to include that code.

Sole Source

The fourth class of opportunities is sole source. Under certain circumstances, agencies may award contracts without having a competition. Typically, KOs have the right to award contracts, especially but not exclusively to small businesses, on a sole source basis. What that means practically is that the KO has determined that a specific company, and only that company, has the experience and expertise, the people, the assets, or whatever to perform the work. The regulations of each agency are different, and the legality of awarding sole source contracts depends on the circumstances. The size of the contract in dollars or full-time employees is an important factor. The urgency, such as an emergency as declared by an agency head or the United States President (or a state's governor or local mayor), is another important factor. Perhaps there isn't enough time to conduct a competition, so a sole source contract is allowed.

Here is a short list of the justifications the KO uses to justify awarding a sole source contract (FAR references are given for each):

- **Unusual and Compelling Urgency (FAR 6.302-2).** When an agency needs a specific service or product because of urgency and any delay could reasonably mean serious injury, KOs are permitted not only to limit the number of sources to be solicited but also to award quickly to meet the situation. In fact, the solicitation may never be formally released to anyone other than the awardee. There is a requirement to publicize the award, so that other potential offerors for that type of work may identify themselves to the KO against any future similar requirements.

◆ **Specialized Knowledge or Expertise (FAR 6.302-3).** When a specific candidate contractor has intimate and unique knowledge or expertise in creating the standards of other advanced work for the customer and awarding to another company could result in undesirable duplication and waste in, for example, training costs or unreasonable delays, a sole source award is then justified.

◆ **International Agreement or Treaty (FAR 6.302-4).** In some cases, the government has agreed to limit competition for certain goods and services. A logical reason could be that a third party, such as another government, is paying for that service or goods and has a preferred contractor in mind; then sole source is justified. Moreover, for international transactions, where the source of funding is a foreign government, that government may well specify a source from its own country.

◆ **Authorized or Required by Statute (FAR 6.302-5).** Some law or regulation may have within its terms the requirement to procure from a certain source or class of sources. In some cases, the law actually specifies the particular source for some purchases.

◆ **National Security (FAR 6.302-6).** The needs of our three-letter agencies (such as CIA, DIA, NSA) may preclude soliciting in unclassified documents, so it is necessary to award a contract to a sole source. However, classification *alone* is not a justification for sole source. Many companies have the right clearances to submit competing offers. In fact, in recent years, more and more of the less-sensitive contract work has been solicited using an unclassified solicitation. This has allowed the procuring agency to enjoy the benefits of competitive bidding for some work previously awarded on a sole source basis.

What's the lesson here? If you want a sole source contract, you're in a much better position if you use face-to-face contact with the customer (see Chapter 4). Being in the right place at the right time is important to getting that type of contract. You'll be way ahead of any competition if you've already built name and face recognition with the decision-makers in the customer organization. That decision-maker can then work with the KO to achieve a sole source contract.

Government Insider

A useful website for finding out about government opportunities is www.FedBizOpps.gov, which can also be accessed through www.fbo.gov. You need to become familiar with the power of this site.

Multiple-Award Contracts

Many government solicitations result in a single winner. There can be only one contractor to manage the mailroom at the National Institutes of Health and one contractor responsible for managing the Nevada Test Site for the Department of Energy. But the single-award model does not fit well for some government needs, such as providing technical services for the Department of Commerce (DoC) or supplying personal computers to agencies for the next five years. First, the exact needs of the DoC are not known at the time of contracting. Second, the needs over the life of a contract—say five years—are even more highly uncertain. So the government has developed a different format, the multiple-award contract, which means that a single solicitation can result in many awards to different companies. So if you, as a small business, bid on that type of solicitation, you need not win out over everyone. You can be one of several and maybe even many awardees. That's the good news.

The Real Scoop on Multiple Awards

But here's the bad news: winning a multi-award contract typically guarantees you nothing—or almost nothing—and is instead a sort of hunting license—a license to hunt for work. Why? Typically, but not always, there is an award minimum, but that minimum is often very low in relation to the total possible value of the awards under that contract. The award amount could be, say $250 million, and an award minimum something very low, like $100,000. An awardee would be very disappointed with a total award of $100,000, over the say 10-year life of the contract, especially when the company has spent four times that in risk money just to get the contract. So your award, when it's a multiple-award scenario, means what you've won is a license to hunt for work.

What You Provide

What is contained in this type of contract? What are you committing to do as a winner? Typically, in the contract, you provide the customer a schedule of rates and products. For contracts for man-hours of labor, the customer's solicitation includes a list of job categories by function and by skill level, such as Programmer I, Programmer II, Systems Analyst, or System Architect. In response, you then provide the KO with the labor rates for each category. For multi-year contracts, and these ID/IQ contracts typically are, you give labor rates by year (calendar year, government fiscal year, or contract year). This means that if you're awarded a *Task Order* under this contract, you will provide people with those skills and skill levels at no more than the rates stated in the contract for that period. It is always permissible to offer and then provide people at rates lower than those shown on the schedule, but you're not allowed to offer and then provide people at higher rates. The process is similar for products. You can offer to provide products at a lower price than the schedule shows, but not a higher price.

def•i•ni•tion

Once the government has awarded a contract, whether a multiple-award or single-award, and the customer wants a specific task to be done under that contract, the KO issues a request to respond to a **Task Order.** This may be competitive (multiple award) or not (single award).

Advantages of Multiple-Award Contracts

The good news is that once you have a basic contract under a multiple-award solicitation, it's always possible to suggest more categories at a newly provided price. For an example that goes way back, consider the original award for personal computers that may have been given to IBM for their 286 machine. Two years into the contract, no one was buying 286 machines; everyone wanted the 386 machines instead. So all those winners had to do, under the contract modification clause contained in the original contract, was to go back to the government KO and ask for a new *line item* (the 386) with a new price and new performance specifications.

def•i•ni•tion

Contracts contain **line items,** typically in Section B of the solicitation and therefore in the contract. Each line item specifies a specific deliverable (a product or service) and a cost/price associated with it.

Unsolicited Proposals

Another way to get a sole source contract is to give the decision-maker in the agency an unsolicited proposal, usually through the KO, if possible. An unsolicited proposal is one your company creates and submits to the customer but not in response to any specific solicitation.

To be successful with an unsolicited proposal, you should have at least these three things going for you:

- ◆ Technical Discriminator(s) (You're better at this than any other offeror.)

- ◆ Customer Knowledge (You know what the customer has the means and the motivation to buy.)

- ◆ Proposal Knowledge (You know how to discover and communicate the best case.)

Chapters 16, 17, and 18 provide detailed information on how to write a proposal that addresses those three areas. For now, just know that an unsolicited proposal might be the way to go if you've done your homework on what a potential customer needs and can build a good case for why you're the business to meet those needs.

Following are the basic elements of a proposal:

- ◆ Identification of parties

- ◆ Authority to commit

- ◆ Addresses

- ◆ Statement of Work (SOW)

- ◆ Type of contract

- ◆ Relationship of parties

- ◆ Duration of contract

- ◆ Termination

- ◆ Verification of deliveries and liquidation

- ◆ Payment terms and methods

- ◆ Conflicts of interest

- ◆ Rights in data

- ◆ Patent rights

- ◆ Location of work

- ◆ Agreements not to disclose proprietary data

- ◆ Disputes

- ◆ Interpretation of the contract

Make sure any proposal you submit is thoroughly vetted by not only your own contracts manager but also your legal counsel. Failure to do so will certainly get you in trouble, either with program execution or in offering something that cannot really be done the way you propose it.

Your prospects of getting a contract from an unsolicited proposal are greatly enhanced if you have a champion with the customer. Usually, this person has a pressing need and sees your solution as being a good one.

Thirteen Contracting Mistakes to Avoid

If you do not now have any government contracts but are exploring the opportunities in this market, it is entirely possible that one or more of these unlucky thirteen applies to you and your company.

Lack of Detailed Cost Records

Opening your books to the government is the exception rather than the rule. Usually, and especially for small contracts, the government gets all the competitive information it needs and is entitled to through the competitive procurement process. So it's usually not necessary to reveal your cost or your margin. Of course, for larger contracts, especially those involving services, the buyer *is* entitled to see your costs and margins. Don't be afraid to bid on opportunities that don't entail revealing your own costs and margins.

Not Speaking the Language

You can't get past all that stuff that *real* government contractors already know—the jargon, acronyms, contract terms, red tape, and more. Certainly, jargon is involved. But every sub-set of our society has its own "tribal customs" and vocabulary, which are usually easy to get a basic understanding of. Use the glossary of this book to learn the lingo.

Fear That You Won't Get Paid Promptly

That the government is slow in paying is a myth. You worry that you could go broke waiting, but this is absolutely not true. In fact, the government is exemplary in its payment procedures. Yes, before the Prompt Payment Act of 1996, government was notoriously slow in paying. But the Congress realized that the slow-pay policies were counterproductive to encouraging small businesses to be suppliers to the government. So the current law makes it so painful for government agencies to pay in more than 30 days, that it rarely happens now.

Further, a signed government contract is rock-solid collateral to banks. The banks love lending you money until the government pays you. Lenders know you're going to get promptly paid.

Worry About the Competition

You may feel there's too much competition, and skilled competitors at that. This is simply not so. A very large percentage of the smaller opportunities go to the one and only bidder. So you can't win if you don't bid.

Not Knowing Where to Turn for Help

Many sources inside and outside of government are willing and able to help. At the national level, the SBA website (www.sba.gov) offers a great deal of information on how to succeed. And in general, KOs are in the business of encouraging, not discouraging, bidders. At the local level, you can find Procurement Technical Assistance Centers through www.dla.mil.

You've Never Won Before

You've been trying but have never actually gotten a contract award, and you have no idea why. Someone else might be able to say this more politely, but "Shame on you for not knowing why you lost." It's easy enough to find out why—just ask the KO. Also go to the website that had the solicitation and look for "awards." Usually you can find out who won and at what price.

Too Small for Government Work

Some small companies and many one-person or fractional-person companies (those with only part-time help or a single person spread over many different niche markets) actually win government contracts. In fact, within the SBA, there's a specific category of small business called "Very Small Business Concerns." These are businesses with no more than 15 full-time employees during the last three years and average annual receipts less than $1 million.

Caught in the Middle

You may think the small jobs are not worth your while and you can't afford to fund the larger ones. However, remember any contract you win can be profitable. Once you have a contract, you establish some presence and momentum with the government. The government is slow to get started, but it's also slow to make any turns and even slower to turn entirely around. If you treat your government customers with the respect they are due and cultivate those critical personal relationships, history shows that government customers are at least as loyal as commercial ones, and in many cases more loyal.

You're Not Distinctive Enough

Maybe your products are all commodity products. You have nothing to distinguish yourself from many others, and your competition has the market all wrapped up. While it may be true that the KOs already have preferred sources, it's also true that right-minded KOs have the best interests of their government employer in mind and, therefore, consistently seek more competition, new sources of supply, to achieve better quality at a lower price. If you can catch your competition taking a customer for granted and being lazy in fully servicing him, you have an opening to take that business away and make that KO *your* customer.

Not Made in the USA

If your products are made outside the United States, you assume the Buy America Act prohibits the government from buying from you. But just having products made outside the United States is not in and of itself a disqualification. The more than a dozen exemptions to this act are largely common sense and based on the nonavailability of products within the United States. Who would dispute that a government buyer would have a difficult time in obtaining cobra venom from a domestic source? See FAR Section 25 for the details. In addition, as long as your delivered product has at least 51 percent of the cost of the finished item incurred in the United States, Mexico, or Canada, it is *not* considered an imported item.

The Commercial Market Is Just Fine

Maybe the government market has sounded good to you, but you've been putting off getting involved because you're doing just fine in the commercial market. How many of your commercial customers are required, by law, to pay within no more than 30 days? How many often pay on receipt of the approved invoice, instantaneously, via electronic transfer of funds? How many have a sterling credit rating and therefore allow you to go to the bank with rock-solid collateral if you need the money in less than 30 days? Isn't it worth at least trying for government contracts because the government would be such a good customer?

Difficulty Finding Specifications

The government posts the specifications publicly as a part of the solicitation. Do your commercial customers do that, or do they make you guess at the specs? Government business is transparent. Many agencies now are posting such things as travel expense reports, submitted by and paid to their employees. Such transparency is unheard of in the commercial world.

Lack of Experience

You can quickly overcome the lack of experience through getting a small contract at first. Then build up to the larger ones, with a higher buy-in cost and larger pay-offs in winning. No guts, no glory.

The Least You Need to Know

- Small business is really big business.

- Successful small businesses demonstrate staying power and patience.

- Getting yourself qualified as a small business, and then one or more of the special categories of small businesses, opens doors for selling your products and services.

- Explore all available opportunities, including set-asides and sole source contracts.

General Services Administration Schedule Contracts

In This Chapter

- ◆ Understanding GSA and its jargon
- ◆ Reasons you'll want to get on board
- ◆ Registering your company
- ◆ Discovering your place in this huge marketplace
- ◆ Deciding to go it on your own—or not

"The sun never sets on the British Empire." This saying refers to the fact that Britain once had colonies all around the world. So as the earth rotated, the sun continually shone on British territory. Similarly, the sun never sets on the array of opportunities for you to sell your products and services to the federal government (and state and locals, too!) through General Services Administration (GSA) contracts. This set of contracts is without end and (generally) without closing dates.

In this chapter, discover why you should be interested in this way of selling your products to the government, how to register your company as a seller, and how to figure out where you fit in this wide and varied marketplace. Also explore the pros and cons of using your own internal resources to get on the schedules or outsourcing to one of several firms specializing in getting companies on schedules.

Why the General Services Administration?

The General Services Administration (GSA), www.gsa.gov, is what amounts to the government's "designated purchasing agent." GSA buys virtually anything you can imagine and undoubtedly some things you have no idea even exist.

The role of GSA (rarely "the GSA") is to bring order and efficiency to the acquisition of all the products and services the government requires to carry out its mission.

def·i·ni·tion

Indefinite Delivery/Indefinite Quantity (ID/IQ) contracts allow agencies to purchase products and services, using the baseline contract as a starting point. At the time of contract award, the delivery dates and quantities are unknown, but there will surely be some demand for the items listed in the contract.

GSA acquires its products and services through a variety of contracting vehicles. For example, it has helped government agencies of all stripes buy telecommunications services through a series of three long-term *Indefinite Delivery/Indefinite Quantity (ID/IQ)* contracts. These were and are highly prized as they allow the winners an inside track in delivering telecom services. Beware, however, that an ID/IQ contract is just that. The quantities and the delivery dates are indefinite. Therefore, getting an ID/IQ contract is simply a hunting license; it allows you to hunt specific transactions. But note, having a license is much better than not having a license!

If you think that's all GSA is, wait! There's more! GSA is the government's landlord and leases 7,100 buildings for use by various government entities. GSA is also at the forefront of the acquisition of "green" vehicles. So GSA is a lot more than just schedule contracts.

Speaking GSA Jargon

The formal name for this set of contract vehicles is "General Services Administration Schedule Contracts." But you won't hear that mouthful in the halls of any company with success in this area. You may hear GSA or schedule or similar terms. They are also known as Multiple Award Schedules and Federal Supply Schedules, but they all mean the same thing.

Your prospective customers may ask you, "What's your GSA?" "Do you have a GSA?" "Are you on GSA?" These questions are asking if your company can provide your products or services under an existing GSA Schedule Contract.

The fact is that small businesses are attractive not only to the large prime contractors (see Chapter 9 for goals for small business participation) but also to government buyers of all types. Be aware that they usually have their own targets for getting small business participation. The single best way is to "get on GSA."

You'll know you've arrived as a legitimate participant in this way of converting "maybes" into revenue dollars when you can follow the lingo and customs without missing a beat.

Beltway Buzz

Many government agencies—and there are more than 1,200 of them in the federal government—contract for their special needs through their own contracting officers (KOs). For example, the United States Army buys tanks and rifles directly using its own KOs. But for those items used by many agencies, GSA is the preferred purchasing agent.

GSA's Vast Array of Transactions

The variety of transactions under this family of contracts is truly staggering. Imagine you're working at a government installation under a contract with Agency XYZ. As you came into the building this morning, most likely, there was some sort of security, either industrial security or special security, because of the nature of the work at that facility. The guard at the door, who either signed you in or verified that you had a picture badge, is probably hired under a GSA contract. The building is probably leased by GSA. The computer on your desk was probably bought under a GSA Schedule Contract. The telecom services were obtained under a GSA contract. Almost everything in the building was bought under a GSA contract. The variety of products and services is as wide as all outdoors.

Beltway Buzz

The common perception is that most of the deliverables under GSA schedules are products, and although that was once the case, the majority is now for services, not products. GSA has schedules for many different kinds of services, especially technical services.

Here are some facts about the enormous GSA market:

- Total GSA Schedule purchases are now in the $40 billion range.

- The volume of all government purchases, including those through GSA, has been going up steadily for the last decade.

- There's no sign that the pace of increase is slowing down anytime soon. As a matter of national policy, government purchases are headed upward.

- Government contracts (for all the government) are awarded at a rate of 75,000 per day.

Minimal Competition for GSA Contracts

Your competition is often not savvy about operating in the GSA world. Here's a stark statistic: of the approximately 46 million businesses in the United States, only about 400,000 are registered to do business with the government. That's less than 1 percent of total businesses. Compare that with the variety of products the government must buy and the volume with which they must buy them, and you'll likely ask, "Why?"

One reason is that these businesses don't know how good the government can be as a customer. Another reason is that they don't know how to get started. But now you do.

State and Local Governments (S&L), Too!

Getting a GSA schedule has another advantage, which is coming into play more each year as the government opens up its buying power, including quantity discounts, to purchases by other governments. State and local governments account for about 14 percent of the Gross National Product.

Beltway Buzz
Yet another staggering fact should tell you this is a good thing to get into: a lot of contracts are awarded on the basis of only a single offeror. Only one company bid, and that company won! How good is that! The winner didn't have to beat anybody.

State and local government entities are now eligible to purchase from GSA schedule contracts under the Cooperative Purchasing and Disaster Recovery Purchasing programs. If you're selling to S&L, they need to know to review the conditions under which each program may be used. If you're experienced with these restrictions, you can make a real friend with your S&L customer and help him buy from your GSA schedule.

Low Cost and Low Risk with GSA

As if you needed more, one final reason why you need to get into the GSA game is: low cost and low risk. Experienced leaders of small businesses agree that the single best, most cost-effective way to break into the government market is via the GSA schedule route. You can and should try other ways, such as being a supplier to a prime contractor or a subcontractor to a prime contractor. Those other ways can work. But day in and day out, the vehicle of choice of savvy small businesses is the GSA schedule route.

Getting Registered to Do GSA Business

There is a clear path to getting your company registered as one eligible to do business with the government. This list is as of the publication date, so don't be discouraged if the now-current list isn't exactly like this one. "Persistence is the essence of success," so be persistent in getting your company registered. Use the GSA website, which is very user-friendly (once you have the jargon down pat).

To do business with the government, you must first register with the Central Contractor Registration (CCR). Go to www.ccr.gov to begin. You'll be asked to enter a series of numbers to identify yourself. There are seven numbers unique to your company, and you'll need four other numbers which come from a master list of possibilities. A description of these numbers follows.

Numbers from Standard Tables

Let's start with the four numbers you'll choose from a master list for each type of number.

- ◆ **NAICS Codes.** This is the North American Industry Classification System, which is a table of 6-digit numbers that classifies businesses by type. See www. naics.com. For example, if your business is Mobile Food Service, your NAICS Code is 722330. You can easily find your NAICS Code (or codes) by using this website. Write down any codes matching your business; you'll usually have more than one code, but perhaps not.

- ◆ **SBA Size Standards.** This is a table look-up from the SBA site. The size standards are subject to change, so get the current version from the SBA site to verify that your business qualifies as a small business. Do a search for the phrase "size standards," and you'll be directed to a table of size standards by NAICS Code. Verify that the size of your business, by NAICS code, qualifies as a small business. But large or small, carry that information forward.

- **FSC Codes.** These are Federal Supply Classification Codes, and each product and each service has a code. You can find your code by going to the Federal Business Opportunities website (www.fedbizopps.gov or more simply www.fbo. gov). Go to "Advanced Search," and scroll down to "Search by Procurement Classification." Then follow "Additional Information on Classification Codes." These codes are a little more difficult to understand because some are two-digit numbers and some are single alphabetic characters. Scroll down until you find the classification or classifications applying to your business. Record these for later use, along with the two other numbers you've already found.

- **SIC Codes**. These are Standard Industrial Classification Codes, which is an older system of business classifications that will eventually be replaced by the NAICS Codes. The Occupational Health and Safety Administration (OSHA) maintains this list, which is found at www.osha.gov. Visit this site, do a search for "SIC", and you'll find the list. You'll need to find your business in these codes, also. As with the NAICS Codes, record all codes applying to your business. You must have at least one to complete your registration.

Numbers Unique to Your Company

Now here are the seven (whew!) numbers you'll need to register with the CCR.

- **DUNS.** This is the Data Universal Numbering System. For this number, either call 1-866-705-5711 or get one from the website: www.ccr.gov.

- **TIN.** This is your Taxpayer Identification Number. If you're a sole proprietor, this will be your Social Security Number (SSN). If you're incorporated, it will be the number given to you by the Internal Revenue Service when you first formed your company.

- **TPIN.** This is your Trading Partners Identification Number. The TPIN is a confidential number issued by the CCR of the Department of Defense and assigned to organizations that already are or intend to be contractors to the federal government. You are consistently advised to treat the TPIN as if it were a password and not reveal it to others not directly involved in your business operations.

- ◆ **MPIN.** This Marketing Partners Identification Number is a password you create yourself; it is 9 digits long, with at least one alphabetic character and at least one numeric character. As with the TPIN, do not reveal this to others not directly involved with your business operations.

- ◆ **CAGE Code.** This is your Commercial And Government Entity Code. The Defense Logistics Information Service (DLIS) has sole responsibility for assigning and maintaining the CAGE Code Master File. The CAGE Code is a five-position code that identifies contractors doing business with the federal government, NATO member nations, and other foreign governments. The CAGE Code is used to support a variety of mechanized systems throughout the government and provides for a standardized method of identifying a given facility at a specific location. The code may be used for a facility clearance, a pre-award survey, automated bidders lists, identification of debarred bidders, fast pay processes, etc.

- ◆ **ORCA Registration.** This is your Online Representations and Certifications. Thankfully, this electronic submission allows you to be awarded contracts through submitting individual representations and certifications documents. This type of representations and certifications is typically required in response to Requests for Proposals. Using the ORCA means that you don't have to submit those "reps and certs" each time. But this does not relieve you of the responsibility of living up to the certifications you make.

- ◆ **CCR Registration.** You'll get this number at the end of the registration process; safely record it somewhere that's always accessible.

Registering with the CCR

First get all eleven numbers from the previous section, because you'll need all of them to complete your registration.

Then go to the CCR website, www.ccr.gov. Begin the registration process by following the instructions on the home page. At press time, this first step was in the upper left corner and labeled "Start New Registration." From here, follow the clear instructions the site provides.

Government Insider _____

There's good news in the registration process. You need not complete the entire process at one sitting. If you get called away by a fire drill or simply run out of time at a single sitting, you have chances along the way to suspend your registration and resume at that point at a later session, which is good to know. The registration system is forgiving of your dropping connectivity. You can resume later, and pick up where you previously left off.

Finding Your Niche in the GSA World

With all this volume and all these different products and services, how can you ever find your niche? The short answer is the same as the answer to, "How do you get to Carnegie Hall?" Practice, Practice, Practice.

There is no substitute for experience. No matter how long you sit and watch other companies be successful in getting government contracts, you'll never get your own unless you try. Get off the sidelines, and get into the game. A very wise person in this business, someone who's forgotten more about government contracting than most of us will ever know, observed, "You can't win unless you bid." Take that as a serious, if completely obvious, observation.

Begin by getting registered as a government contractor, as described earlier. Start exploring the www.fbo.gov website for opportunities. Search by geography; search by NAICS Code; search by agency; and focus on an agency you think could use your products or services.

Talk to other companies (preferably not your direct competitors) and see how they have been successful. Offer to share your knowledge in exchange for the same from them. Find a company you're comfortable dealing with and share the one-time expenses of getting started.

Red Flag _____

If you're going to "partner" with another company, know enough about that company to feel confident that you practice the same ethics. Don't wake up one day and realize you're somehow associated with a company of notoriously bad ethics. You can easily be tarred with the same brush that blackens your partner.

In-Source or Out-Source?

This last question is a thorny one. Do you rely only upon in-house resources to obtain your GSA schedule contracts, or do you cry uncle and turn over at least part of your marketing efforts to outside sources?

Appendix B contains a selected list of the providers of services. Among those providers you'll find the "Assist with GSA Schedule Contracts." Remember to rely on prudence when selecting any company from this list. Specialists providing assistance in getting GSA schedules, who have been in business for a while, have demonstrated value to their customers. They could not be in business after 10 or 15 years unless they've earned their fees. Whether those same companies can earn their fees for you is for you to decide. Nevertheless, do your homework before paying any fees, and let the buyer beware!

The Least You Need to Know

- ◆ For small businesses, GSA schedules are an excellent entry point to government business.

- ◆ Getting "on GSA" is a necessary condition, but it's only a hunting license so you can start hunting.

- ◆ When going through the complicated process of registration, remember all your work will pay off and that all current contractors have had to go through the same registration process.

- ◆ Getting your company registered is a good first step, but it's only a first step; you must then put your opportunity finders into high gear.

Part 4

Kicking Off the Proposal Process

It's time to dive in and develop a proposal. Starting with strategy development, you learn the tricks of the trade for creating proposals that will knock the government evaluators' socks off. This part then turns from the strategic to the tactical with an overview of the documents you'll need to create, find, and store and tips on setting up a proposal center to house all these documents and the people who create them. Then you'll learn what to do in the first five days after setting up shop to ensure a smooth proposal development process in the many days to follow.

The Strategy Behind Your Responses

In This Chapter

- ◆ The rules you can't break
- ◆ Offering solutions, not just responses
- ◆ Getting the team's and top management's commitment
- ◆ Current trends in procurements

As with any major undertaking, starting with a strategy for winning is a critical first step toward a win, so that's why this chapter is all about basic principles for creating winning responses to customers' solicitations. Here, you'll find a list of rules you must follow to learn what to do and not to do. You'll also learn how to offer a solution that can make a difference to the customer, rather than just going through the motions of a response. And you'll learn what to expect of the leadership and management of your team and how trends in the procurement process affect your strategy.

The Rules You Shouldn't Bend or Break

Getting government contracts is much easier if you know and obey the rules the government contracting industry has established. Just as a failure to obey traffic laws has consequences, failure to obey the rules of government contracting has consequences, so let's look at the absolute rules you must follow in creating your response to a government solicitation.

Answer the Mail, or You Might Fail

The mail is the solicitation that gives you directions for how to answer. You've probably already learned the life lesson that following directions will get you far. Well, contracting is no exception. For example, when the solicitation has four sections numbered one through four, your solution must conform to that same order. Reordering your solution may seem like common sense to you, but the customer may see it as nonsense.

One of my former bosses had a great analogy for this: "When you come into my house, don't rearrange the furniture. You may not like the furniture, and you may have better furniture in *your* house, but that's irrelevant. Don't rearrange the customer's furniture either. Rearranging can confuse the scorers and can't improve your ranking." The customer evaluators' scorecards, used to compare your solution with the solicitation, are in the same order as the solicitation, *not* your "better" order.

Speak the Customer's Language

Use the customer's terminology rather than substituting your own. If the customer's term is "Management Volume," don't use a "Management Approach" and vice versa. There may be no significant difference between the two terms, and either could apply, but the customer sets the rules, and you have to play by them.

Government Insider

In proposal writing, creativity doesn't have a place. You can get creative with how you develop a unique solution and build a case for why your solution is the best, but when it comes to the format of your response, don't get creative, and keep your writing focused and clear.

Consistent terminology is also important when describing the roles of people in your organizational charts. Use titles that reflect the function of that person in the program you are proposing. For example, if Clyde Clodd is a senior scientist in your organization who is going to be your program manager, use "Program Manager" as Clyde's title, not "Senior Scientist." The internal title doesn't mean much to the customer when evaluating Clyde's ability to do the Program Manager's job.

Here's another example. Let's say the customer's solicitation clearly states the desire for a product featuring a certain level of quality and reliability. Translated into the automobile arena, let's say the customer wants to buy a Buick. Your winning solution should demonstrate that you know about Buicks and you have a plan (included in your proposal) to deliver the best Buick possible at a competitive price. Nowhere should your proposal speak to the advantages of either a Chevrolet or a Cadillac, which the customer doesn't want to buy.

Red Flag _____

Just because you shouldn't use internal titles in your proposal organization charts (unless they're relevant to the project) doesn't mean you should hide someone's internal role. A senior scientist's credentials may be relevant to the customer, so be sure to include a description of why you chose that scientist to be program manager.

Have the Customer's Idea, Not a Better Idea

In your solution, at all costs avoid describing something that doesn't fit the customer's wants. If you took the opportunity to submit a draft solicitation or other pre-competition customer document or briefing (see Chapter 7), then you've already had your chance to put forward a different technical or management solution. Your immediate task now is to show that you understand the customer's problem and that you have a plan to achieve a solution to that problem with the minimal (or at least bondable) amount of risk.

Anything else offered is not only an example of technical (or managerial) arrogance but is also unlikely to be accepted by the customer's evaluators. The time for you to put forth a somewhat different solution is as the winner, not as an offeror.

Imagine you are a government evaluator and an offeror submits a solution radically

Government Insider _____

When all else fails, discuss risk—all three kinds: technical, schedule, and cost. Evaluators need to know how you're going to manage the risks you've identified. See Chapter 16 for a detailed discussion of risks.

different from the terms of the solicitation. The solution is clearly superior to those of the other offerors. What would you do? Would you scrap the entire procurement and start again, giving the other offerors an opportunity to resubmit their offers using those new specifications? Not likely. The most likely course for the evaluation team is to reject the radically different offer as being nonresponsive. That offer shows how to solve the problem, but it's not what you, the customer, have said throughout the solicitation.

Speak to the Customer, Not to Your Team

Make the customer the center of attention. Beginning every section or subsection of your proposal with, for example, "The Acme solution gives …" puts the focus on your team. Instead, begin sections with, "The (Agency's) requirements drive our solution to be …"

Another way you can break this rule is by putting the names and functions of people in your organization who have no relationship to the customer into the organization chart. Listing the business development department is an example of making an internal proposal reviewer happy (proud to see his or her own name shown in the organization chart as the Vice President of Business Development), but that position is not likely to have relevance to any customer during the execution of the contract.

Know the Score

The customer's Source Selection Evaluation Board (or similar team of evaluators) compares the incoming proposals with the score sheets that the KO or someone representing the KO has provided to them. These score sheets come directly from the solicitation and combine the elements of the three major solicitation sections: C (Statement of Work); L (Instructions to Offerors); and M (Evaluation Factors for Award).

These are the traditional solicitation elements. Not sure we need to deviate from them. However, today we are seeing solicitations that do not have the traditional sections C, L, and M. In fact, we are receiving SORs (statement of requirements) or SOOs (statement of objectives) that do not have separate sections C, L, or M.

The *theory* of evaluations is that the evaluators judge each proposal against the score sheet and evaluate each of the incoming proposals on its own merits rather than against the other proposals. The theory has been known to break down as the evaluation process devolves into a head-to-head competition among or between offers. If this is to your advantage, you may be able to induce such a comparison through the inclusion of anti-competition themes. For example, assume you're in competition with a certain known competitor. You know your competitor is going to propose a Windows-based operating system (OS), so you propose a Macintosh operating system, OS-X. Each of these systems meets the specifications without question. But you know that Mac OS-X has several additional features at no additional cost that are not included in the evaluation criteria, and that these features are not available under a Windows-based OS. Further, you know these extra features are of great value to the customer. So a strict interpretation of the solicitation instructions does not require you to include a discussion of those features in your proposal. But it's certainly optional for you to include the advantages of those extra features.

Now here's the tough judgment call: do you use valuable page space to do so or just ignore your advantage? If you do include a discussion of those features, it casts doubt on the competitor's solution and could cause the evaluators to favor your solution. It's a judgment call, but I usually favor including it if you can spare the pages.

There are almost as many scoring methodologies as there are contracting offices in the government. Buyers tailor their scoring processes to fit their own needs and biases. So be aware that the scoring process shown here is only an illustration.

A Typical Scoring Process

The customer's score sheets should not be a mystery to any experienced proposal process person. This is typically not an issue. However, there can be, and often are, subtle spins on "what counts as good" to that customer. These considerations often correspond to the "hot buttons" for this particular customer.

Adjectival ratings (This is from an Army document.)

Rating	Color	Score
Outstanding	Dark Blue (A)	3.5 to 4.0
Excellent	Purple (B)	2.5 to 3.49
Good	Green (C)	1.5 to 2.49
Marginal	Yellow (D)	0.5 to 1.49
Unacceptable	Red (F)	0.0 to .49

Giving Customers Solutions Instead of Responses

The industry standard term for your answer to the solicitation is "response." We use this term throughout the book to conform to industry standards, but a better term to use is "solution." A solution is what the customer is seeking. A solution goes beyond a response, telling how your company plans to provide what the customer wants to buy. Here's a good test: if what you've written to the customer does not read like a solution, then you probably have a response. Go back and rewrite it, reconsider the text, and restate it as a true solution.

Getting at What the Customer Wants

In responding to government solicitations, the proposal team must determine what the customer wants to see in the proposal and thus really wants to buy. Here are some considerations in formulating the proposal:

- The members of the customer's organization likely have more than one point of view, more than one preference, and more than one agenda. The ones that matter most are the ones actually *participating* in the proposal evaluation, so finding out who they are and what their interests are can help you create a winning response.

> **Red Flag**
>
> Using previously submitted texts from your company's files of previous proposals can be a helpful timesaver, but don't make your proposal too boilerplate. Avoid a quick cut-and-paste, and instead take time to tailor the materials to fit the solution required for *this* competition.

- People in your organization bringing you information will interpret the client differently—project managers, business developers, executives, and others all come with a different bias. The request for proposal (RFP) must, by law and regulation, tell you what the customer wants, but the evaluators have a hand in writing it. This means that what the customer asks for is not what the evaluators actually want.

◆ Assuming the RFP is accurate, it may be incomplete. It's not unusual to see RFPs with extremely detailed specifications for computer equipment that give no clue whether the client is trying to centralize IT management at headquarters or empower its field offices. You might get a different answer depending on whether you talk to someone at headquarters or at a field office. But the opinions that count are those of the evaluators. Getting the wrong opinion can lead to your offering the wrong solution.

A major reason why you should talk with the customer before solicitation release is that the client may not talk to you at all once the RFP hits the street. If they do answer your questions, you can be sure it won't be on a level that provides real insight. To effectively give the evaluators what they want, you must have a real understanding about the client's environment, goals, and agendas.

In the vast majority of proposals I have worked on, the proposal team desperately wanted to give the evaluators exactly what they wanted. Giving them what *you* want them to have is a recipe for losing, and most teams understand that. The problem is that knowing what the customer wants requires insight above and beyond what is in the RFP. The only way to gain this insight is to understand your client—what are their goals, what problems do they face, do they have an internal consensus or competing factions, do they have preferences or bias, do they have constraints they have to work within, standards to comply with, or anything else that may affect their decision and may or may not be in the RFP?

If the solicitation has just been released and you've never worked with the customer before, your chances of getting this kind of insight are slim. Therefore, your company's job is to get to know the customers well before the solicitation release. Using the considerations, develop a list of questions, submit them to the KO, and study carefully the KO's responses. When the solicitation is released, you can look for ways to demonstrate your insight and stand out from the pack.

The Role of Top Management

You know from Chapter 6 that top management (TM) ought to be involved at more than just a figurehead level and that you need to find ways to engage TM in your proposals. This person (or group of persons if a committee is holding this role) is singularly important to winning. The number-one reason for losing competitions is the lack of TM involvement in the proposal creation process. Getting and keeping TM committed is of the utmost importance.

Why is TM's support and involvement so critical?

- Only TM has the ability and authority to commit the critical resources, at critical times, to this effort.

- A famous former boss said, "I can't solve your problem if I don't know about it." TM can solve major problems only if TM knows about the problem.

- We've all had at least a few bosses, including some in TM, who were less than stellar. But the general rule is that people in TM positions are there because they are *good* people—intelligent, resourceful, and knowledgeable.

- Because of the position of responsibility, TM has knowledge and perspectives that their staff simply does not have. When such knowledge and perspectives are truly important, the TM can make a unique contribution to winning.

- In addition to helping the proposal team create the winning proposal, TM can help influence the customer's evaluation of your proposal if the customer's perception of TM is positive.

There are some specific ways you can keep TM engaged in the process. Invite and encourage TM to visit the regularly scheduled meetings to see, firsthand, the issues and activities of the staff. They don't have to come to every meeting, but showing up occasionally is an important demonstration of support. When you create early versions of your response, show these to TM for their review and feedback. And if no other mechanism is effective, send regular notes to TM on the highlights of the good and bad events in the life of the proposal team.

Getting Commitment from All Team Members

Have you heard the story about the hen and the pig passing the church on a Saturday morning? They see a sign for "Bacon and Egg Breakfast." The hen suggests they go in and help out. The pig refuses, saying, "I don't mind making a contribution, but my commitment is a lot greater than yours!"

So the question is, how committed are your team members? Commitment is an often misused word. For example, marketing materials, sales brochures, and formal letters from TM to government officials may claim that your company is "committed" to a certain type of work or a certain program. But unless accompanied by hard evidence of a real commitment, such claims are just that—claims. Avoid the word commitment unless you can provide proof.

Real commitments are made real by tangible, verifiable actions. See the entries on the left. Anything else (see the entries on the right) are not verifiable, and are therefore of far less value to the proposal team.

Commitments vs. Understandings

Best	Not Good
Formal	Informal
Written	Verbal
Acknowledged	Sent
Negotiated	Imposed
Specific	General
Public	Private
Recent (or reverified)	Ancient
Current Management	Previous Management
Mutually Beneficial	Just Fulfills a Promise

Recent Procurement Developments

The landscape of getting government contracts has changed drastically in the decades I've been doing this. So to craft an effective strategy for your response, it's important to understand recent developments in procurement.

Multiple-Award Schedules

One significant trend is the increased use of relatively broad, multiple-award schedules. The General Services Administration (GSA) awards the most common multiple-award contracts. The formal name for these contracts is "GSA Schedule Contracts," and the casual names are "GSA Schedules" or just "getting on GSA." They all mean the same thing. GSA Schedule Contracts are discussed in more detail in Chapter 12.

This type of contract fits best the case of the government wanting to acquire a spectrum of products, usually over a long period of time and when there are many qualified suppliers. One good example is the GSA contact for telecommunications services.

In April 2007, GSA awarded Networx Universal contracts to three (of four submitting) offerors. These contracts are for 10 years and have a total estimated value in the tens of billions of dollars. They include about 40 different services, covering virtually all the possible government requirements in telecommunications for the length of the contract. These contracts were highly competitive, and each of the offerors spent millions of dollars to secure a contract for this work.

There are many other examples of multiple-award contracts. The Department of Commerce has awarded multiple winners to contracts in the NETCENTS series. Instead of the three winners of the GSA Networx Universal contract, there were more than 40 winners for NETCENTS. Each "win" of a contract was in effect a "hunting license," the right to market to the ultimate customers using that contract as a vehicle. This allows the government to acquire goods and services in a much more efficient way as compared with a discrete solicitation for each and every requirement.

Typically, the KOs at, for example, the Department of Commerce, release a solicitation for responses under that contract. These solicitations are called "task orders" and go to either all awardees or often a small subset of those awardees—those judged as qualified to perform the work described in the task order. The resulting winner of the task order competition then performs the work under a task order. These awards are an addendum to the master multiple-award contract.

Your interest in this type of contract is twofold. The good news is that, if you can get a multiple-award contract, you are an eligible offeror for a long period of time, often years.

The bad news is that, if you are NOT an awardee, you are mostly shut out of that market (at least as a prime contractor) for that same length of time. Your only chance at that point, and it may be a good one for small businesses with a strong niche market, is as a subcontractor.

Longer Terms for Contracts

The Budget and Accounting Act of 1921, which established the Bureau of the Budget (since 1970, the Office of Management and Budget), held a tight rein on government spending. It recognized and enforced the Constitutional requirement for congressional authorization (Article I, Section 7, 8, and 9) of any funds expended.

Until the late 1970s, the government typically limited contracts to a single fiscal year. Multi-year contracts were rare. However, this restriction became increasingly burdensome and costly because effective program management required commitments over many fiscal years. Therefore, government contracts now are typically for many years, and multi-year authorizations and appropriations are used where warranted. Such multi-year contracts remain subject to the Congress' annual authorization and appropriation processes and to oversight by the Office of Management and Budget within the Executive Office of the President.

Increased Use of Electronic Submissions

The days of 20 hard copies of a 500-page technical volume and 15 hard copies of a 200-page management volume are largely (but not entirely!) gone. Governments are increasingly taking advantage of the Internet's power and allowing responses to be submitted electronically. You can often submit by e-mail, with proposal documents attached, and increasingly can even post your proposal documents directly onto a secure customer website. Electronic submission is a great time and money saver for both the offerors and the government evaluators.

Increased Reliance on Oral Presentations

Offerors are increasingly requiring that respondents make oral presentations as a way of making final decisions among offerors.

See the discussion of the use of oral presentations. See also Appendix B for sources for fee-for-service help with your oral presentations. See also a discussion in Chapter 6 of the government use of oral presentation on making award decisions.

The Least You Need to Know

 ◆ Make real solutions, not just canned responses from previous proposals, the heart of your proposal.

 ◆ Know and obey the rules for replying to solicitations, especially those on following directions and using the same terminology as the customer.

 ◆ Include anti-competition materials that cast doubt on the competitors' solutions.

 ◆ Get and keep top management involved in the process of proposal creation.

Proposal Management Documents

In This Chapter

♦ Contents of the proposal plan and attachments

♦ Core documents that go into every proposal plan

♦ Noncore documents—the optional parts of your proposal plan

♦ Customer documents

♦ Documents from the public domain

Now that you have a strategy to guide your response, your next step is to launch the formal proposal creation process. The proposal documents you create will communicate your response to the customer. It is your strategically crafted case for why your company offers the best solution. This chapter focuses on the documents that support the proposal effort, not the actual proposal itself. Those are the technical, management, and cost/price volumes found in Chapters 16, 17, and 18. These documents are the ones you need to develop at the start of the effort so you can effectively and efficiently develop the proposal.

Here, you learn about developing a proposal plan that serves as a guidepost of sorts for the proposal itself. A proposal plan usually has several attachments, some of which are provided as samples in Appendix C. You also learn about documents you need to find in your company's records or create, as well as materials you get from the customer or the public domain that you need to keep.

What Goes in the Proposal Plan and Attachments

The proposal plan is the first formal document your team should create because it is the control mechanism for your proposal team's activities. Without a proposal plan, you'll surely get chaos.

Government Insider

The best way to manage all the documents connected with a proposal effort is to use a file-sharing system on your company's intranet. SharePoint is one common application. (See www.microsoft.com/sharepoint.) Others are on the market, but SharePoint seems to be one of the preferred solutions.) This enables you to control access to your documents; you certainly don't want your competitors to know what you're doing.

The proposal plan is a living document that evolves during the proposal creation process so don't feel you have to get it completely right the first time. As you create the plan, you'll make estimates and wild guesses and sometimes even enter incorrect information without realizing it, all of which you can replace as you go along with the latest-and-greatest data and ideas.

Red Flag

Not keeping up with your proposal plan, that is forgetting to make changes to it or believing that you're just too busy to do so, is a serious mistake. A proposal effort is too complex and too expensive to take a fly-by-the-seat-of-your-pants approach. "Ready-fire-aim" is no way to run a proposal effort.

This proposal plan outline gives you a high-level view of what should go into the plan.

Proposal Plan

TABLE OF CONTENTS

Section	Title
0.0	Opportunity overview
0.1	Philosophy of the plan to capture this opportunity
	0.1.1 The procurement
	0.1.2 Your win strategy
0.2	Description of the customer
0.3	The proposal team
1.0	Introduction
1.1	Purpose and scope of this plan
1.2	Scope and importance of this program to the customer
1.3	Time as a proposal team asset
1.4	Kickoff meeting
1.5	Strategies and winning themes

Solicitation-driven plans and schedules (2-7)

Section	Title
2.0	Proposal volumes plan
2.1	Organization of the proposal
2.2	Individual assignments—proposal team
2.3	Proposal's numbering system and physical appearance
3.0	Topical outlines
3.1	First-level detail
3.2	Second-level detail
3.3	Third-level detail

continues

continued

4.0	Proposal development plans and schedules
4.1	Time schedule
4.2	Resource application
5.0	Resource requirements of proposal development
5.1	Summary of internal resources
5.2	Summary of technical services resources (outsource resources)
6.0	Work breakdown structure (WBS)
7.0	Solicitation-to-proposal cross-reference matrix

General-purpose materials (8-9)

8.0	Style guide
9.0	Training objectives—kick-off training course(s)
9.1	Training course performance standards
9.2	Schedule for training of team members

Attachments:

(End of Table of Contents)

To bring the proposal plan outline to life so that you can envision how your own team's might look, we provide the elements of the proposal plan, and discuss each item.

Once you create your plan, you're ready to pull together the core documents to support it.

The Must Haves of a Proposal

The core documents are materials every proposal, without exception, must have. They form the heart of the proposal plan because they play critical roles in keeping you on track and focused for a successful proposal effort. You'll see how this plays out as you read about each of the five documents, which are:

- 01 Contact List
- 02 Proposal Development Schedule

- ◆ 03 Executive Summary

- ◆ 04 Proposal Drivers

- ◆ 05 Proposal Outline and Responsibility Assignment Matrix (RAM)

Each of these attachments has a two-digit index number at the far left. These numbers are very useful, so retain them in your own work. One large advantage to using these numbers is that the file structure within the folders lines up automatically, from 01 to 23. Any index numbers that are missing will show up immediately, making quality control easy.

You should use these document labels consistently, including the leading index numbers, across all the proposals you create. Consistency enforces discipline on your proposal teams and increases the efficiency of the teams.

01 Contact List

The contact list is a list of all proposal team members. It is vital that each member of the proposal team, including any and all sub-contractors, be on this list. Each member listing should have the company name (if more than one company is on the team), the individual's name, their proposal team function (don't use company job titles; use proposal team role title), work phone number, mobile phone number, home phone number (if you can get it), and e-mail address.

Government Insider

Keep the five core documents on file after you complete a proposal submission so that the next time you begin a new proposal effort you don't have to create the documents from scratch.

02 Proposal Development Schedule

This document shows the milestones for each of the important events in the development schedule. Show milestones and not activities. If you show milestones, the activities will be clear. Show both historical (that is, achieved) milestones to put those in perspective to members who may be joining the team late and to show how many steps you've already taken to get to this point. The table that follows shows a sample proposal development schedule.

Sample Proposal Development Schedule

Milestone	Players	Date
Draft RFP	Customer	
Solicitation Analysis, DRFP	All	
Identification of Long Lead Items	Proposal Manager/ Capture Manager	
Bid/No-Bid Review #3; Positive "bid" decision	TM and selected Proposal Team	
Finalization of Nondisclosure Agreements with team members	All, led by Contracts Manager	
Request, Accomplishment of Open Bid & Proposal (B&P) Account	Each company	
Last round of pre-RFP contact with Government	All	
Creation of Detailed Proposal Plan	Proposal Manager	
Submission of "Comments" on DRFP	Contracts Manager, for all the team	
Kickoff Meeting version, Proposal Plan	Proposal Manager	
Kickoff Meeting (if resources make this possible)	Proposal Manager	
Responsibility Assignment Matrix, with page targets	Proposal Manager	
Just In Time Training: Solicitation Analysis, Proposal Writing, Evaluations Teams	Proposal Manager	
Black Hat Team	Black Hat Chair and Members	
Green Team Evaluation— Cost/Price Alternatives	Green Team Chair and Members	

Milestone	Players	Date
Consider Requesting Extension	TM and Proposal Team	
Selection of Evaluation Teams' Members, Chairs	Proposal Manager and others	
Final RFP	Customer	
Solicitation Analysis	All	
Pre-Proposal Conference	Hosted by the customer, for all prospective bidders	
Pink Team (mixture of storyboards, outlines, and text)	Pink Team Chair and members	
Red Team	Red Team Chair and Members	
Purple Team	Your TM and subcontractors' TM	
Red Team Recovery	Proposal Team	
Team Regrouping and Planning	Proposal Team	
Conference call on Management Plan, Staffing Plan	Proposal Team	
Gold Team Review	Gold Team Chair and members	
Pricing Review	TM, with selected others	
Final sign-off by Top Management and release to Production for completion	TM	
Production at Which Location?	Production	
Delivery of Proposal Documents to Customer	Capture Manager; Contracts Manager	
Award	Customer	
Contract Start	The Program Team	
Victory Party	Everyone Involved!	

The last two entries in your schedule, the contract start date and the victory party date, are important. Never put out a proposal development schedule without both a contract start date (probably just an estimate) and a date for the victory party, even though these two dates may seem a long way off and might never even come to pass. But always put out a schedule that plans for success!

03 Executive Summary

The only document in the proposal plan that is likely to be something you'll also hand over to the customer with your final proposal submission is the *executive summary*.

def•i•ni•tion

The **executive summary** reviews your solution and communicates with the executive level within your customer. This answers your customer's implicit question, "Why should I award this contract to you?" It also communicates with your proposal team and helps the team involve TM in the process.

Some solicitations require an executive summary. In that case, you must follow the instructions of the solicitation and deliver the summary exactly as required. However, more often, there is no specific requirement for an executive summary, but it's a good idea to create one anyway both for your internal use and to submit to the customer. A well-constructed, communicative executive summary serves three purposes:

◆ Its primary purpose is to have a positive influence on the customer's decision-maker(s). It builds your case to help them understand why *you* should win the competition.

◆ It focuses your own top management on the task—helping them get a handle on the effort so they can see their role in helping to build and communicate the case.

◆ It communicates the most important aspects of the competition to the proposal team, including any subcontractors.

To create an executive summary, you can use templates from other proposals, archived photos or other visuals, action captions to show why you've included a text or visual in this document, and anticompetition themes wherever possible. Do not use any anti-competition themes you're unsure about.

Beltway Buzz

Photos are a powerful element of your submission, but if you are not already doing the work of this contract—you're not the incumbent—you may wonder how you're going to submit photos of your people doing the work of this customer. Well, you can't; instead use photos of your folks doing similar work for similar customers.

Further, if the solicitation *does* call for an executive summary, you can use the following outline to create something with a different name so as not to confuse the customer with two documents having the same name. Call it "Solution Overview" or "Our Commitment to (the customer)" or something creative fitting that specific opportunity.

Perhaps you'll never actually formally deliver this version to the customer as a part of the proposal, but you may still have an opportunity to use it with the customer, subject to the rule that everything be given to the customer through the customer KO.

The following list shows the typical format of an executive summary. All elements listed here may not be right for your proposal as this is only a recommended checklist. This list of components is just illustrative and not definitive. It is a starting point for your really creative people to build you one for a specific opportunity.

1. Cover page

   Features customer's logo (obtain permission from customer for use) and photographs or other representations of your people performing the customer's work.

   Red Flag

   Always obtain the permission of your customer to use its logo in your proposal. Some customers, especially those in the intelligence community, are very sensitive about such use.

2. Inside cover

   Lists the four to seven best themes of your solution and case. The inside front cover is a good place to answer the question "Why us?"

3. Commitment letter

   Combined with the cover page and the inside cover, addresses the important discriminators—particularly good anticompetition themes—without lapsing into meaningless, generalized sales slogans.

4. Schedule for Delivery of Products (Program Schedule)

    Shows deliverables, de-emphasizes activities, contains enough detail to demonstrate technical competence.

    Ideally, provides the customer with a better program summary, using a powerful graphic, than is available from any other source.

5. Organization Charts

    Reinforces the positive name and face recognition you've built; shows simplicity of reporting relationships; speaks to the customer's wants, not your own internal organization. Simple is better.

6. Product Flow Diagrams

    Shows, using visuals, that you really know the sequence of steps occurring in delivering the customer's products.

7. Material Addressing Customer's Known "Hot Buttons"

    Overcomes any uncertainties you know the customer has about dealing with your organization, such as accomplishing the task on time and within budget. Re-enforces the idea that you understand what the customer really wants to buy.

04 Proposal Drivers

As covered in Chapter 8, proposal drivers are a topic in your early strategy meetings when you discuss the opportunity and the possibility that your company will become a candidate for bidding. This document has four simple questions about your solution. If you can give good answers to each of these four questions, you'll likely be able to build a strong case for a contract award. If you have partial or weak answers, you must either take steps to improve your answers or seriously consider whether you can create a winning solution.

05 Proposal Outline and Responsibility Assignment Matrix (RAM)

This document not only contains the outline of your proposal, as driven by the Section L instructions, but also assigns the responsibilities for each piece of the outline to an individual. (This applies when there really is a Section L. If the solicitation does not have a Section L, then substitute whatever instructions provided that dictate how your proposal must be organized.)

Make these assignments as specific as possible, to individuals rather than to organizations or groups of individuals. Proposal management should have a single point of first-line responsibility for each piece of your solution.

This document is perhaps the single most important one in the attachments to your proposal plan. This matrix accomplishes three distinct, but related, purposes:

♦ Demonstrates that your proposal, when submitted, is in fact compliant with the solicitation;

♦ Gives an outline of your proposal, fully conforming to and compliant with the solicitation;

♦ Details just who, by individual, carries first-line responsibility for that section of the proposal and how many pages you have allocated for that part of your solution.

To develop this outline and matrix, you'll need to know the nitty-gritty details about the various sections of the solicitation—how a solicitation is typically structured and what it's asking for. See Chapter 14 for introduction to this material and then details in Chapters 16, 17, and 18.

Noncore Documents of Your Proposal Plan

Noncore documents are optional ones depending on what's needed for a specific opportunity. This list, in rough order of importance from most important to least, gives all the noncore documents in the proposal plan. The importance is always a matter of judgment and taste, and therefore the right answer varies from solicitation to solicitation. For example, for some solicitations, the Commitment Letter is very important, which moves it up the chain. For others, perhaps the Hot Buttons rises above its normal rank.

In this list, the items with an asterisk (*) are those derived from the solicitation. The content of all others is the proposal team's choice.

♦ 06 Action Items

♦ 07 Evaluation Factors for Award*

♦ 08 Roles and Responsibilities

- ◆ 09 Asking Questions and Log of Q&A (Questions and Answers)

- ◆ 10 Past Performance Template*

- ◆ 11 Kick-Off Meeting Agenda

- ◆ 12 Call-In Process

- ◆ 13 Formatting*

- ◆ 14 Conventions and Ground Rules

- ◆ 15 Customer Hot Buttons

- ◆ 16 Commitment Letter

- ◆ 17 Transmittal letter

- ◆ 18 Fact Sheet

- ◆ 19 Resumé Template*

Note that four of these noncore documents are driven largely by the solicitation. These are the attachments indicated by an asterisk (*). They must appear in the proposal plan because (sadly) no matter how many times proposal managers ask, request, cajole, entreat, beg, or threaten some members of the proposal team to read the important sections of the solicitation, that proverbial 10 percent fails to get the message. Including them or excluding them is a judgment call by the proposal management team.

06 Action Items

The action item list tracks the items the proposal team needs to resolve. It is a living document that changes every day. And it's the main document supporting the proposal team's *daily stand-up meeting*.

def•i•ni•tion

Proposal teams usually have regular—often daily—short meetings of all team members, referred to as **daily stand-up meetings**. "Stand-up" emphasizes that the meetings should be short enough that the attendees remain standing (but they can sit if they wish!), ready to leave as soon as the meeting is over.

The action list has seven columns:

- **Index numbers**   Start with number one and count up to however many you need. As the team identifies issues for the list, use the next available index number. The list has two parts: open items and closed items. An open item is closed at the resolution of that issue (that is, you get an answer to the question). Then the person with version control (typically the proposal manager or perhaps the capture manager) moves that entire row below the line into the closed part. That way, only the open items remain at the top, highly visible, yet you have a complete record of all those issues you've closed. It's very handy when new people join the team because the new individuals can see where the team has been and what they have accomplished.

- **Issue**   These are always in the form of a question. Issues not in question form, such as "order paint," are not as amenable to be resolved as in the form of a question, such as, "When can we confirm that the Sky Blue Orange paint we need has been ordered from our supplier?"

- **Raised by**   The item shows the name of the person raising the issue. This is important because that person and only that person can declare the issue closed (unless for some reason that person redelegates the authority to close it).

- **Assigned to**   You assign the action (that is, first-line responsibility for answering that question) to one individual. Group assignments usually don't work here. You want one person to do the job. As soon as there is more than one person, it's too easy to point fingers. If there is more than one assignee, then the person listed first is the first among equals if that's an issue.

- **Date Assigned**   This is the date the issue was first raised and documented.

- **Date Due**   Items without a due date are always suspect. How will you know when an item is overdue for no good reason? Always assign a due date even if it's only a rough estimate. You can always change it later as events unfold. If you change it several times, indicate that it's a new, revised date by replacing "10/30" with "11/07r", where r stands for revised.

- **Results**   This is a better, more accurate term than status. It can show some intermediate progress (that is, something of interest even though the issue is not yet closed).

Government Insider _____

The owner (the one with version control) of the 01 action items should repost the current version of the list within minutes of the close of the daily stand-up meeting, so anyone who did not attend the meeting can see the now-current version. It gives an excellent summary of what came out of the meeting.

07 Evaluation Factors for Award*

This is a sometimes simplified version of Section M. Moreover, these can be value-added through your own team's notations on the factors. For example, the owner of this one can solve the word problem as discussed in Chapter 14. This solution shows your own team's best guess at the relative weights of the proposal parts, and this set of weights then influences the allocation of the (usually limited) page count.

08 Roles and Responsibilities

As you have already formed the proposal team with assigned roles and responsibilities (see Chapter 6), now you are documenting the current version of those roles. Often, you will see changes in personnel during the proposal creation process as individuals take on new assignments and new folks come on. It is important to reflect these changes in this document and to change the contact list, correspondingly.

09 Asking Questions and Log of Questions and Answers

All solicitations let the offerors ask questions of the KO. The FAR requires that the KO respond to these questions (within reason) and to share both the questions and the answers with all prospective bidders. The companies asking the questions are never identified by name.

Red Flag _____

When asking the KO a question, always mask your identity. Although the KO is required to withhold the questioner's identity, sometimes companies inadvertently disclose their identity in the question. Don't ask the KO, "Did you really mean to exclude our patented Left-Handed Framazoid paint?" That's a tip-off to all the other offerors that the holder of that patent asked that question. Figure out some way to ask the question without revealing the company of origin.

10 Past Performance Template*

Most of the time, the solicitation contains a very clear format for the *past performance* submissions. Unfortunately, there is a frustrating inconsistency among agencies in these requirements. One agency asks for contract dollars but not manpower. Another procurement shop, within that same agency and sometimes within that same procurement shop, will ask for an entirely different set of statistics. This phenomenon causes an unnecessarily large burden on the offerors. In fact, large companies typically have staff members whose only function is to respond to requests for past performance. And even small companies must spend a lot of time and money tailoring their responses. So to solve this problem, at least partially, you should develop a comprehensive folder on all your contracts. This folder can then serve as a source document for these responses and cut done (but not eliminate) the necessity of data mining for each response.

def•i•ni•tion

Past performance is a citation of work you've done in the past. The customer wants to know how well your company has done work, typically for another customer. If you're new to government contracting, you can cite commercial work, using this format if the work is similar.

11 Kickoff Meeting Agenda

The kickoff meeting is typically held about three to five days after the release of the solicitation. Sometimes there is more than one meeting: one upon release of a draft solicitation and another upon release of the final. For details see Chapter 14, but for now know the agenda for the kickoff meeting should be part of this set of documents.

12 Call-In Process

Communication among team members is critical. For major efforts, the industry standard practice is a daily stand-up meeting. These are mostly held in the early morning, but when team members are scattered over time zones, set the time to accommodate as many members as possible.

The call-in process should involve at least an audio link, if not also a video link, which allows team members to see the same screen desktop available to the members in the meeting room. The prices for teleconferencing services allowing desktop sharing among team members are coming down rapidly. Both hearing and seeing the materials under discussion is best.

This document gives complete instructions for the call-in number and the required participant code. Limit the distribution of the host code to only a few individuals to minimize the danger of compromise of these meetings. But do make sure more than one person knows the host code in case the primary host can't chair the meeting.

13 Formatting*

For major opportunities, the customer specifies a page limit by major section. Part of that page limitation is the specification of text margins, typeface and size, and which pages do and do not count against the page imitations. This formatting document must match the solicitation requirements. Where it is silent about formatting requirements, the proposal team makes its own decisions on format. For example, you may determine all visuals must have two labels: a horse title—which means if you show a horse, label it "Horse"—and an action caption or text that tells the story of the visual. (See Chapter 15.)

14 Conventions and Ground Rules

In long and complex proposals, written by many individual authors, this document provides helpful guidance on how the proposal team responds to certain solicitation requirements. For example, is the bidding team "Team XYZ" or "the XYZ Team"? This is simple enough, and either is correct, but mixing the two in the same proposal shows a lack of team discipline that is unsettling to the evaluators. And it's unnecessary. It's up to someone on the team, usually the proposal manager, the capture manager, or a senior editor, to provide top-down guidance.

Here's a common situation. Let's say the XYZ Team has four members: XYZ, Acme, Bluenose, and Cardiff Technical. On page 4 of the technical volume, the proposal speaks to the team members in that order, but on page 17 of the same volume, the order is: XYZ, Cardiff Technical, Bluenose, and Acme. And the visual in the management volume shows a third order. Any order can be correct, but using different orders is unnecessarily sloppy and can confuse the customer.

There are two logical solutions to this problem. After XYZ, the prime (always listed first), you can go either alphabetically (least likely to be offensive to any company) or in the pecking order of the subcontractors. Let's say that Cardiff Technical is a company known and loved by the customer and your XYZ Team was really lucky to attract

Cardiff Technical to your team. That's a good reason to list Cardiff Technical first, followed by Bluenose (second most important), and then Acme (least important but on the team).

15 Customer Hot Buttons

Your meetings with the customer (see Chapter 5) and other sources (such as the customer's previous unhappy experiences) should tell you which subjects are of particular interest to them. For example, in telecommunications contracts, there has been a great deal of unhappiness among many customers with the way a new contractor takes over from the old (outgoing) contractor. When the customer suffers service discontinuities during the transition from the old to the new contractor, they lose valuable resources. The aggravation to the customer then becomes a hot button.

The responsibility for identifying those hot buttons lies mostly with the relationship manager and the capture manager. If your team knows the customer hot buttons and addresses your plan for mitigating the risks present in those activities, the evaluators will have a warm feeling about your plan. It's good to turn the customer's anxiety into confidence.

16 Commitment Letter

This letter is related to, but different from, the transmittal letter. This one is also seen by your customer. The substance of the letter is that you and your company or team is committed to the success of the program. It is addressed to the decision maker at the customer organization from his or her counterpart in your own organization, and TM signs the commitment letter. It is to your team's advantage to obtain the signature of the highest-ranking individual possible in your company. If you are the CEO, it's your job to sign the letter on the important bids.

This letter is optional but a good idea. It gives a name and face to the commitment of your company to solving your customer's problem. People (your customer) buy people (you and your company) and not just companies.

17 Transmittal Letter

The transmittal letter responds to the solicitation and is one of the few attachments to the proposal plan your customer sees. Typically, the letter responds directly to any concerns shown in the solicitation. Your contracts manager (CM) signs these letters.

The best letters are brief and focused on the customer's concerns, as expressed in the solicitation. Typically, the CO points out any deviations or exceptions you are taking to the requirements of the solicitation. It's best to avoid taking deviations and exceptions at all. However, if you feel compelled to ask for exceptions and/or deviations from the specifications, you should do so only with great reluctance and humility and explain them in the letter.

Make this transmittal letter very formal, stating that you, the offeror, are now submitting these documents for the customer to review. For example, if the solicitation requires your offer to be open for 180 days, state here that your offer will, in fact, be valid for 180 days. The objective of this letter is to demonstrate compliance with the solicitation.

18 Fact Sheet

In proposals with multiple volumes and multiple authors (and all large proposals qualify on both counts), you'll need a fact sheet. This document keeps track of specific facts used in the proposal. My favorite example is the number of employees in your company and the total number of employees on the team as a whole. Left without adult supervision, these quantities will appear in different volumes, and sometime within the same volume, as wildly different figures:

◆ "XYZ has 16,345 employees worldwide."

◆ "Team XYZ's companies have a total of over 22,000 employees."

◆ "Our program manager has over 17 years of experience in managing programs having more than 25 people."

◆ "Our program manager has nearly 20 years of experience in managing programs with 25 people."

To resolve this through top-down proposal leadership, have a short meeting of knowledgeable and concerned individuals and get the facts straight; then communicate those to all involved.

19 Resumé Template*

Your customer wants to know the background and qualifications of the important individuals named to lead your program team. The evaluators want to do an apples-to-apples comparison of, for example, your program manager with the program managers of your competition. So giving a resumé template in the solicitation simplifies the evaluators' job.

Unfortunately, formats vary greatly from solicitation to solicitation, so there is no standard resumé format. Your company may have a standard format, which is good news. The bad news is that you can almost never use that format in a proposal.

Furthermore, even if there were a standard format, you should at least consider tailoring the format you'll use for a specific opportunity to match the characteristics and terminology of the resumé content to this specific opportunity.

Here's an example. Let's say the solicitation has four requirements for your program manager. Your program manager-designate has 31 years of experience and has held a wide variety of jobs involving a dozen major technologies in his career. The solicitation requires 15 years of professional experience and specific experience in any 3 of a laundry list of 15 categories. So from the list of 15, you pick this individual's strongest 3 then rewrite the resumé to highlight the 3 chosen specific experiences.

I'm not now or ever advocating that you rewrite the resumé to include statements that are untrue or misleading. That is never a good idea. That said, it is fair and proper to emphasize the three specific experiences matching the solicitation. The idea is to make it easy on the customer's evaluators to find the experience and to give your person a high score on meeting those requirements.

Documents That Come from the Customer

Customer documents are items you receive from the customer or that you find about the customer. These help your team keep track of everything you know about the customer and about the opportunity they're offering. Customer documents typically include the following:

- Website materials, showing such important information as the mission, the vision, and the location of the customer.
- Pre-release briefings.
- Requests for Information (RFIs) for this opportunity.
- Draft solicitations.
- Answers to question coming from any of these.
- Final solicitation.

- ◆ Amendments to the solicitation.

- ◆ Lists of attendees at any bidders' meetings regarding this opportunity.

Do not mix any of your own documents with the customer documents. You'll find yourself tempted to mix briefings you've given to the customer, say right after you submitted your response to the RFI. *Don't do it.* If you do, you may never be able to find it in all that snowstorm of customer documents.

Documents to Pull from the Public Domain

This category, usually the smallest folder, has clippings from newspapers, trade journals, and professional journals. The most common other type of documents is the results of studies provided by third-party vendors.

The Least You Need to Know

- ◆ Have a proposal plan, abide by it, and publicize it to all proposal team members.

- ◆ Use a secure capability for document control, such as SharePoint on your company's intranet, to give access to all proposal team members, as authorized, and to no one else.

- ◆ Carefully track all customer documents, and especially amendments to the solicitation.

- ◆ Be aware of what the world knows, through public documents.

Chapter 13

Setting Up a Proposal Center

In This Chapter

- ◆ Getting "butts in seats"
- ◆ Finding the right physical space
- ◆ Security issues

The creation of a winning proposal requires the coming together of the right resources—top management (TM) support, qualified, motivated team members, electronic tools, and physical facilities. In Chapter 6, we talked about the people you need to have on your proposal team to cover the various functions. And in Chapter 12, you learned about all the documents you need to develop, collect, or store. So where are all these people going to sit, and what equipment and systems do you need to create and store these documents? This chapter describes the resources—electronic and physical—you need to carry out a proposal effort efficiently and effectively.

We begin with a discussion of location, including amount of office space set aside for the proposal team's use, configuration, and special amenities of the space and end with the security measures necessary to protect your proprietary data.

Who Needs to Work out of the Proposal Center

Communities of professionals working together virtually from some combination of home-based offices, corporate headquarters or field offices, or hoteling situations has become so commonplace in many enterprises that it's become almost the exception to have all employees in one place. Industry experts agree, however, that the best circumstance for creating winning proposals for government contracts is to have all proposal team members in the same physical location for the duration of the proposal effort. Further, the consensus view is that the team members handling critical functions (this varies somewhat with each proposal) should be able to spend the equivalent of full-time on the proposal, and therefore need a place to work out of full-time.

Determine Who Needs a Spot

The first challenge is to get the right people, for the amount of time, required to complete the task. Not every team member needs to be present full-time during the duration. For example, the writers of the technical sections should be able to come and go as needed for the proposal because they often have other jobs. The proposal manager—who does need to be there all the time—is typically confronted with team members who have conflicting priorities between the business development efforts (that is, the proposal creation that will bring business into the company's future) and other responsibilities (execution of another program, the company's current business). In fact, because responsibility gravitates toward demonstrated competence, the team members who are valuable to the proposal team are also valuable to existing programs.

There is very often a conflict between your company's short-term goals and your long-term goals. Do you assign your best people to existing projects, where their efforts produce immediate revenues and profits, or do you assign them to proposal efforts? Every company has an "A Team", and the members on the A Team are typically managing or supporting the important programs you already have in hand. But how do you best achieve your growth goals, if not by using the A Team to get new business?

If the conflict is serious, possibly affecting both the ongoing programs and the proposal effort, then the only way to resolve the conflicting priorities is to call on top management to resolve the conflict. TM cannot solve problems it does not know about. Therefore, having TM close to the proposal effort makes it easier to make the correct call and resolve the conflict between these individuals' "day jobs" and the proposal effort.

Every solicitation is different, and therefore every proposal is different, so you may find it either advantageous or necessary to pull in an individual to work full-time on the proposal effort when you had not originally anticipated that need. For example, if the technical champion and the program manager-designate are the same person and this is a highly technical program, the person carrying both functions will probably be putting in all available time (which may mean all waking hours!) to your proposal. At the other end of the spectrum, you have the orals coach, the legal counsel, and the evaluation team members. These functions are very likely as needed only. The remaining functions are somewhere in the middle, again depending on the character of your response.

To get an idea of how much space you may need, here is a sample list of those functions needing full-time workspace:

Capture Manager

Proposal Manager Functions Needing Space Part-time, Occasional:

Top Management

Relationship Manager

Pricing Manager

Program Manager—Designate

Technical Champion

Proposal Coordinator

Production Coordinator

Evaluation Team Member(s)

Here is a sample list of those functions needing space on a part-time or as-needed basis:

Orals Coach

Contracts Manager

Legal Counsel

Subject Matter Experts

Remember these functions (defined in detail in Chapter 6) might be carried out by one person per function or, in large projects, by multiple people handling each function. So as you estimate office space or workstations needed, try to forecast as best you can the number of offices needed per person, not just per function.

The Challenge of Togetherness

The ideal circumstance is for proposal team members to be able to see the other team members, face-to-face, and not via teleconference. But realistically, for most large proposals, this is very close to impossible to achieve. The important proposal team members are likely to be from different divisions of your company or from companies serving as subcontractors. Typically, these people work at locations away from the proposal development site and may even live or work in different time zones.

The Physical Space for Central Development

When building—or rebuilding—a physical space for proposal development, the factors to consider fall into three categories:

◆ Top-level issues

◆ Personnel issues

◆ Physical facilities issues

Top-Level Issues

These issues will require you or your top management to sponsor any of the actions coming from answers to these questions. In very large companies, the answers to these questions may involve high-level officers from throughout the company.

◆ Will this capability be a cost center (that is, funded by a high-level organization and therefore part of the cost of business development, for example) or a profit center (that is, funded by the parts of the organization requiring assistance, through back-charges to individual users)?

◆ Will there be a single location of this capability (centralized), or will there be perhaps a single central location, with additional locations closer to the users of the services (decentralized)?

◆ Will the capability include some version of SharePoint or other text management software that facilitates version control and allows easy access from more than a single location?

Physical Facilities Decisions

Choosing the right physical facilities is important to functional success. Considerations are:

◆ Physical security—Facility should be easy to isolate from other activities within the customer's location to prevent prying eyes from obtaining competitive information.

◆ Undesirable location—The less desirable, the better because if you occupy prime office space, other parts of the organization will covet this space and perhaps figure out ways to displace your capability even in the midst of the creation of an important proposal.

◆ Central *production facility*/secure, separate work areas for specific team(s)—The best complexes developed in recent years feature a central production facility surrounded by proposal-specific team rooms. This allows all teams to use the central facility without exposing the work to the other teams; often the other team has teammates who are partners on a specific proposal but serious competitors on other proposals.

def•i•ni•tion

The place where you produce the final versions of the proposal is called the **production facility.** This facility often doubles as a support facility for any other documents you create in support of your project work.

◆ Printers/copiers—The central production facility should have a truly capable and flexible set of copiers, from high-speed black-and-white to color and special-purpose copiers to produce out-size displays.

◆ Paper-handling machines, such as those that fold outsized (for example, 11 by 17 paper) for inclusion in the submitted proposal, and accurate, heavy-duty hole punches to ensure a professional look to your proposal documents.

◆ *Burn barrels*/shredders—Encourage the daily use of these, and discourage the discarding of proprietary materials by way of trash and garbage. Impress on your proposal team members that normal trashcans are really the entrance of a very long pipe leading directly to the in-basket of your most serious competitor.

def•i•ni•tion

A **burn barrel** is a trash receptacle that segregates everyday waste paper and trash from the papers containing proprietary materials. The maintenance of these barrels is typically outsourced to a specialty vendor, who supplies the specially marked barrels and takes away the proprietary papers for proper destruction.

◆ Daily sweeps area for all work papers—See previous point. Nothing good happens to work papers left out overnight, and they can be subject to possible theft.

◆ Free, good coffee—It's a small price to pay for improving morale among the authors. Figure out how much it costs in lost time when an author or other proposal contributor takes 23 minutes to visit the local Starbucks, and compare that to the cost of providing good coffee in the workplace. Providing good coffee is peanuts.

◆ Lunches provided on site—Along the same vein as providing coffee, lunches, especially during periods of intense activities, allow the members to remain on site and be productive for the entire business day. Provide dinners, too, if and when proposal activity goes beyond the normal work hours by about an hour.

Special Audio and Video Equipment

Your facilities should include at least one conference room, capable of handling the proposal team's daily stand-up meeting. The room should contain a speakerphone of better quality than the typical desktop telephone. There's no point in spending money on personnel, and then having remote team members get frustrated and not be able to contribute because they cannot hear what's going on in the daily meetings because of poor audio equipment.

You'll also need a projector and a screen. The projector can be driven by a computer to show the attendees your daily broadcast material and other documents you want them to see.

Web conferencing tools are a great help. These tools allow all participants, even those in different physical locations, to see, in real time, the documents you are discussing. Then everyone has a chance both to receive current information and to contribute to the discussion.

Somewhere (often but not always, in the largest conference room available) you need wall space to show the then-current versions of the proposal documents. The presence of these current document versions is a rapid and reliable reflection of where the team is on individual sections and helps stimulate the laggards (if any) to keep their sections up to par with the other parts. And it helps TM view the state of proposal completion. The real benefit is that Joe, writing the management plan, can see what Teresa is writing in the technical plan and can spot any similarities or, more importantly, differences in the company story. There is no substitute for such a feedback mechanism. Even in well-run proposal efforts, individuals concentrate on their own parts but need to see what's going on concurrently in other parts of the proposal.

Electronic Support

Of course, each team member must have his own computer or at least free access to one. Sharing computers is a bad idea if this results in any team member having to waste time waiting for a computer to free up. And software support should load each computer with the same versions of software.

Government Insider

Strive to have all computers used in the proposal creation loaded with the same version of the text processing software, such as Microsoft Word. Incompatible versions will drive the production team nuts when trying to overcome incompatibilities at the last minute.

Keeping Your Proposal Effort Secure

You must take steps to secure the proposal team's work from slipping into the hands of your competition. Industrial espionage is a fact in today's competitive world. As in a game of Bridge, "a peak is worth two finesses." If a competitor can get its hands on even preliminary versions of your proposal, then counter-strategies become easy. This could be enough to tip the scales away from your solution and into the hands of another company.

Electronic Security

Have your information technology support people, helped by the security staff, configure a secure network for the proposal team's use. The complexity ranges from very simple to massively complex, so your security measures will vary accordingly. This is very basic but can be overlooked in the enthusiasm to get the proposal out the door.

One way to reduce your security exposure is to prohibit the use of memory sticks and other portable storage devices within your proposal development center. For classified proposals, you surely must obey government restrictions while handling data classified by the government (Official Use Only, Confidential, Secret, Top Secret, and above). The detailed requirements vary greatly, depending on the sensitivity of the data.

Of all the parts of the proposal, the most sensitive is the data in the cost proposal because if it falls into the hands of your competitors, they can do great damage. You can only imagine the damage you would suffer if your competition knew your cost models and cost figures. Therefore, you must apply the most stringent restrictions to your cost proposal.

Physical Security

Your central development space should have access control, limited to only those people who need to know what's going on with the proposal. This prevents unwanted access to materials by people who have no business reason to be in a space with proprietary data.

It's a good idea to have a designated security sergeant with the job of patrolling the proposal area several times a day, looking for security violations. The common violations are discarding proprietary materials in the normal wastebaskets and having meetings with nonteam members in the proposal space. Discuss security issues at least once a week at the team's daily stand-up meetings.

The Least You Need to Know

- ◆ Have a physical space dedicated to your proposal effort.
- ◆ Determine how many people need full-time office space and how many additional offices or workstations are needed for the part-time or occasional, as-needed personnel.
- ◆ Don't scrimp on equipping the central proposal facility with good special-purpose equipment.
- ◆ Make security a top priority on a proposal site, including limited access to the facility, careful disposal of confidential papers, and tight controls on file sharing and electronic data storage.

Chapter 14

Getting Down to the Business of a Response

In This Chapter

- ◆ Actions to take the first five days
- ◆ The sections of the Uniform Contract Format (UCF)
- ◆ Focus on Section M
- ◆ The kickoff meeting
- ◆ Bid Decision Point #3

The first several days of the formal proposal effort are critical for ultimate success. By this point, you've planned an overarching strategy for your response; you know what documents you need; and you've set up a home for the proposal operations. Now you're ready to get down to the serious business of creating the proposal.

This chapter gives you specific actions to take at this early stage of the process, including what to do in the all-important kickoff meeting.

The First Five Days Start with Day One

When planning your initial activities, start with the first five days as they are critical to proposal success. Of course, each proposal is unique in terms of complexity, total amount of time it will take, and size and makeup of the proposal team, but certain activities are inevitably going to be a part of nearly every proposal process.

The most important task in the first few days is a serious reading of the solicitation. This starts on day one and lasts as long as it takes. For complex solicitations, you'll be fortunate to complete this in the first five days.

On day one of the first five days, you have 10 tasks to focus on. They are:

1. Do a thorough, critical assessment of your own strengths and weaknesses as a proposal team.

2. Ban the term "boilerplate" from your vocabulary.

3. Strategize about the customer relationship.

4. Create a schedule for delivery of products or services.

5. Do a detailed analysis of the differences between the draft and final solicitation.

6. Create the "60-Second Justification" for your win.

7. List four ways to keep the cost/price folks involved.

8. Load the electronic bulletin board with contact info.

9. Confirm the leadership roles and reporting lines.

10. Prepare for the tasks to come.

Don't worry if you're not sure how to go about doing some of these things or aren't exactly certain what they mean. I offer this list as a handy reference and will provide more details on each activity in the following sections.

Assess Your Team's Strengths and Weaknesses

I'm often asked to help to rescue proposal efforts that are in trouble. The reasons for the need to rescue an effort are varied. It's enough to say that the progress toward submitting a winning proposal is disappointing, and a change in direction is necessary, and the sooner the better. When I arrive on the scene, I ask three questions:

- ◆ Where's the executive summary?

- ◆ Where's the proposal outline?

- ◆ Where's the capture plan?

These three documents, the executive summary, the proposal outline, and the capture plan, give a rapid, accurate assessment of the proposal team's readiness to begin a serious proposal effort. Unless all three exist and are in a reasonable amount of detail, the proposal team is not ready to proceed at full speed. You must immediately begin a remedial action to create these or increase the amount of detail in them.

Ban the Boilerplate

Every solicitation is unique, and every proposal should be, too, so from day one help everyone recognize that this process is not going to be about simply recycling old proposal material with a cut-and-paste effort. Instead of *boilerplate*, encourage the team to think of the proposal content as being made up of new materials as well as some carefully chosen old materials on file, all tailored to the customer's wants as expressed in this solicitation.

Every team member should know both the usefulness of boilerplate materials and their potential misuse. Such materials can be useful as a starting point for describing your solution, but the danger is that those materials will be simply adopted from previous work without the proper analysis of the direct applicability. You will need to modify or tailor just about all materials to your new solution.

def•i•ni•tion

Boilerplate is the text and visuals used in a previous proposal or other presentation for another purpose. These materials may be out of date, incorrect, or otherwise not applicable to your solutions for this new customer.

Strategize About the Customer Relationship

Review what you know about the customer and who on your team knows the customer, and figure out how you can capitalize on the name and face recognition you've built. Involve the program manager-designate, technical leader, and business manager in this process.

Create a Schedule for Delivery of Products or Services

This schedule should demonstrate your knowledge of the customer's program and serve as a valuable communication tool with your own creation team. It should be a joint product, with the technical people and the management people working together to show what will be available when. The best schedules of this type show the delivery dates of the customer's important products or services. This schedule answers the ustomer's implicit question, "When will I get my products?" If this is good, your customer's working level evaluators will use your schedule to explain the program to others on the evaluation team.

Analyze the Draft vs. Final Solicitation

There isn't always a draft solicitation. Sometimes a customer just issues a final solicitation. But even if there is no draft solicitation, you may be able to identify a previous solicitation from that customer, perhaps even including enough detail about what the customer might have in mind, to serve as a stand-in for a draft. But if there is neither a formal draft, nor something to substitute for a draft, you may just skip this section.

Task two of your smartest people to create a detailed analysis of the differences between the draft solicitation and the final solicitation. Remember those differences separate winners from losers within the customer organization, and therefore greatly influence your own decisions on proposal creation.

Create a 60-Second Justification of an Award to Your Company

All this is just conjecture and will never be delivered to the customer, but create a short statement in the form of a brief press release. This is an announcement your customer might very well use to announce the award of this contract to your company. (Extra credit: pretend you're writing that corresponding statement for your toughest competitor.)

Get the Cost/Price Folks Involved

List four ways you intend to keep the cost/price experts intimately involved in the proposal creation process. Include in your list where those individuals will sit with the other members of the proposal team during the creation effort. Deduct points if the chief technical guru is sitting closer to either the proposal manager or the capture manager than the cost/price folks. These folks are an integral part of the proposal team and so should be physically close to the proposal team leaders, such as the proposal manager and capture manager, and not off in another building or on another floor.

Load the Electronic Bulletin Board

Gather and record information on all your proposal team members. Include names, phone numbers, beeper numbers, cellular phone numbers, and e-mail addresses. For the relationship manager and the capture manager, also include their home address.

Confirm the Leadership Roles and Reporting Lines

Observe the official end of democracy with a formal ceremony at your first stand-up meeting. The proposal manager officiates, and the capture manager takes note of any nonbelievers. Seriously, it's important to establish the leadership hierarchy from the get-go so that everyone understands who's in charge and who has the ultimate say, without, of course, squashing the morale and contributions of those not in leadership roles. It's a team effort, with the team leadership roles and responsibilities clearly described.

Brace Yourselves

You and your team are about to embark on a wild ride as you begin devoting full effort to winning this government contract. Plan on devoting whatever work hours are necessary to get the job done, and if at all possible, postpone any scheduled vacations. If that's not possible, make sure the team knows of those absences and has sufficient back-up through shared responsibilities.

Days Two Through Five

Having begun the solicitation analysis on day one, the next four days (or perhaps longer for complex solicitations) will find you continuing to do this difficult and even tedious task. If you've been able to do a comparison, publish and discuss the results of the analysis of the differences between the draft solicitation and the final solicitation. There's no point in paying for a serious analysis and then failing to make the results available to all team members.

By now, you should have a good, solid 05 Proposal Outline and Responsibility Assignment Matrix (RAM).

By the end of day five, you should have a robust set of questions to ask the customer. These questions will help you further get a handle on the solicitation and will continue building your name and face recognition with the customer.

Ask Good Questions and Get Good Answers

Not even the most highly skilled customer procurement shop issues solicitations that are perfect the first time out. Some content is always subject to interpretation, and in a complex solicitation, usually a lot of content requires clarification. Therefore, you are allowed to ask questions of the customer. Solicitations typically state the format, timing, proper addressee, and schedule for agency response to these questions.

Red Flag

The customer's answers to questions have no effect on the solicitation. It's usually okay to rely on those answers in creating your proposal. But be sure the KO changes the solicitation. Changes are legitimate *only* through a formal amendment to the existing solicitation.

Each company usually submits these questions in writing directly to the Contracting Officer (KO). If there is a pre-proposal conference (sometimes called Bidders Conference), then you'll have a chance to ask questions of the KO. The KO usually solicits those written questions in advance and sometimes also offers to take live questions from the attendees at the conference.

An important part of a winning strategy is to have the right people ask the right questions, in the right way, at the right time. The customer's responses to your questions give insights into exactly what he wants to buy.

Formulating Good Questions

Asking questions is as much art as science. Avoid simply making a list of questions and submitting them under the terms of the instructions in the solicitation. That said, though, there are only guidelines and principles and no hard-and-fast rules for asking good questions. One route to success is knowing the KO. If you've followed the scenario of the technical and marketing interchange, then you know the KO by name and face, and the KO knows you. This makes the process easier.

Formulate your questions so that the answer you really want from the customer is "yes" or at least begins with "yes." This establishes a positive frame of mind with the customer. Customers would rather say "yes" than "no."

If you plan to ask questions about internal inconsistencies, incorrect citations, reference to obsolete standards, or similarly negative, even embarrassing, features of the solicitation, seek TM's guidance in handling what could be a delicate matter. Not only is their wise counsel useful here, but this is also an opportunity for your proposal manager or capture manager to get TM participating in the proposal process.

> **Beltway Buzz**
>
> The customer's answers do not identify the name of the company asking the question, so you have anonymity.

Finally, remember, as discussed in Chapter 3, the customer limits any communication, including your questions, from you as an offeror to its own KO. A corresponding rule is that your own contracts manager, your CM, should be the single point of contact with the customer KO. This customer rule applies strictly to any communication after release of the solicitation, and it's a good idea for your side to limit itself to using your own CM to communicate internally as well.

Changing the Customer's Mind

In some cases, what you really want to do is try to bring about changes in the solicitation. Try phrasing a question that casts doubt about the way the solicitation currently reads, and then suggest an alternate formulation. This can be particularly effective if the solicitation now favors a technical solution different from the one you're planning to put forward. Justify your requested change in the solicitation in terms that could benefit the customer. Similarly, avoid the perception that you're just whining about something you don't like.

> **Red Flag**
>
> Refrain from asking questions for which you can't stand the answer. Sometimes, it's better to ask forgiveness (after submission) than permission (as you're writing the proposal). As scientific and technical people, our training tells us to have all the answers, but that's not necessarily so in this case. For every tough question, at least consider not asking it because someone else might or for other reasons. This is a really tough judgment call.

The customer's answers are often very helpful to your proposal team. The KO can give you and your competitors answers to important, pressing questions and can answer questions rather quickly if that's required. But making amendments to the solicitation can be much slower because amendments may require the review of other influential parties within the customer organization. Be aware, however, that the one and only way the solicitation can be changed is through a formal amendment to it. So unless and until the government makes formal the customer's answers by changes in the solicitation, the solicitation of record stands.

Questions for Your Own Team

You'll also need to develop some questions for your proposal team. Here's an example of a question a team might pose to itself:

The detailed analysis of the differences between the draft solicitation and the final solicitation seem to indicate that our solution is not favored. The changes in Section M are not in our favor but in the favor of our strongest competitor. So what should our next moves be? Which of these actions should we take?

- Ignore the changes, and move on with the proposal effort?

- No-bid this one with the no-bid letter to the customer?

- Consult with another competitor and be willing to team with that competitor, with us as either the prime or perhaps as a subcontractor?

- Change our own solution to be more in line with the way the solicitation has changed?

This question is clearly not the type you want the customer to see and would be answered only by the proposal team. This is also another good way to involve TM in the process—bring the thorny questions to them!

Should You Request More Time?

By the end of day five, you may have the sinking feeling that a very large amount of activities and milestones lie ahead of you and your team and not enough time to create a really good, winning proposal. For any number of reasons, you may see the need to request an extension of the due date for your proposal.

If you do request an extension, strive to craft your request so that it appeals to the customer, not just your organization.

> **Red Flag** _____
>
> Avoid asking for more time as a knee-jerk reaction. Request an extension only if it benefits you in relation to the competition and only after careful deliberation. Sometimes you'd like to have more time, but that would just give the competition a chance to catch up, too.

Sample Extension Justification #1

At the 09-06 conference of (prospective offerors) (Agency KO) estimated that answers to questions submitted by the due date of 09-07 would be answered in about two weeks. It is now 09-28, which is three weeks past that conference, and one week past the estimated time for response to questions. The delay in answering the initial set of questions has caused this offeror to delay completion of critical portions of our solution and therefore critical portions of our own response.

Sample Extension Justification #2

This offeror has experienced difficulty in relating the data on site locations, as provided by the (service provider), to physical locations. Efforts to engage service provider and other sources to resolve this problem have proven to be unsuccessful and have required much more time than we had planned. At this time, we have significant risks associated with this problem, and we require more time to resolve this issue and to allow accurate planning and pricing.

Sample Extension Justification #3

Below are the same three paragraphs we submitted earlier to the government, to justify a one-time, large extension:

1. As against the (redacted) design requirement of (previous submission) (which was derivative of the previously issued redacted procurement), (XYZ Opportunity) requires TWO complete designs: one for the Commercial (shared) (capability) and another, separated design for the Dedicated (redacted).

2. Unique to (XYZ Opportunity) is the requirement to develop (several) unique (redacted) responses.

3. The (XYZ Opportunity) submission is a response to a Statement of Work and not for an entirely new contract. But we must write to and price to a complexity and level of detail (redacted) that is greater than that required of (redacted). Further, we must develop two—not one—technical solutions and the accompanying (description of work). And the design complexities must be balanced against the ability to deliver competitively priced solutions.

These three separate, but related, requirements compete for the same (fixed) resources within all (prospective offerors) and represent a significant effort to prepare responsive proposals as compared with requirements of previous proposals.

In light of the above, we believe that a significant extension in the due date is in the best interests of the government, as well as all the prospective offerors.

On the basis of the above, we request an extension in the due date for (XYZ Opportunity) to 3:00 P.M. on Friday, 11-06.

Understanding the Uniform Contract Format

All solicitations don't follow the Uniform Contract Format. However, many do, and so it's important for you to understand the details of this format.

Invitations for Bids (IFBs) and Requests for Proposals (RFPs) must use the *Uniform Contract Format (UCF)*. This format has stood the test of time, and experienced individuals know this format like the back of their hands. It includes 13 sections from A to M.

def•i•ni•tion

Uniform Contract Format (UCF) is the format (Sections A through M) that must be used for invitations for bids (IFBs) and requests for proposals (RFPs).

Here are the sections of the Uniform Contract Format (UCF):

A: Solicitation/Contract Form

B: Supplies/Services and Prices/Cost

C: Descriptions/Specifications/Work Statement

D: Packaging and Marking

E: Inspection and Acceptance

F: Deliveries or Performance

G: Contract Administration Data

H: Special Contract Requirements

I: Contract Clauses

J: List of Attachments

K: Representation, Certifications, and Other Statements

L: Instructions, Conditions, and Notices

M: Evaluation Factors

Don't be distracted by slightly different names for the sections of your first solicitation. For example, Section L may be called "Instructions to Offerors"; Section M may be called "Evaluation Factors for Award"; and Section C may be called the "Statement of Work (SOW)". It's all the same thing.

Let's look at each section in more detail.

A: Solicitation/Contract Form

This is a standard form, such as an SF-1449 or SF-33, and contains all the really important information about the competition proper: issuing office, contacts, due dates, solicitation number and type. All proposal team members must read and understand this page, at least to know what's there. Some of the terms have specific meanings that are fathomable only to experienced proposal gurus and/or contracts managers.

B: Supplies/Services and Prices/Cost

This section is your opportunity to describe your costs/prices. The format varies with the type of products being bid, but this section shows the offered costs/prices by Contract Line Item Number (CLIN). Again, this is a form best understood by the contracts and pricing staff. Don't worry too much if you don't understand the fine details.

C: Descriptions/Specifications/Work Statement

This section lists the stuff to be procured under this contract. This is often abbreviated as the Statement of Work (SOW) or the Statement of Objectives (SOO). This is typically detailed and says as precisely as possible what the contractor will be required to deliver or provide.

D: Packaging and Marking

This section tells how the deliverables are to be packaged and marked, whether to commercial or military specifications. This is of little importance to most proposal team members.

E: Inspection and Acceptance

This section as well as Section F gives the details of how the government will receive the products. This is particularly important because once the contractor has complied with the details of this section and has a formal sign-off from a government agent, this can be a trigger for the customer to pay the contractor for its work, in accordance with the other provisions of the contract. Without a definitive sign-off process, it could be difficult to determine just when the contractor is allowed to bill and collect from the government. After all, it's not about getting the contract or performing under the contract, it's about getting paid!

F: Deliveries or Performance

This section specifies the requirements for time, place, and method of delivery or performance. This may include a formal Delivery of Performance Schedule.

G: Contract Administration Data

This section says exactly how the government will pay the contractor. In recent years, the act of payment has been greatly simplified and streamlined, and the government now pays by electronic means, into the proper bank account. This paperless process avoids the problems of the past, with hard copy checks being lost, then found, and getting all messed up. The current system is far superior.

H: Special Contract Requirements

This section is where the government sticks any contract requirements that apply to this contract. Someone should read all of these during the first few days of the release of the solicitation. The contracts manager and the company counsel are obvious choices. There have been cases in which the right people did *not* read them with understanding and really bad things happened to the contract awardee.

I: Contract Clauses

This section contains clauses that apply to this contract. Some contract clauses are incorporated by reference, and some are stated in their entirety. See comment on Section H, above.

J: List of Attachments

This section is a grab bag of attachments to the solicitation. Whatever doesn't fit anywhere else, but is essential to the solicitation, ends up here. Again, someone should read these attachments very carefully and hope there are no unpleasant surprises.

K: Representation, Certifications, and Other Statements

This section is often tagged Reps & Certs. Here, you are asked to assert many things about your company. You could be asked to certify that you have not been debarred from getting government contracts, that you are not owned by a foreign company or organization, and the like.

L: Instructions, Conditions, and Notices

This section is the most important to those responsible for creating and submitting a compliant proposal. Its importance means that the proposal manager in particular must read and understand every word. This section is either the most complex or at least among the most complex in the solicitation. You'll find that a large percentage of the questions to the KO comes from this section.

M: Evaluation Factors

This section says most clearly what the customer really wants to buy. This is "what counts as good." Second only to Section L, this section typically is the origin of the most questions. The good news (for the customer) is that the customer can make (almost) any rules of evaluations and awards. The bad news (for the customer) is that once the rules are in place, the customer is bound by those rules. Many successful protests of awards rely on the failure of the customer to follow its own rules.

Section M

Chapter 1 introduced the concept of the word problem, a description of how the customer plans to evaluate the offers. Rather than give a straight quantitative weight to the various factors for award, the customer may say something like the example provided here, which is from an actual USAF solicitation, with some identifying, non-essential information replaced by "XXX"):

F. EVALUATION FACTORS (SAMPLE)

1. Proposals:

Award will be made to the offeror proposing the combination most advantageous to the government based upon an integrated assessment of the evaluation factors and subfactors described below.

Factor 1: Technical

Subfactor 1: Management

Subfactor 2: XXX Training Program Development

Subfactor 3: Courseware Development

Subfactor 4: Classroom/Simulator Instruction

Subfactor 5: XXX Mission Simulator/XXX Operator Support

Subfactor 6: Registrar's Office Management

Factor 2: Past Performance

Factor 3: Cost/Price

2. Order of Importance:

Technical acceptability is a prerequisite to the trade-off between cost/price and past performance. The Order of Importance is used to explain how the other factors will be traded off on technically acceptable proposals.

For all technically acceptable proposals, Factor 2 (Past Performance) will be evaluated on a basis approximately equal to Factor 3 (Cost/Price). Cost/price will contribute substantially to the selection decision.

3. Evaluation Methodology:

Initially, the government technical evaluation team will evaluate the technical proposals on a pass/fail basis, assigning ratings of Acceptable, Reasonably Susceptible of Being Made Acceptable, or Unacceptable. The proposals shall be evaluated against the subfactors listed in paragraph (4) below.

Past Performance will be evaluated on all technically acceptable proposals as described in paragraph (5) below. Cost/Price will be evaluated as described in paragraph (6) below and will be listed from lowest to highest cost/price. The SSA will then assess the price and past performance ratings for all evaluated offers to make an integrated assessment for a best value award decision.

Using the nonquantitative evaluation process described above, it is possible for the government to award to just about any of the bidders. Note that the six subfactors under "Factor 1. Technical" are not explicitly weighted. Are these in order of decreasing importance? (Sometimes the customer gives you at least that helpful hint.) You don't know from this text. If this was a solicitation you were considering bidding on, I would recommend at least you *consider* asking a question in an effort to obtain more details about this method. You could ask the KO to provide a relative weight, at least among the six technical subfactors, and then (and this might be a stretch) the relative importance of past performance and cost on the one hand and technical on the other.

> **Government Insider**
>
> Sometimes, the solicitation reflects an uncertainty or confusion by the customer between past performance, which is "How well did you do YYY?" and experience, which is "What kind of work have you done?" If the solicitation is unclear, ask a question.

Note also that management is a subfactor within technical. This is not unusual or contradictory to my general process of separating the technical and management solutions.

People experienced in the proposal creation game are creatures of habit and usually know which sections of the solicitation are of greatest importance to them. I have been more than slightly amused by this experiment. I take a hard copy of a solicitation, bound in a three-ring binder and properly tabbed, A to M. I place the solicitations before a group of individuals, ask them to spend five minutes with the solicitation, and give me at least two questions that occur to them and are perhaps worthy of asking the customer. Without further conversation or hints, I can, without fail, determine each individual's interest. The technical people, who have an interest in what would actually *be done* under this contract, study Section C, Statement of Work. The proposal manager and others on the team who must deliver the proposal documents study Section L, Instructions to Offerors. And the business development folks, with their compensation package at least partially dependent on winning contracts, study Section M, Evaluation Criteria.

> **Beltway Buzz**
>
> Even for programs involving high technology, the factor discriminating the winning proposal from the losers is the quality of the management solution. Sometimes, all competitors offer a similar technical solution. Then the winner is the company with the best management solution.

The General and Specific Parts of a Kickoff Meeting

Chapter 12 introduced the kickoff meeting with the meeting agenda. The kickoff meeting has two parts: the general and the specific.

The general part features the items that are of interest to all the participants. Your challenge here, as the prime contractor, is to have a representative of each of your subcontractors in attendance. Aim for as high in the subcontractor organization as possible. This is to convince the subs that you know what you're doing and that you have a specific, detailed Proposal Development Plan.

Under the best of circumstances, as the prime, you will probably be able to hold the attention of your high-level audience for only a short time. Once you've shown the subcontractors' top people what they need to know, then dismiss perhaps half of the room and get down to a smaller group for the specific part.

The specific part of the meeting is limited in participation to those who are actually going to assist with the proposal creation. This includes, very importantly, the three modules of Just-In-Time training of the SMEs and authors.

The following table is a sample agenda for a kickoff meeting.

Team TBS Kickoff Meeting

Agenda
April 22, 2010, 9:00 A.M.

Time	Activity	Responsible
9:00	Opening remarks, introductions	Capture Manager (CM)
9:10	02 Proposal Development Schedule	Proposal Manager (PM)
9:15	08 Roles and responsibilities	PM
9:20	09 Asking questions & Log of Q&A (for government and for Team TBS)	PM / CM
9:25	05 Outline and Responsibility Assignment Matrix (RAM), with page allocations	PM
9:30	The Process (daily meetings; configuration control; final production)	PM
9:50	Methodology for and achievement of allocation of billets among TBS members/CM/all	
10:00	Pricing	Pricing Manager
11:00	RELEASE of NONWRITERS Just-In-Time training for authors and writers	PM

(NOTE: numerical references are to the Proposal Plan Attachments)

Just-In-Time Training at the Kickoff Meeting

Use the following three training modules during the final part of the kickoff meeting. This part of the meeting typically lasts between 20 and 40 minutes, depending on the experience and interest of the attendees. Each module has specific importance to the tasks immediately ahead. This training is consistent with the standards for training, as described in Appendix E.

◆ Solicitation Analysis   Every important proposal team member should do a thorough analysis of the solicitation; the more eyes, the better. This training focuses on *how* to analyze the solicitation.

◆ Proposal Writing   This training puts all the authors and the available SMEs on the same page. The training stresses simplicity and directness and cautions against convoluted sentences, which confuse the evaluators.

◆ Evaluation Teams   The reason to include this module is that the subcontractors are present at the kickoff meeting, and this is an excellent opportunity to set your expectations for their people's participation in the evaluation teams. For you, the prime contractor, this has a double whammy: 1) you build team spirit by the requirement for using some of their people on the evaluation teams, and 2) you reduce your own cost, by sharing the cost of the evaluation teams with your subcontractors.

Three Critical Decisions for Bid Decision Point #3

Now that the final solicitation is available to you, begin replacing estimates or guesses about the three critical sections, C, L, and M, with the real content.

This is an excellent time to make final decisions on the subcontractors you'll use for this effort. If you're a subcontractor, it's a great time to make final decisions on which team you'll join (if that's still uncertain) and to begin establishing yourself as a *preferred* subcontractor, through the actions described in Chapter 9.

The Least You Need to Know

◆ Careful analysis of the solicitation pays large dividends.

◆ Although the entire solicitation is important, Sections C, L, and M are *the* most important.

◆ By the end of the kickoff meeting, the proposal team membership, roles, and responsibilities should be largely complete.

◆ When given the formal opportunity, ask good questions to learn more about the customer's wants.

◆ As a subcontractor, seize any opportunity to help your prime contractor and thereby improve your standing on the team.

Part 5

Creating a Winning Response by the Volumes

Proposals are typically made up of three sections, called volumes. These cover the technical solution you're offering to solve the government's problems and meet its needs, the management approach you'll take to yield that solution, and a volume on cost and price where you show you're worth the money you're asking for. There aren't any aardvarks or lutes, but lots of text to be written, visuals and graphics to be created, and versions to be tracked and stored. This part tells you everything you need to know about all that, plus what to do to improve upon your first proposal submission and how to keep marketing your business to the government after you turn in your proposal.

Controlling Text Creation

In This Chapter

- ◆ Proposal writing standards and conventions
- ◆ Intermediate documents to create
- ◆ The role of evaluation teams
- ◆ Track questions and answers
- ◆ Bid Decision Point #4

The proposal your team will create as a solution to a customer's solicitation can number in the hundreds or even thousands of pages, and those pages will go through many draft versions before everyone is satisfied with the final document. Proposals vary greatly in length, but a typical technical portion is 75 pages and the management portion, 50 pages. The cost portion is usually not limited. The customer leaves its length to the judgment of the offerors.

The final creation you submit to the customer is likely to be one hefty document. This means that keeping track of the various pages and parts and iterations during the creation and writing process can be a challenge. You also must work within page limitations set by the customer and can't create a document so hefty that it's too much to read. You must use those pages carefully. Creating proposals is inherently inefficient and expensive, so it's important to keep focused on the process.

This chapter offers several ways to ensure tight text control, including creating and enforcing writing standards and conventions; using the dreaded intermediate documents; getting reviews from internal evaluation teams; holding another bid decision meeting; and tracking questions and answers you exchange with the customer.

Standards and Conventions of Proposal Writing

The first step toward reining in the process is to assign someone on your team the responsibility of establishing and enforcing proposal creation standards. Usually the proposal manager takes on this responsibility, but anyone willing and able can do it. The typical large proposal has many authors, each with a unique style and idea of what makes a good proposal. So to create a *one voice* proposal with the appearance of one author requires the application of uniform standards to the entire proposal document.

def•i•ni•tion

A proposal with a **one voice** quality reads as if a single person wrote all parts, when in fact, a proposal is the creation of many people. Proposals with one voice use consistent terminology across sections, the same verb tenses, and generally a similar tone.

Proposal Plan Attachments

In Chapter 12, two documents support good proposal writing. These are attachments to the proposal plan:

- 14 Conventions and Ground Rules
- 18 Fact Sheet

From that same list of attachments to the proposal plan, three other documents also act as guideposts to proposal writing standards and conventions:

- 10 Past Performance Template
- 13 Formatting
- 19 Resumé Template

Each of these helps you achieve the consistency among proposal sections that is a hall-mark of a well-written proposal.

The late Bud Wilkinson's Oklahoma Sooners put together a winning streak of 47 football games between 1953–1957. Legend has it that someone asked the president of the University of Oklahoma what his own contribution was to the university. In reply, he said something like, "I'm trying to build a university that our football team can be proud of." Correspondingly, you'd like to build a company that's as good as the one described in your proposals!

Government Insider

The customer has the right to expect, and does expect, that the quality of work in the proposal is indicative of the quality of the work that will be delivered under the awarded contract. So build a proposal your company can be proud of.

Proposal Language

The language you use in proposals is important, so another early step in setting writing standards is to identify some wording you should or should not use. Especially in page-limited circumstances, both precision and economy of words are necessary to make your case.

Here is a list of some "No-No Words" and the corresponding "Yes-Yes Words" you should use in their place:

Don't Use	Use Instead
committed	full-time
dedicated	full-time
research leader	program manager
in order to	to
proposal	plan
proposed	planned
consists of	includes
utilize	use
overall	total; high level
basis	something else
try, intend, purpose	anything else

Some offerors try to use these words to describe the amount of time a specific individual is going to give to this program, which is especially important when you are designating an individual with positive name and face recognition with the customer. This could be the program manager-designate, a senior engineer, or some other individual in a conspicuous position on your program team. "Committed" means nothing unless it is backed by the willingness to spend risk money (funds not provided by a contract but from company margin or profit). "Dedicated" is similarly not well defined. What does it mean? If you mean this individual is planning to work on this program and this program only, then say "full-time."

Research leader—The no-no word is a description of this person's function within the company. If the research leader is the program manager, then call him "program manager," and don't confuse the customer. The important thing to the customer is this person's function on your program team.

In order to—The "in order to" contributes nothing except more words to this text. Do a word search for "in order to" and strike this phrase from your proposal.

Proposal, proposed—It may strike you as strange to take out "proposal" (in any form, such as "proposed") and replace it with "plan." The reason is simple: the *whole thing* is a proposal; what you're submitting is a proposal. Using "proposal" leads to an unnecessary tentativeness in your writing. Good proposals *are* plans, and good plans *are*, in effect, proposals.

Consists of—Most often when you are tempted to say this, you really mean you're not going to list everything in the text that follows. That's why you're much safer and more accurate to say "included." You can do even better if you really do know all the elements in the list, in which case you can say, "The following seven items …."

Utilize—This is a truly awful word. It's pretentious and belongs on another planet. Just use "use."

Overall—Where I come from, overalls are made of denim, and you put them on one leg at a time. You almost always mean either "total" or "high level" or even "overarching."

Basis—The most common misuse of this word is something like, "meeting on a daily basis." So just say, "daily meeting" or "meeting daily."

Try, intend, purpose—As in, "we'll try to …" or "we intend to … " or "the purpose of this hardware …." Never "try" or "intend" to do something. "Plan" to do it. The hardware doesn't have a purpose; it actually *does* something, at least in your plan.

Physical Appearance Standards for Proposals

Whether the evaluators see your proposal by hard copy or electronically, the physical appearance is an important indicator of quality. So bring your team to agreement on the expectations for how the finished product will look. Most of the guidelines below apply to proposals submitted by hard copy, so if you're submitting electronically, just disregard the points that don't apply (such as weight of paper the proposal is printed on). Be aware, however, that even if you submit on a website or as an e-mail attachment, you'll usually end up printing copies of your proposal on paper. You might submit copies to the customer along with the initial electronic version, distribute copies within your company, or take them with you to any oral presentation.

Government Insider _____

First impressions count. You have only 30 seconds to make a favorable impression. There must be a feeling of substance to the proposal as if to say, "We have something of substance to say in this proposal."

Use color sparingly. Don't "Disney-fy" your proposal with too many colors or too much flash, as this can detract from the seriousness of your content. On the other hand, usually no requirement in a solicitation says the proposal must be dull! Some touches of color are fine.

Use high-quality paper and notebooks. Nothing cheapens the appearance of a proposal like the use of run-of-the-mill copier paper and flimsy notebooks. You don't have to go overboard with leather covers and 60-pound bond paper, but do invest in high-quality notebooks with pockets inside the front and back covers and paper that's slightly higher weight, such as 24 pound or even 28 pound bright white, for presentations.

Organize the notebooks well. Use foldouts, inserts, tabs, and cross-reference matrices to make the notebooks easy to navigate. Consider adding "zingers," such as a clever, perhaps oddly shaped, insert to further distinguish your proposal from the others.

Proposal Writing Principles

Many books have been written focused solely on principles of good writing. But when it comes to writing proposals for government contracts, a few key pointers stand out above all others:

◆ Write in the present tense wherever possible. Avoid "when we win, we will …." State instead, "Our policy is to …" or "The plan includes …."

Government Insider

Strive for this reaction by the evaluators: "This proposal will be our baseline proposal, against which all others will be measured."

♦ Use first person plural: "we manage …," "our plan includes …."

♦ Sound certain, not tentative. The customer wants to hire an organization to take charge, not hang back and wait for interminable analysis or detailed instructions from the customer. The customer is usually buying products, not effort or good intentions.

The JIT training your team will go through as part of the kickoff meeting includes these and other principles.

Using Visuals

Visuals show your solutions in a vivid and attention-getting way. Your objective is to have the evaluators quickly grasp the features and benefits of your solution. Then, the text re-emphasizes those points and seals the deal with the evaluators.

Every visual has two labels: a "horse title" (if it's a picture of a horse, say "horse") and an "action caption." The action caption says, in words, the message the visual gives. Unfortunately, many SMEs begin their response to a request for describing an important point in support of the proposal creation with a hand-drawn visual. They sketch something out and then begin to explain the meaning. This is conceptually wrong. The right way is to start with the action caption and build the visual around that, because it's the message that's important, not the sketch.

Why do we even use visuals? Let's start with the old saying, "A picture is worth a thousand words." That's one reason. Another is that you're almost always page-limited, and you need to use every trick in your book to get your message across within the fewest number of pages. But the rule is that you use visuals to reinforce the materials in the text and vice versa. It's at best confusing and distractive to have one set of messages in the text and another in the visuals. They should match and complement each other. Be aware that different evaluators work differently; some are visual learners and some are text learners. Your messages should be consistent for either type.

Training for Writers

Your proposal team members are likely to bring different skills and interests to the table when it comes to writing proposals. But many of them will have writing included as a part of their responsibilities. Some may even have little or no experience in proposal creation. By the time you and your team are ready to start writing, the members should have had at least the Just-In-Time (JIT) training included in the kickoff meeting. That is actually only the minimum amount of training needed to do the job. Many team members are going to need additional guidance in order to be solid contributors to the proposal creation process.

Your technical people are often only reluctant participants. These folks would rather be doing what they are good at: engineering, scheduling, finding the best network solution, building something no one else thought could be built, or working at almost anything other than proposal writing. So your team's task, and maybe your task, is to encourage those reluctant participants. But remember to be reasonable about your expectations concerning their writing abilities.

Leverage their contributions; exploit their strengths, and ignore or shore up their weaknesses through other personnel, such as professional writers. Encourage these individuals to do the thinking, and create versions of visuals to tell their story. Don't expect nonprofessional writers to deliver Pulitzer Prize–quality writing. It's just not going to happen.

Progress toward a complete version of the proposal is not a smooth process. It's a complicated process that doesn't typically go smoothly.

Plan before you write. Don't be deceived by thinking you can just start writing without a plan. If you do, you can be surprised by the difficulty of finishing the task, in spite of apparent easy going early.

Let's say you have a 60-day time frame for your proposal. Your inexperienced author has 20 pages to write. At the end of the sixth day, he has two pages written. That seems good. Ten percent of the time has passed, and he has 10 percent of the text done. He's right on track. Hardly. What he's done is the easiest 10 percent. What happens at the 50 percent mark when the going gets rougher? The fifth and sixth pages are not so easy. The lesson here is to plan and then write.

Be quick to praise, and slow to criticize the writer's work. Limit the writer's time responsibilities, and focus his attention on activities he can understand and embrace, even if not enjoy. Have the authors help create graphics, with the help of a graphic artist, or explain a relevant technical point to a technical writer. The result can be much better than relying solely on technical people to "write." No one does anything right the first time. Remember, proposals do not spring forth from nothing into final form, but are created a page at a time.

> **Government Insider** _____
>
> Even though the writing of words is, obviously, a big part of proposals, today's proposals are actually created more than they are written. When you think, gather, collaborate, assemble, and upload or e-mail, that's not really "writing," and yet these all contribute to the creation of the proposal.

Creating Intermediate Documents

There are two classes of proposal plan documents (see Chapter 12):

♦ *Customer documents:* only three are candidates for submission: 03 Executive Summary, 16 Transmittal Letters, and 17 Commitment Letters. A fourth one, 05 Proposal Outline and RAM, is used to generate the proposal outline but is not itself delivered with the proposal.

♦ *Intermediate documents:* All other attachments to the proposal plan are for the use of the proposal team only; the customer never sees them.

def•i•ni•tion _____

Intermediate documents are documents used by the proposal team in the preparation of the proposal but are *not* delivered to the customer.

No one likes developing intermediate documents. Many team members, particularly those relatively new to proposals, are frustrated by the requirement to build the proposal through a structured process. These folks want to jump right in, write their sections, and go on their way. Unfortunately, this simply doesn't work. That would be like trying to build an extra bedroom on the second floor of a new home without worrying about the basement, the foundation, and all the supporting structure.

Storyboards and Text Outlines

Before launching into the creation of text solutions, the authors (see The Responsibility Assignment Matrix in Chapter 12) must first devote time in planning their part of their solution by producing a document for review by other team members (peers, supervisors, and other reviewers).

Some sections of solutions will be better suited to an outline, and others to a storyboard form. The common element is that your authors should begin by creating a review document (outline or storyboard) matched to their individual assignments.

> **Beltway Buzz**
>
> The great majority of individuals involved in creating a proposal fall into one of two camps: they really *like* it, or they really *dislike* it. Few individuals are in the middle.

The storyboard is a great tool for converting an idea to a source document to guide a response. These come in a variety of forms, all designed to allow the storyboard creator to describe the required response (or better, "solution") using bullets, graphics, tables, and other devices. Upon review and approval of the storyboard, the authors then have the go-ahead to convert those ideas to text.

Various Document Versions

Creating proposals is an iterative process. You begin with a high-level outline as supplied by 05 Outline and RAM, a proposal plan attachment. Using that framework, you and your team develop more detailed outlines and/or storyboards. Immediately, your team will experience problems with the control of these various documents. Someone will ask, "Who has the latest *version* of Section 3.12?" This can be a serious problem unless your team practices good version control.

def•i•ni•tion

Version is the preferred word to describe documents (text or visuals) at some stage in the evolutionary process. Avoid "draft" as every version is a draft until the final version is submitted. As important, using "draft" can be a poor excuse for failing to create the best text or visual you can at any one time.

Evaluation Teams and Their Roles

It's a rare achievement to do something right the first time, so your proposal will likely go through many versions until it's a quality finished product ready to submit. One way to ensure a great finished product is to have qualified people review and evaluate various versions as you go along. The trick is to get the right kinds of evaluations at the right time by the right evaluators to achieve an increase in the quality of the versions.

Evaluation teams come in six types, each of which we describe in the order it is typically used. These teams usually work on a 60-day turnaround time basis, with days being calendar days, not work days. (By the way, we use the terms "review" and "evaluation" interchangeably here. Different teams use different terms, so get used to hearing both.)

The Black Hat Team

The black hat team plays the role of the "bad guys." They can do a review at any time but certainly should do one either just before or just after the release of the final solicitation. Members of this team know the competition, and their objective is to assess the competitors' strengths and weaknesses regarding technical management, past performance, and price range. Using this knowledge, the team then compares these strengths and weaknesses with your own strengths and weaknesses. The result of the evaluation should be strategies you can use to make a convincing case that your own solution is not only different from but also better than those of your competitors.

The Green Team

The green team evaluators focus on the financial, cost, and price aspects of the proposal, thus the name "green" for money. Their review usually begins five to seven days after the solicitation is released. This team is interested only in how the cost volume is progressing, giving only passing consideration to the technical or management aspects. It looks for opportunities to cut costs while still meeting specifications. In large companies, individuals from other divisions with cost knowledge and responsibilities are particularly effective members of this team.

Members of the green team should include the following people:

- ◆ Proposal manager (facilitates the effort and reports the results)
- ◆ Relationship manager (salesperson)
- ◆ Capture manager (if different from the relationship manager)
- ◆ Program manager-designate (helps with any management volume issues)
- ◆ Cost/Price manager (to supply ROM estimates on relative costs)
- ◆ Contracts manager (CM)

In addition, the team may take a look at about a half-dozen alternative technical and management approaches and decide (or at least provide analysis for a decision) which of these is the best approach to use for this opportunity.

The heart of this review is the creation of a seven-column table. Each column in the table represents a different case, which is a management, technical, or others (such as logistics or build vs. buy decision). In the stub column of the table, list and describe the characteristics of the solution. The final entry stub column is "Relative Cost." In the first, or baseline, column for cost, enter "1.00" to signify that this is the column that will provide the nominal value of 1.00. Other entries in this row will be assigned numbers indicating an (imprecise) estimate, or guess, of the cost of that column, in relation to the base column. Be aware that these are often very rough estimates and not based on lots of detailed cost analysis.

At the top of each column, name the alternatives, the first case column being "Baseline." The next column might be "Decentralized Program Management Office" or "Juniper Equipment" (for example, if Cisco is in the baseline case).

Think creatively long enough to develop as many as five to nine cases, each with a relative Rough Order of Magnitude (ROM) cost. Then on the basis of your best judgment of what the customer really wants to buy, choose the *real* company solution.

Assuming this is thoughtfully done, it is highly likely that one of the discarded cases is the solution of one of your competitors. If you know that, then you're in a position to "ghost" that competitor's solution and show that your solution is not only different from, but also better than, theirs.

The Pink Team

The pink team is called pink because they're not ready for red, as in a proposal that's not ready to have the red pen put to it for a heavy-duty edit. This team usually does their review about 15 days after the solicitation release, and its members are typically in-house people at your organization but not members of your main proposal team for this effort.

This team's review is at the storyboard or outline level. Typically, there is no text to review at this time. In fact, if there is text, that's usually because it has been mined or borrowed from a past proposal. Upon the conclusion of the pink team's review, the various authors should have an approved outline or storyboard and be turned loose to convert the ideas and approaches into full text.

The Red Team

Even though the red team's review may be done mostly electronically with editing marks that may or may not show up in red, this team takes its name from the tradition of editing a document with a red pen. Or you can think of the name as representing the blood spilled at their review!

This team conducts an evaluation about 10 to 12 days before the proposal is due. Your desired standard for the red team version is that the version should be good enough to go to the customer, with some cleanup of visuals and resolution of minor conflicts between or among sections. The Red Team is also the last major opportunity to ensure compliance with customer requirements.

The Purple Team

With purple being the traditional color of royalty, this team's title is fitting for the top management (TM) reviewers. The purples review the proposal concurrently with the red team. The near-final version of the proposal is given both to top management in your own organization and the top management of your subcontractors. This team does not meet formally as the others do. Instead, you bring TM into the process in this way without allowing their membership in the concurrent red team. Having this team accomplishes two things: you keep TM off the red team (their presence on the red team can be so powerful it dominates the team, which you don't want); and TM has the benefit of the then-current state of the proposal version, so that TM is fully prepared to help the proposal team take into account the red team comments.

The Gold Team

The gold team is made up of important people who have the authority to approve the submission of your proposal. They may not be the very top management individuals but are usually the trusted lieutenants of TM. Their review is done two or three days before the proposal is due. This is well after the red team comments have been incorporated into the proposal version. This is the absolute last chance for your company to make changes before submission and typically includes last-minute decisions on cost issues. The trick is to make those decisions cascade through the balance of the proposal document, to ensure consistency among the volumes, and particularly to ensure that the cost figures match those in the other volumes.

How to Track the Questions and Answers

You must keep careful track of the questions your CM has submitted to the customer, along with the customer's responses to your questions as well as to those of your competitors.

Here's a checklist of tips for why and how to track the answers:

♦ Tracking your own questions tells you which questions you've already asked and prevents the embarrassing circumstance of asking the same question twice.

♦ Using your own questions, you can then compare the customer's summary answers to your own questions. This analysis could well tell you important facts about your competition.

♦ For complex solicitations with lots of questions and answers, keep an electronic log of all these actions and a detailed crosswalk between your own questions, your competitors' questions, and the customer answers. Identify any unmatched items, and do a running analysis of why there are unmatched items.

♦ If your questions are not answered in a timely way, you do have the right to point that out to the KO and ask him why your questions have not been answered in a timely way.

Bid Decision Point #4: Proceed or Cease Efforts?

In Chapter 4 we introduced you to the concept of bid decision points. The first three points came up in Chapters 4, 8, and 14. Now that you've read Chapter 15, you might find it surprising that you could get all the way to the process of starting to write the proposal and still be considering not bidding. But remember, the process of creating a solution and a proposal to submit is such a lengthy, expensive endeavor, that even if you bow out at this point after having invested considerable time and some money, you are still ahead of the game.

Now, as you're on the brink of committing the bulk of the time and money required to create a large proposal, you face Bid Decision Point #4. Do you proceed with the plan and bid to win, or do you cease all efforts and try again another time?

TM is the final decision-maker on all bid decisions, including this one. At each bid decision point, TM decides: go or no-go. Sometimes these decisions are easy, and sometimes difficult. The best TMs listen carefully to all relevant proposal team members, but in the end, TM makes the decision.

The Least You Need to Know

- ◆ Proposal creation can easily become inefficient and expensive, so keep a tight rein on the process with text creation controls.

- ◆ Intermediate documents are an absolute requirement for winning proposals.

- ◆ Use evaluation teams to review and improve your work.

- ◆ Proposal authors must think, plan, and have peer reviews at the storyboard or outline level before creating solutions using text.

- ◆ Keep careful track of the questions you and your competition ask the customer and the answers you get.

- ◆ TM ultimately makes all the bid decisions, but proposal team members' inputs are important influences.

Chapter 16

Creating Technical Volumes

In This Chapter

◆ Defining technical volume

◆ Organizing the technical volume

◆ Stating your solution

◆ Showing as well as telling

◆ Common mistakes to avoid

Every opportunity for a government contract begins with a problem to be solved, and every good proposal created to win a government contract must offer a solution to that problem. The technical volume is the portion of your proposal that describes that solution.

The technical volume says not only what you're going to do but also how and when you'll do it. Working in consort with the management volume (explained in Chapter 17) and the cost/price volume (covered in Chapter 18), the technical volume is where you build your case for why your company can not only do the work and offer the product or service needed but can also do it better, faster, smarter, or in any other way that blows the competition out of the water.

How Do You Organize Technical Volumes?

The first question in creating the technical volume is, "How are we going to organize a solution to the customer's technical problem?" Your first reaction might be to organize your response in the way it's laid out in Section C of the solicitation (see Chapter 14). But this is not a good path to take, because the correct answer is that you need to stick with your proposal plan. Pay particularly sharp attention to your attachment 05 Proposal Outline and RAM. This shows that the correct precedence is: First by Section L (Instructions, Conditions, and Other Statements), then within L, by Section M (Evaluation Factors), and then within that, by Section C (Descriptions/ Specifications/Work Statement).

Red Flag

Having sketchy knowledge of customer requirements before the solicitation is released puts you at a disadvantage when you create the technical volume. With gaps in your knowledge of what the customer really needs, you have only the solicitation's statement of need to go on, which usually isn't enough. Work with your relationship manager to complete the gap analysis worksheet early to discover the gaps between your company's current capability and the customer requirements.

Team Members for the Technical Volume

Your technical people are typically the leaders of the technical volume as they are the ones who create technical solutions and have responsibility to describe that solution. Technical writers and others who are not subject matter experts may assist them, but your technical people are in charge of the technical content.

Beltway Buzz

The black hat review and the green team review (see Chapter 15) are great sources of input on how your solution is far better than the alternatives offered by the competition.

The technical team does not work in a vacuum, however. Coordination among the different volumes is a must as your solution in each volume must match your solution in the other volumes. So cooperation across teams is an absolute requirement. This coordination is best achieved by having everyone physically working in the same location. Rubbing elbows, having impromptu hall conversations, and seeing each other's outlines and storyboards are all part of the process that is only possible when everyone's in the same place.

Expect Some Resistance

Unfortunately, but typically, the technical experts from your team will resist following the proper order. They would like to give solutions organized either in the Section C order or in some other way that they think makes better sense. However, neither of these is correct. You *must* use the outline provided by Attachment 03, as created by the proposal manager and the PM's staff.

Government Insider _____

If some team members resist following the prescribed organization of the technical volume, tell them that making it easy for the evaluators to find your solution is half the battle to a good score. Stick with the plan!

Stating the Solution

The leading paragraphs of your technical volume should describe the conceptual level of the technical solution that is a part of your program plan. So before you launch into a detailed response, give enough of an overview of your solution that the readers and scorers can have an idea—a road map—of where you're going. Using a clear, but simple visual is a start. (Don't overwhelm your evaluators with the nitty-gritty details at this level.) A succinct, powerful summary of the technical solution goes a long way to getting a high score on this volume and ultimately a contract award.

Stating Your Solution as Problem-Solving

Remember, also, that your technical volume is not only about how you are going to carry out the solution but also when you will do it and over what time frame with what sort of schedule. That's why your "Schedule for Delivery of Products" is so important. This schedule answers the customer's implicit question, "When am I going to get my stuff?" (See Chapter 12 for a discussion of the 03 Executive Summary and the "Schedule for Delivery of Products," an important part of the executive summary.)

Your Solution in a Broader Context

When presenting your solution, you're not simply responding to what's in the solicitation, but rather you're crafting a response that reflects the procurement, that is the bigger picture context of what has led the customer to the point of having this opportunity—the *real* problem to be solved. (See Chapter 8 for differences between the solicitation and the procurement.) You'll be able to describe your solution in a broader context of the procurement if you've gained that insight through many pre-solicitation contacts with the customer, including most prominently the technical and marketing interchange.

Writing to Your Audience

Two audiences, not just one, will read your proposal, so you must win over two different sets of readers. Those two will be reading and reacting to your proposal in two different ways.

The Decision-Maker Audience

Your first audience is the decision-maker or team of decision-makers, the people who will make the award decision. These decision-makers are interested in concepts and leave the detailed scoring work to others. The impression you must make with a decision-maker is that you do understand the customer's problem and have a well-planned, comprehensive solution described in your proposal. In the best case, the decision-maker knows the top management of your company. Let's say your top management is led by Pat. The reaction you want to elicit in the decision-maker after reading your proposal is, "Good ole Pat came through for me."

> **Government Insider**
>
> When referring to your solution, use the word "the," not "a," as in "We have the technical solution." This establishes the mind-set among reviewers that your company offers not just any solution but the only solution that meets the customer's requirements.

The decision-maker is interested in concepts, not details. That's why, in the opening paragraphs of your technical volume, you "describe your solution using both words and graphics or visuals. Your plan is to have the decision-maker understand your solution, embrace it, and like it.

The Proposal Scoring Audience

The proposal scoring audience members are the individuals charged with evaluating proposal submissions in great detail. Some evaluation teams are made up of "scores of scorers," with many people doing the evaluation. But for smaller opportunities, there may be only a small handful of scorers on the team.

The mechanism for evaluation is a set of scorecards or score sheets. Each section of the incoming proposals has a matching scorecard, which the customer evaluation team has created in accordance with the solicitation. These cards are not opportunities for creativity but are products of brute force, matching the solicitation to the incoming proposals and weighted consistent with the stated evaluation factors.

The reaction you want to illicit from this audience is, "This is the proposal against which we will judge all others." You can get this reaction *only* by strictly adhering to the solicitation sections and in the L, M, C order. Anything else will be inconsistent with the scorecards, and will therefore mean more work for the evaluators. More work for them will undoubtedly result in lower scores for your team.

Beltway Buzz

Already is the most powerful word in proposals. If your company is now engaged in activities similar to those of this opportunity, then you can legitimately say you are *already* doing whatever it is you now propose to do again. Because of the evaluators' wish to avoid risk, the word *already* gives the evaluators a warm feeling about your solution. "Hey, this offeror is already doing this kind of thing!"

Putting the Show in Show and Tell

Anyone can claim they're going to do something. They can describe a solution and use fancy words and impressive language to claim that they can do it. But if you go on to show, not just tell, you can be much more convincing. Showing can be in the literal sense with visuals that feature your products or service process or demonstrate the flow of your program plan. But showing can also mean describing how you will carry out the solution, not just what the solution is.

Use Visuals

The mind thinks in pictures, so use a picture of the device you're delivering if your solution is complex. Show a high-level system architecture diagram of a large network, or show a flowchart of processes you're using. What is the most prominent feature (and benefit) of your solution? What characteristic of your solution makes yours stand out above all the noise and details? All these are candidates for helping to explain your solution in terms easily understood by the evaluators.

You can almost say that the proposal that communicates the technical solution most clearly, in visuals, is the one the evaluators will reward with a contract.

Government Insider _____

Engage SMEs and other technical and management gurus early and often, especially for doing a gap analysis in the pre-RFP stage. Strive not only to discover your own weaknesses but also to influence the customer requirements away from your company's weaknesses toward your strengths.

Show *How* You Do It

A good proposal is a good plan, and vice versa. So your technical solution should show not only *that* you plan to do something but also *how* you plan to do it.

This list suggests possible ways you can use to describe just how you plan to do it, where "it" is the customer's work. All these are simply placeholders, examples of the form of your themes, so it's unlikely you will be able to lay claim to these exact phrases in your own technical volume:

- We have a rolling start on the customer's program as a result of our current and recent work at (another customer).

- We leverage our experience (processes, personnel, lessons learned) from these customers we've served. (Say whether this is through horizontal or vertical integration.)

- Our quality program conforms to XYZ national/international standards.

- Our subcontractors (call out by name) contribute XYZ to the technical solution offered by our team.

- Our technical solution is based on To Be Supplied (TBS) trade-off studies, which have caused us to select this specific technical solution, because of (TBS).

- Our technical solution integrates To Be Supplied (TBS) individual components, each of which has passed rigorous subsystem tests.

Position Your Company as the Least Risky Choice

When you're really stuck as to how to describe your solution and all else has failed, you can always turn to risk assessments. Very often, those speaking or writing about "risk" are guilty of fuzzy thinking as the term "risk" by itself is unclear. Because there are three distinct *types* of risk, it's important that speakers and writers be clear about which type or types of risk they mean.

- ◆ Technical Risk—Will this work as described in the work statement?

- ◆ Schedule Risk—Can this be completed within the time frame contemplated by the solicitation?

- ◆ Cost Risk—Can this product be delivered within the cost constraints of the contract?

In an old urban legend, a contractor was asked, "What can you deliver?" and the answer was, "Quality. Schedule. Cost. Pick any two." There's certainly truth in that response as trade-offs are often made among these three. If a customer is pushed to the wall, it's then necessary to choose which of the three to sacrifice. For example, if the program is in trouble and is unlikely to be completed satisfactorily (the product works as specified), on time (consistent with the program schedule), and within budget (for the money stated in the contract), a reasonable way to solve this would be to have the customer choose among these alternatives:

- ◆ Accept a lesser performance

- ◆ Accept that the product will be late

- ◆ Add money to the contract

Making that choice is not something you want to force your customer to do. So your technical solution should address these three types of risk individually and then as a set. This will give the customer confidence that you truly do understand the seriousness of the work and that you are fully prepared to achieve the desired results, on time and within budget.

Avoid Common Mistakes

Whatever else you do in creating the technical volume, take care to avoid the mistakes discussed in the following sections.

Presenting the Zero-Content Solution

A "zero-content solution" means that when stripped of the fancy words and all the fluff, your proposal doesn't say *how* you'll do the work or that you have any idea about the work (except what's in the solicitation). It only says you'll *do* the work. Then you fill up space by embellishing the response with claims of previous successes, which might be interesting, but the customer really wants to know how you're going to do *this* job.

A well-written solicitation might contain a phrase, usually in Section L, that specifically admonishes the offerors to avoid this mistake. The phrase to look for is something like, "Responses stating that you understand and will comply are nonresponsive." Even if the phrase isn't in this particular solicitation, pretend it is, and avoid at all costs solutions that are high on verbiage and low on specifics.

Red Flag

The danger of zero-content solutions is not only that they can earn a very low grade by the scorers but also that if your proposal is riddled with too many instances of zero-content response, you run the risk of being judged as "nonresponsive" and are made ineligible for a contract award.

Using Your Terms, Not the Customer's

Among the most common and most serious mistakes is the gratuitous substitution of your own terminology for the customer's. If the customer calls the head person on this contract "Project Manager," then you call that person "Project Manager." Never mind that, in your company, project managers get promoted to program managers, and therefore someone who is—within your company—a program manager may resent being "demoted" to a project manager. Again, play back the customer's language in everything you do in the proposal. Absolutely nothing good happens when you change labels, because changing labels is a sign of technical arrogance, which will be punished by the customer evaluators.

Writing as if the Evaluators Know It All

Don't assume all the evaluators know as much as you do about the subject matter, as the evaluators will come from many different places in the customer community. Some evaluators may be very highly technical; others may be simply someone not on an alternate assignment with a higher priority. You may get entry level evaluators or ones with management expertise. Make your writing simple enough to resonate with all the evaluators. An evaluator who can't understand what you're saying is very unlikely to give you a good evaluation.

The Least You Need to Know

- Your technical volume has two different audiences: the decision-maker and the evaluators.

- The best solutions are in the context of the procurement, not just the solicitation, and address the customer's problem as you understand it.

- You must organize the technical volume in the L, M, C order of precedence, unless for some unusual reason the solicitation specifies otherwise.

- A good technical proposal is a good plan and vice versa.

Creating Management Volumes

In This Chapter

◆ The management volume is critical

◆ Three questions your management volume must answer

◆ Showing you have a program plan

◆ The makeup of a management plan

◆ Common mistakes to avoid

The management volume is your chance to show the customer how you actually plan to manage the program you're proposing to carry out. Your technical volume as described in Chapter 16 might lay out an impressive solution to a problem the government is facing, but unless you can deliver on that solution, the technical volume may as well be used to line bird cages. So it's critical to know what goes into the management volume, how to organize it, and how to avoid common mistakes. This chapter helps you deal with these things.

As you read this chapter, you may want to refer to Appendix C to see a sanitized (all identifying information removed) version of a real solicitation for the management volume. The requirements included in that sample solicitation are what drive the response suggestions we describe in this material.

The Importance of the Management Volume

The evaluators of your proposal will find it moderately interesting that you have successfully managed programs of this size and type before. The evaluators think it's great that you can cite past performance on contracts similar in size, scope, and complexity. If you have no significant past performance citations, it's often acceptable to cite the past performance of your subcontractors. However, read the solicitation carefully because it's not always acceptable to use your subcontractors for past performance citations.

The crucial question you must answer is how you are planning to manage *this* program. Do you know enough about the peculiarities of this program to give the evaluators confidence that you have a grasp of the risks found in this program? The management volume is your opportunity to convince the evaluators that your team can deliver the products on time and at or under the budgeted cost.

Beltway Buzz

Let's say you're the prime of a small company, and you have no "standard processes," such as quality assurance, configuration management, document controls, and cost accounting systems. Then it's perfectly acceptable to adapt and adopt the corresponding processes of a team member—such as a larger, more experienced company—to be the processes of your team. This is an easy way for your small company, still lacking your own well-developed processes, to compete on an equal footing with larger companies.

The management volume is often the difference that separates winners from losers in the competition. Solicitations often appear to focus on who can offer the best technical solution. In fact, these are often really management competitions, just disguised as a technical shoot-out.

Multi-Yea...

The r... ...ou describe it in the management
volu... ...l last over many years. The custom... ...
me...

Th...

...rships with their contractors, espe-
...ance your chances of winning the
...ion high in well-defined processes
...at you will bring the customer into
...or example, solutions that base the
...ases are covered, the offeror makes no
...immingly, are simply not believable.
... Winning plans are based on the real-
...hrough an open partnership and spirit
...return to the desired track. So the real

◆ How does... ...am quickly identify any unfavorable
detours from the program plan?

◆ How does the team create and then execute a believable catch-back to that plan?

If you can answer these important questions clearly and convincingly in your management volume, then it will serve you well on the road to a win.

Telling the Evaluators How You're Going to Do the Work

The details of the solicitation dictate the content and organization of your management volume (see Chapter 14 for a full discussion of this process). Whatever else the customer requires, how you plan to organize your program is of keen interest to the evaluators. So let's take a look at a convenient and efficient way of describing that "how." (Again, the organization of your response must be in accordance with the solicitation's instructions.)

In many different ways, the customer asks about how you plan to organize your people to achieve the customer's goals. In some solicitations, the customer may not care or want to know how you're going to do the work. But except for very simple programs, the customer wants to know, and needs to know, how you're going to do the job. So a nearly universal request is to show how you plan to manage the program. In other words, they want you to describe your management plan. You'll find two common clues in a solicitation that should trigger you to write about your management plan:

- ◆ Show an organization chart.

- ◆ How do you plan to organize this program to achieve the program objectives?

Each solicitation is different, and therefore your response (or better, your solution). But the vast majority of solicitations want to know that you have a plan for accomplishing the work. The language used in the solicitation you're responding to might be different, and the exact request will be tailored to the specifics of the solicitation, but the resulting, net request remains the same. The customer simply wants to know you've got a plan, and what your plan looks like.

Red Flag

If asked to provide an organization chart in your management volume, stick to job titles that are easily understood outside of your company. The easiest way is to play back the customer's own job titles. I've never figured out whether a Senior Analyst III is higher or lower than a Senior Analyst I. Have you?

Describing the Management Plan

If you've found the clues and know you need to lay out your management plan, then you need to structure it around three main topics. These topics are usually presented with visuals that answer the three questions the government evaluators have about your management plan. These are:

♦ Does this offeror really know who's in charge? (The right answer is that the government's program manager will be in charge.)

♦ Where, within your own organization, does this program manager report? (That is, how high in your company does this person reside, so that I, the customer, don't have to go through layer-upon-layer of bureaucracy to get to someone who can fix the problem if I'm unable to do so through the program manager?)

♦ How does your program manager plan to organize the program resources to accomplish the government's mission or objectives? (That is, who reports to whom, within the program organization, and does that organization mirror the government's own organization, if that's desirable?)

Answering these questions requires you to include three visuals in your management volume. These are:

♦ Reporting Responsibility

♦ Our Organization Chart

♦ Program Organization

The point here is that there is a flow-down from Top Management to the Program Manager and his or her team. The Program Organization describes, in some detail, just how the program manager's organization is well suited to accomplishing the program objectives.

Include the first two visuals as part of a standard management solution. The third visual presents the real solution for how you plan to manage this specific program. The details of this visual must tie closely to the technical solution you are offering, so creating this visual requires close cooperation from, and coordination with, the authors of the technical volume.

*Our Program Manager,
Clyde Clodd, reports to, and
takes direction from, the
government Program
Manager.*

Reporting Responsibility

Government Program Manager
XYZ Program

Company Program Manager
XYZ Program
Clyde Clodd

*Clyde Clodd, our Program
Manager, reports to Steve
Strong, the XYZ Program
Director.*

Our Organization Chart

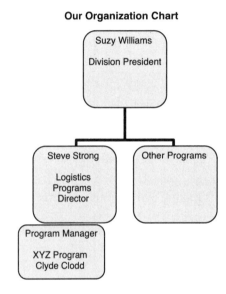

Suzy Williams

Division President

Steve Strong

Logistics
Programs
Director

Other Programs

Program Manager

XYZ Program
Clyde Clodd

Program Organization

Program Manager
XYZ Program
Clyde Clodd

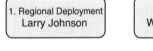

1. Regional Deployment
Larry Johnson

2. R & D
Walter Whitlock

3. Quality Control
Frankie Larson

4. Logistics Support
John C. Lee, Jr.

5. Network Change
Analysis
Janie Towers

6. Vendor Interfaces
Leslie Brooke

7. Program
Management
Tammy Jarrett

Clyde Clodd organizes his program in accordance with the statement of work.

Showing You're Off to a Rolling Start

Your management approach is very likely based on the management processes of a similar program. Or perhaps you are planning to rely on the management processes of a subcontractor to use in this program. In either event, you can legitimately claim that you have a "rolling start" in the execution of the management plan. You can strengthen your case by, for example, pointing out that you have *contingency hires* for certain critical positions. (Critical positions is a generic term; the term the government uses most often is *key personnel*.)

def•i•ni•tion

Individuals who, upon award to your company, have already fully committed in writing (provided with the proposal) to come onto your payroll and fill a specific need within the organization are **contingency hires**. You may have plans to go outside the personnel currently in your organization to use one or more new-hire individuals with sterling qualifications. This can be a very good idea, especially if the customer could view your company as being too small to handle this contract on your own, with the people you already have on the payroll.

Key personnel are the limited number (usually about three to six) of people the customer wants you to show as being available very early in program execution. Typically, this includes the program manager, a technical lead, and perhaps a deputy program manager. Less frequently, but also possible, are management lead, logistics lead, manufacturing team lead, and quality assurance manager. However many, you must pick these people carefully. Their suitability and availability are sure to be major evaluation factors. Include these individuals, by name, in your O2 Proposal Drivers in the proposal plan.

Make a Chart of the Rolling Start

As part of this rolling start, you can prepare and show a visual displaying the characteristics, for example, of the work statement across the top (horizontal axis) and the personnel, by name, on the left column (vertical axis). Then show a crosswalk relationship between these individuals and the elements of the work statement. We call this a meatball chart because it looks like meatballs in the squares.

	Regional Deployments	Research and Development	Quality Control	Logistics Support	Network Change Analysis	Vendor Interfaces	Program Management
SOW Elements	1	2	3	4	5	6	7
Our Personnal							
Clyde Clodd	1	2		2		1	2
Larry Johnson	2						
Frankie Larson			2		2		1
Leslie Brooke	1			1		2	
Tom Truesdell	2	1			1		1
Dave Russett			1	2	1	1	
Walter Whitlock		2				1	
Tammy Jarrett	1		1				2
Anna Mari Stephenson		2	2			1	1
Lynn Willingham	1		1		1		
John C. Lee, Jr.		2		2		1	1
Janie Towers		1	1		2		1
Legend:							
blank = no exerience							
1 = journeyman							
2 = expert							

Our Team Has Both Breadth and Depth of Experience in All
Seven Elements of the SOW

Our available personnel are at least three-deep in each of the eight parts of the statement of work.

We Have a Plan

A good plan yields a good proposal and vice versa. So correctly and prominently saying that you have a plan—specifically a *program plan*—is a real plus for your proposal. Being realistic about how programs really go, the probability that you will be asked to execute that specific plan in all its glorious detail is nearly zero. However, don't let this dissuade you from presenting a detailed plan as a part of your submission.

def•i•ni•tion

A **program plan** describes, in as much detail as possible, how you will bring the right resources together to achieve the objective of your customer's program.

As a practical matter, one of the first milestones in your program execution is to meet with the customer and verify or reverify all the plans you've submitted.

Post-Award Requirements and Opportunities to Change Your Plan

One of the first activities in a new program is a meeting with your customer to discuss the details of your management plan. No matter how well you planned your program (and you did well enough to win!), there will be changes that reflect the differences between your management plan as a basis of award and the management plan you'll actually execute. This is now an opportunity for you and the customer to begin to operate as a cooperative team to replace the offered plan with the real plan. You improve the plan, as a team, by replacing the best guesses available at the time of the solicitation with the best data now available. So the customer will require that you make changes in your plan.

Now is your chance, as the winning bidder, to suggest a "better idea," insofar as you have truly better ideas. Yes, this is directly contrary to my previous admonition to avoid having a *better* idea and instead discuss *his* idea. That was true at offer time. But now that you're the winner, it's not only acceptable, but expected, that you come forward with at least some alternative approaches to accomplishing the work. Just remember that anything you recommend, and is accepted, must be followed by a change in the contract to reflect that change. And of course, if this is a more costly activity, you are entitled to an *equitable adjustment* in the contract.

def•i•ni•tion

Equitable adjustment is the compensation or price adjustment to which a contractor is entitled upon the occurrence of a constructive change or special event.

It's Really Plans in the Plural

The earlier reference to "we have a plan" is only partially correct. More often, your proposal will include the one program plan but also a list (sometimes short, sometimes long) of other plans. For a complex or large proposal, these plans could include a quality plan, technology refresh plan, logistics plan, configuration management plan, and deployment plan.

The really good news is that there's now a requirement, and an opportunity, to replace each of these plans with a revised plan. These revisions will be based on better data provided by the customer. And it is also your own opportunity to improve the plans through tailoring to this specific customer's wants. Again, now is the time to talk about any "better ideas" you may have to yield better results.

Here are two differences between having a better idea as an offeror, and as the winning contractor:

◆ Having a better idea as the offeror can cause you to be judged noncompliant with the solicitation, because you have not described how you plan to do the work required by the solicitation, and instead do some other work. This is a possible cause for rejection of your proposal.

◆ Having a better idea as a contractor can make you look good in the eyes of the customer, and perhaps even make the customer look good, by using your better idea!

Do you see the difference between having a better idea as the offeror and a better idea as the contractor?

Other Parts of the Management Plan

Now that you've learned about the two most common high-level questions:

◆ How do you plan to organize your program?

◆ Can your choices for important people on this program really do the job?

Let's discuss the other parts of the management volume as set out in the addendum.

Capacity of the Team

Your response must show how your team, including all your subcontractors, has the ability to "step up" to the amount of work this contract might require. This necessitates your listing the subcontractors by roles and responsibilities. Your best solutions would have no single point of failure, which means your team has built-in redundancy—you plan to compete (on the basis of price and availability and quality) among your subcontractors for pieces of the work. And your subcontractors (at least some individuals within each company) should have the same kind of name and face recognition with the customer that your program manager has.

Subcontract Management and Related Plans

There are three major types of subcontract plans, and they are sometimes confused. The confusion may result from a poorly constructed solicitation, which could reflect the customer's own confusion. The three types address three distinct objectives:

◆ Subcontract management asks how you, as the prime, plan to manage all the subcontractors on your team.

◆ Small Business Subcontracting Plan asks you how you plan to conform to the FAR subpart 19.7. This subpart covers the Small Business Subcontracting Program. However, if you're a small business yourself (as called out in FAR 19.702(b)(1), you may claim an exemption from the requirement to include this plan with your proposal. Don't worry too much about this one. The details are important in the context of a specific proposal, but these vary significantly from case to case.

◆ Small Business Participation Program is how you'll be measured, during the execution of the program, against the goals you've committed to in your proposal. Watch out; because even if you are a small business and therefore not required to submit a Small Business Subcontracting Plan, you may nonetheless be required to submit *this* plan. This plan has goals for subcontracting with (other) small businesses.

The above discussion is in the context of a specific proposal. You may well be required to submit other plans or give answers to other questions. You're on your own for these, but always work in the context of what is by now an old friend: the Section L–Section M–Section C precedence (assuming, of course, these sections are a part of the solicitation).

Avoid These Mistakes

As you prepare your management volume, consider this list of tips to follow and pitfalls to avoid.

◆ Your management volume in general speaks to your own company and not to the customer. For example, your organization chart shows several people who are important within the company and are shown on your chart because they were on an evaluation team and wanted to be shown. But the marketing vice president is undoubtedly of no interest to the customer and should not be present on the visual.

◆ Use labels that tell the function of the individual in the organization chart and not the level within the company. For example, if Susie Creamcheese is a quality assurance staff person, label her Quality Assurance Representative, and not Senior Analyst III.

◆ If your organization charts change over time, show these different charts, and label them as applying to a certain period. For example, during contract start-up (see Chapter 21), you may have more people on the project than later on. Perhaps you have start-up specialists, but only for the first 45 days. Showing this is a real plus with the evaluators as it demonstrates you've really thought about how to execute this program and not just pulled some materials from a previous proposal and changed the names.

The Least You Need to Know

◆ Your program organization must answer the customer's three implicit questions.

◆ Proving you have a rolling start is a major plus for your proposal.

◆ Know about, and take measures to avoid, the three common mistakes in management volumes.

Chapter 18

Creating Cost/Price Volumes

In This Chapter

♦ Ways cost and price fit into the decision mix

♦ Believable and realistic pricing

♦ Make your pricing competitive

♦ Integrating cost into the other proposal teams

♦ Checklist for creating cost volumes

Your technical volume tells the customer about the products or services you're offering as a solution to their problems, and your management volume explains how you're going to make it all happen. So the next question on the customer's mind is, naturally, "How much is it going to cost us?" That's where your cost/price volume enters the picture. In this portion of your proposal, you name your price, hoping the government entity will see that they'll get a good value for their money—better than they'd get from your competition.

So why do you use both the terms "cost" and "price"? How do they differ, and how are they related? And how do we make our pricing both believable and competitive, as well as develop the cost/price volume? These are good questions for you to ask, so let's give you some good answers.

The Difference Between Cost and Price

First, let's distinguish between cost and price, different but related concepts. The term "cost" is used when applied to contracts based on cost, not price. What this means is that the customer is uncertain about the precise nature of the work to be performed or the product to be delivered, and therefore can't expect a bidder to take the risk of naming a price that ends up not adequately covering the bidding company's costs plus some margin. So the customer assumes most of the risk, meaning that the customer goes into the deal without knowing exactly what it's going to cost them. But in this scenario, the contractor is required to report and justify its costs, according to the fine details of the contract.

We use the term "price" for various forms of fixed-price contracts. That is, the customer believes it has provided sufficiently detailed specifications that the bidders should be able to make offers at a firm price. Therefore, the bidders assume the risk of performance, hence the term fixed price. Whatever you offer and have had accepted, you will have to deliver at that price.

This is only a high-level explanation of cost versus price contracts, because many fine details are within these categories. Typically, such details are contained in the solicitation, and all offerors respond to the same requirements.

In this chapter, for simplicity, we will use "cost," but be aware that, subject to the previous distinction, you may substitute "price" and the advice will still hold.

Cost Can Be a Deciding Factor

Cost has always been important in government procurements. As taxpayers, all citizens appreciate that our public servants in the various government agencies are cost-conscious. This is unassailable. But there are other important factors in choosing between or among offerors. Just because you offer the lowest cost does not mean you'll be picked as the winner.

Beltway Buzz

In response to a Government Invitation For Bid (IFB), where the specifications are very clear, contracts are awarded to the bidder offering the lowest price.

The Best Value Factor

The most common process for requests for proposals (RFPs) is to evaluate proposals and make an award on a "best value" basis. You'll hear some common phrases used in the evaluations. "The government reserves the right to award to other than the lowest bidder." However, accompanying that statement is something like, "However, as technical solutions become more and more similar, price becomes more important." Or "The government will not pay substantially more for a small difference in quality." So if you look closely at the Section M Evaluation Criteria (or other solicitation sections giving "what counts as good," in the eyes of the customer), you'll usually see that the government is reluctant to award the contract to any offeror other than the lowest bidder unless they can justify the cost differential. Contracting officers (KOs) often find such justification difficult and will do so only with strong support from the balance of the customer evaluation team and/or the *Source Selection Authority (SSA)*.

def•i•ni•tion

Source Selection Authority is the person (usually a specific individual) with the authority to make the ultimate decision on the winner of a competition. Other staff functions, such as the Source Selection Evaluation Board (SSEB) help with the scoring of the proposals and may make a recommendation on the winner, but the SSA has the final word.

Lesson on Cost Competitiveness

So the lesson here is that if you and your company can't be cost competitive, your chances of winning a contract are not good. This does not mean you must be the low bidder to win, but it does mean that any cost differential must have clear justification. A legitimate question is often asked around this issue: "Is there some way to determine, in an individual case, just how much higher you can be and still win?" How much better must your solution be to justify, say, a 5 percent cost differential? There really is no definitive answer to that question, and the best we can say is that if you're not the lowest bidder (but also see the discussion on "cost uncertainty"), your technical and management solutions must be significantly better along some evaluation criterion that is important to your customer. Your best clues about what is important to the customer are found in the balance of Section M.

The "Should Cost" Factor

There is a strategy that might enable your company to win with a higher offered cost. Particularly for large and important contracts, the government develops an independent "Should Cost" amount," basically an estimate of what the project should cost.

This estimate is important as it gives the evaluators a benchmark against which to measure the cost of all incoming bids, a way to determine how reasonable they are. Equally important is that it helps ensure that the solicitation will result in solutions with prices that fit into the budget set aside for the program. It would surely make no sense for the government to release a solicitation with a "should cost" of $100 million if the budget for the program is only $75 million.

> **Red Flag**
>
> Your customer's program has two different budget numbers. The larger number, the gross budget, includes the government's own cost of managing the program. A smaller number, the net budget, is the amount the customer believes the contractor will need for his costs. Know the difference, or you may be working toward the wrong target budget.

How is this important to you as a bidder? Well, very. If you can find out—legally and ethically, of course—what the customer has as a "should cost," you'll be in a better position to develop your own cost.

Cost vs. Cost Uncertainty

Offerors have some latitude in how they present and justify their cost volume figures. The format of the results is set, but there are still opportunities for differences in presentation. These differences in substance and presentation can then be judged by the evaluators as either being reasonable and accurate or not-so-reasonable and not-so-accurate. Those in the second category are then judged to be high in risk because the evaluators estimate that those offerors will ultimately have higher cost to the customer. So for comparison purposes, the evaluators add some amount to the offered cost to cover the additional risk.

When awarding a cost-type contract, the government is very aware that the risk falls largely on its own shoulders. Therefore, any mitigation or elimination of cost risk you can offer is viewed very favorably. If you use the techniques in the following section, you will improve your chances of winning. By providing details about how you arrived at your costs, the evaluators are likely to accept your costs as stated. Correspondingly, if you fail to provide details about how you arrived at your costs, the evaluators will not accept your costs as stated. They will instead add a "fear factor," or other penalty for lack of believable details, and assign your cost proposal a higher probably cost. This higher cost could make the difference between your bid winning and losing.

Making Your Costs Believable and Realistic

Believability is important. The evaluation rules allow the customer to add to your offered cost if your cost proposal is not believable or if it has an unusually large amount of risk. In contrast, if your competition's cost presentation lacks detail or uses questionable assumptions or logic, the evaluators may well add to those costs, thereby resulting in a higher evaluated cost for those bids.

Providing the required detail is one way to make your cost believable. Here it's best for you to become a strict constructionist. If the solicitation requires detail down to the fourth level of indention, you must provide it. Three levels will not do. If the solicitation asks for a breakout of your subcontractors' costs, you must provide it. Doing an incomplete job of responding to the precise instructions for the cost volume has the same effect as for any other volume: you are in danger of being judged non-compliant.

Realism goes hand in hand with believability when it comes to costs. The best way to show that your costs are realistic is to provide increased details about just *how* you developed the cost estimates. There are two distinct ways of developing cost estimates.

Parametric Estimates

Parametric estimates come from starting with the cost of a similar product and then adding factors based on time, complexity, general cost escalation, and others, depending on the specific situation. For example (a fictitious example), you're asked to price a left-handed framazoid, which you've never built, but you developed a right-handed framazoid last year. To estimate the cost of the left-handed one, you start with your cost of the right-handed one, add a complexity factor for left-handed (everyone knows that left-handers are more complex, so you multiply by 1.125), and add an inflation factor for the year's difference (multiply by 1.035). So the parametric estimate gives you $1.125 \times 1.035 = 1.164$ (rounded) as the factor to use. Last year's right-handed framazoid cost $125.00, so this year's left-handed one can be bid at $145.55 (rounded).

Grassroots Estimates

Grassroots estimates come from a careful build-up of the pieces that go into a left-handed framazoid. Let's say you've never before built a framazoid, but you know it has seven parts. You develop estimates for each of the seven parts, down to the lowest piece you can find. Let's say you can buy five of the parts from outside sources, and you have enough independent bids that you know with a high degree of certainty that you can buy those parts, each at a certain known cost. You know you can manufacture the two remaining parts and the cost of each of those. Add the cost of the components, five plus two, and then add assembly and test costs (these are in-house, and you have good estimates on those). So now you have a good grassroots estimate of the cost of the left-handed framazoid.

In the best circumstance, you can develop a cost estimate using both the parametric and grassroots methods. Also in the best circumstance, your two independent estimates turn out to be close to each other. So now you have the ability not only to choose between them but also to report in your cost volume that you've developed the estimates in two ways. They are very close, and your offer is a blend or compromise between the two results. This type of presentation is comforting to a customer evaluator and allows that evaluator to accept your offered cost as the evaluated cost.

Let's carry this a bit further and say that the competition is not nearly so careful and thorough and complies minimally with the solicitation requirements. This *may* indicate that the competition did not put its own *first team* on this proposal and therefore has not done a good job. The customer evaluator may conclude that if the competition is not putting its first team onto the proposal, then that company will not put its first team onto the program, either. Good for you, and bad for the competition. So even though your offered cost is higher than the competition, your evaluated cost is lower than the competition, and you have an excellent chance of winning.

def·i·ni·tion

A **first team** is the very best a company has to offer. First team members are analogous to the starting lineup for sports teams.

Making Your Bid Competitive

Whatever you decide to submit with your proposal as your program cost, the bottom line is that the offered cost must be competitive. It is very unusual for a proposal to be successful at a significantly higher cost than alternative offers. While it is true that the lowest offered cost does not always win, the SSA is hard pressed to award to an offeror at a cost out of line with other, competing offers.

You must use your best efforts to know what the competition is likely to bid for a specific opportunity. Lack of good information about the competitor's willingness and ability to undercut your own cost is like going to a gunfight with a knife. You are probably *not* going to win.

Appendix B lists some fee-for-service sources with the ability to offer assistance in what your competition is likely to bid. Among the large systems integrators (SAIC, CSC, Northrop Grumman, Lockheed Martin), bidding habits are especially well known and can be calibrated with a fair degree of certainty. This game is not for amateurs. If you don't know what you're doing, engaging an outside, independent competition analysis firm can be very helpful in making cost decisions.

Integrating Cost with Other Volumes

The cost volume must be developed concurrently with the rest of the proposal. The cost volume is an integral part of the proposal, so it is imperative that the individuals for this volume (cost volume manager and contracts manager) be involved as full members of the proposal team. In fact, failure to fully integrate the cost perspectives in the proposal team is an invitation to disaster.

Green Team, Meet the Cost Team

The green team (as described in Chapter 12) looks at a variety of technical and management solutions to the customer's problem and arrives at a preferred solution, which your proposal team will offer. This is an excellent time and place to engage your cost proposal team members to collaborate with the green team on whether this choice will cause problems for the cost proposal team members.

GREEN TEAM TEMPLATE					
Category	You	Competitor #1	Competitor #2	Competitor #3	Competitor #4
Strengths	•	•	•	•	•
Countering Their Strengths		•	•	•	•
Weaknesses	•	•	•	•	•
Countering Your Weaknesses	•				
Opportunities (1)					•
Threats (2)	•				
Defending Against Attacks	•				

1. How can you capitalize on their weaknesses (ghosting)?
2. How will they attack you?

Strengths / Weaknesses / Opportunities / Threats (SWOT Analysis)

The Green Team uses this template to consider alternative technical and management solutions.

Avoid the Last-Minute Panic

A major flaw in any proposal process is to leave out the cost considerations until the last minute. You are then at Day 42 in a 45-day proposal effort. The proposal team presents the technical and management solutions to the cost proposal team (the cost manager and staff and your contracts manager and staff) and says, "Here's our solution. Now go cost it out." So the cost proposal team dutifully does so, burning the midnight oil and giving back a cost.

But it's 25 percent too high, higher than the customer's own "should cost" estimate and higher than anyone had anticipated. What are you to do? Is it possible to get 10 pounds of sand into a five-pound bag? Not likely. So you end up cutting the cost to within view of the should cost, but it's now no longer consistent with the technical and management volumes. At this late date, to meet the required submission date, you have no choice but to submit what you know is an inconsistent proposal. This is not what your team had counted on and not what you want. But the root cause of the last-minute panic and the inconsistent proposal occurred way back at the beginning when you failed to make the cost proposal team a part of the mainstream proposal team.

Match Estimating and Execution

Remember, a good proposal is a good plan, and a good plan is a good proposal. There's a corresponding point about cost volumes. The best cost estimations use the same techniques and same parameters that your accounting system uses for the program execution. Why is that? Well, if you use different models for estimating (which is really "budget formulation") than you do for accounting for actual costs (which is really "budget execution"), you can never compare the two directly. So if you can't compare the two directly, how will you ever know when you're getting better? Or getting worse? The simple and undeniable answer is, "You can't." That's why you must use the same model. Usually, your company is locked into an accounting system that is difficult and expensive to change, so you should adopt your cost estimation processes to match your accounting system.

Checklist for Cost Volumes

Here is a short checklist for developing an excellent cost volume.

- ❏ Develop this volume concurrently with technical and management volumes, including the type of trade-off analyses shown earlier in this chapter.

❏ Include, where you can, anti-competition themes. Of course, this presumes you know of and can articulate the competition.

❏ Provide complete data. Complete data helps raise the believability of your bid.

❏ Distinguish, in your narrative description in this volume, between *low cost* and *low uncertainty about cost*.

❏ Calibrate, wherever possible, any elements of cost/price with previous or known prices. Again, this lends believability to your bid.

❏ Discuss "best value" or other selection criteria, and justify your choice of technical/management solutions in the context of total procurement.

Do these things right, and you're on your way to a win!

The Least You Need to Know

◆ Cost volumes are very important because cost or price is often a primary differentiator evaluators are looking for.

◆ Submit a believable, competitive volume by showing how you came up with your estimates and by providing all the necessary detail to justify your cost.

◆ Know the customer's estimate and the competition's likely submission.

◆ Integrate the cost proposal effort fully into the efforts of the rest of the proposal team.

Clean-Up and Improvement Tasks

In This Chapter

- Factors that take you out of the contest early
- Reworking your proposal's existing version
- Preparing for customer change requests
- Preparing for best and final offer (BAFO)
- Sharpening all the plans

After submitting your initial proposal in all its radiant glory, your proposal team has every right to feel relieved and satisfied. The work of a proposal team can be grueling, so completing the process can be quite satisfying.

Everyone looks forward to the relief of actually seeing that hand receipt, or now more frequently an electronic receipt, confirming your proposal is in the hands of the people who might choose to award you the contract. So it's not only natural but also perfectly acceptable to want to take some time off and release the tension of the proposal process you've survived.

But this was only the first lap of the race, and so begins the second lap and perhaps later a third—and—no, that's too discouraging to contemplate. But you must be ready for more laps, so let's take it one at a time. In this chapter, you'll find out what the major tasks are, those laps between initial submission and contract award.

Ways You Might Be Taken Out of Competitive Range

The bulk of this information presumes you'll make it to final selection and award, but be aware that a *down select* may take you out of contention earlier. There are several reasons why your offer might be declared "no longer in the competitive range."

def•i•ni•tion

Down select is when there are many offerors and either a single winner (contract awardee) or a small number of winners; the government may notify you early in the offer evaluation process that you are no longer in the competitive range. The bad news is that you are no longer in consideration. The good news (if there is any) is that you may stop spending scarce business development funds on this opportunity and turn your attention to the next good opportunity.

Judged Noncompliant

The easiest way to find yourself taken out of the running is to be judged noncompliant, which means you failed to follow all the solicitation instructions. This is a serious shortcoming. Submitting a noncompliant proposal is almost without excuse. Your team should be experienced enough and thorough enough to avoid this disqualification. But if this happens, your next step is to ask for a debriefing by the Contracting Officer (KO) as soon as possible to determine exactly which instruction or instructions you failed to follow. Unfortunately, obtaining the required debriefing may have to wait until the competition is over and a contract is awarded.

Low Scores

Another reason you might be out of contention is that your technical, management, or other scores were so low in relation to other offerors that your offer no longer stands a chance of award. If you are rated fifth best in a field of six for a single award, the KO could easily judge your bid as no longer in the competitive range.

Not Acceptable

Related to the point about low scores is the fact that your offer could be judged not acceptable, and further, "not susceptible to being made acceptable." The difference between "noncompliant" and "not acceptable" is that the first fails to comply with the solicitation instructions. Not acceptable can be for a variety of reasons, including the following examples. The bottom line is that your proposal no longer has an opportunity for award.

An easy example is that you've taken an exception to one of the terms and conditions set out in Section K of the solicitation. For example, if you have taken an exception to the method of payment (probably a silly thing to do, but this is just an example) and all other offerors have not taken exception, then your offer could be judged unacceptable and removed from the competitive range. Another example is that you cannot meet the required 18-month delivery schedule, and you instead base your offer on a 24-month schedule. If the offers of three other offerors meet the 18-month schedule, your proposal will probably be judged, by the KO and the evaluators, as not acceptable.

In some cases, an offer could be judged unacceptable but could be made acceptable through relatively minor changes in the offer. But in other cases, it could be so bad that no reasonable amount of effort could make it acceptable, and you're no longer under consideration.

Pricing Too High or Even Too Low

Perhaps you've submitted an acceptable technical and management solution, but the price you've offered is either much too high (most often the case) or, in rare cases, too low.

Most major solicitations contain language allowing the government to eliminate offers with prices so low as to indicate that the offeror does not understand the complexity of the required work. This prevents an offeror, through its own error, from contracting for work that is far different from what the government really wants to buy. You can decrease the probability of this happening by carefully watching the prices of contracts for similar work.

If your submitted price is too high and judged very high by the evaluators, then there is reason for the KO to rule that you don't understand the complexity of the work, but this time on the high side.

Reworking Your Existing Proposal

Regardless of how well you believe your proposal team has done in creating a proposal, it's highly probable that you know of at least a few defects. Things happen at the last minute. Inconsistencies creep in. The technical and management volumes don't quite match. You had to use the name of a person who resigned three days before the proposal was due, and you didn't have time to change all 13 references to that person, by name, in the proposal. Almost anything that *could* go wrong in the last few hours of your proposal creation *did* go wrong. These glitches are nothing to cause the evaluators to judge you as noncompliant or nonresponsive. But they are things that require correction should the customer give you a chance to change your proposal of record.

One of the first things to do is to create a *tiger team*. This team should have both holdovers from the proposal team and at least a few members with fresh eyes and no ego involvement in the proposal.

This is a good time to engage contractor technical editors or proposal gurus as supplements to your full-time staff. You should also consider enlisting some help from any subcontractors on your team for this opportunity. The tiger team should spend two or three days looking at all aspects of the proposal of record. The holdover proposal team members should list the known deficiencies and errors. The members new to this proposal look for instances of internal inconsistencies, undefined terms, and similar problems. This team's work then gets saved in the electronic files until you have the opportunity to formally submit the changes.

> ### Beltway Buzz
>
> A typical Section L of a solicitation allows the government to award a contract on the basis of the initial submission, and therefore offerors should offer their best price with their initial submission. The reality, though, is that major, complex proposals are rarely awarded on the basis of initial submissions, so this never (okay, almost never) happens.

def•i•ni•tion

> A **tiger team** is a small group of people (usually fewer than a dozen) who come together for a limited time with a focused responsibility. The responsibility can be just about anything within the scope of the proposal effort, as long as the responsibilities and time frame are clearly defined. Tiger teams work hard for a short time, and show tangible results.

Prepare for Customer Change Requests

The customer questions and requests for changes can come in a variety of forms. For some proposals, the customer gives you Clarification Requests (CRs) and Deficiency Reports (DRs). A CR is less serious; it simply asks you to clarify a part of the proposal.

This could be a minor change in wording to make your statement clearer. A DR, in contrast, is more serious as it means the evaluators see a part of your proposal as deficient in some way. If not changed, this could eventually lead to your disqualification for being outside the competitive range, nonresponsive, or disqualifying in some other way. You and your team must take the DRs very seriously, even to the point of having your best senior staff look at these carefully.

Another form of feedback from the evaluators is to provide you with a list of Discussion Items (DIs). DIs are replacing CRs and DRs in more recent evaluations. These can be all over the spectrum, from relatively minor tweaks to major issues. Typically, you'll have time to prepare a response to the DIs by first submitting your responses in writing. Then, if the KO and his team desires oral discussion of these DIs, you will have a chance to discuss them with you and your team on one side of the room and the KO and the KO's team on the other side. These discussions can be pleasant or unpleasant, depending on the circumstances. Hope for pleasant; prepare for unpleasant.

Prepare for Best and Final Offer

After all discussions are complete, the KO may call for another round of proposal submissions. One common one is to ask for a Best and Final Offer (BAFO). This call usually means that the KO is now willing and able to make an award and is soliciting a final round of offers. Often, but not always, the issue is cost or price. This is the one last chance for the KO to attempt to drive down the offered costs and prices. Most KOs find it difficult to skip this round in the belief that offerors will submit more attractive terms with each round of negotiations.

Red Flag

An old hand at proposals has said that there's also such a thing as a BARFO, which stands for Best and Really Final Offer. Legend has it that a customer really wanted to award to Company A. Unfortunately, Company B kept submitting a better bid, including a lower price. So the KO kept asking for "just one more BAFO" and did so until the KO's choice won. So that became the *really* final offer.

Prepare early for such an eventuality, and know how much flexibility you and your company have on the offered cost/price. Here is a very good example of where it's absolutely necessary to have top management on board and fully informed of the issues. TM and only TM can approve any final cost/price concessions. Only TM has the perspective and authority to make this call. In fact, in large companies, the person or persons who have been TM for the proposal team to this point now must go to the next higher level of management to get permission to further reduce cost/price.

Sharpen All Plans

Typically, major proposals require you to submit plans. Examples of plans are:

- Management Plan: Answers the customer's questions, "How do you plan to actually manage this program? Who will be involved, and what functions will each perform? Does the organization you plan follow some logical outline, such as correspond to the Statement of Work?"

- Configuration Management Plan: Answers the customer's questions, "How do you plan to keep configuration control, especially of the critical deliverables? Will you use a board, a committee, or depend on industry standards?"

- Quality Plan: Answers the customer's questions, "Will you use certain standards of quality? ISO? CMMI? Will the individual charged with assuring quality report to the program manager (less desirable), or to a higher authority (more desirable, as this person then enjoys the appropriate amount of independence from the mainline management structure)?"

- Transition Plan: Answers the customer's questions, "How will you accomplish the high-risk activities associated with program start-up, and/or transition from the current contractor to your company? Do you have a specialist in such activities to help out for the first few days and weeks?"

- Security Plan: Answers the customer's questions, "Do you know all the government regulations on security, both document security and physical security? Do your staff members already have the required security clearances, or will there be a long wait while your staff members can obtain the required clearances? Will these important individuals be available in a timely way to support my program?"

Government Insider _____

There is a difference between a "plan for a plan" and a "plan." The customer sometimes wants one type, and sometimes the other. If you can't tell which of these the customer wants, ask the KO. The former requirement asks you to demonstrate your company's ability to create a plan; the latter requires that you deliver, with the proposal, a plan specific to this program.

Typically, you will submit proposals under significant time pressure. Unfortunately, the various plans often get less attention than you would really like. Now that you have more time, it's a good idea to take a look at each plan you've submitted with the proposal, to see if you can improve them. If you've been asked for and submitted a "plan for a plan," now consider whether it's to your advantage to spend a few more hours of effort to create an executable plan; that is a real plan, specific to this program.

For example, if you've submitted a quality plan, which was really more like a "plan for a plan," you may want to spend some time developing a quality plan tailored to this specific customer and this specific situation. You need not achieve a polished plan, but you could develop an outline for what would, upon award, go into the executable quality plan for this program.

The Least You Need to Know

- From the very beginning, your plans should include compliance, including taking no exceptions to the terms and conditions in Section L, to avoid being noncompliant.

- Anticipate the volume of work required after initial submission, and retain the important members of the proposal team as available for this work as this provides continuity.

- Fresh eyes, in the form of fresh outside help, provide a critical look at the proposal of record and can suggest improvements the proposal team is unlikely to find.

- Know what the customer is likely to ask and how you'll respond.

- It's possible to improve all the plans you've submitted now that you have more time.

- Know what flexibility you can get from TM if you believe you should reduce your cost/price when the KO asks for a BAFO.

Chapter 20

Continuing to Market Your Business

In This Chapter

◆ Ways to improve your chances of winning

◆ Using back channels to stay in touch with the customer

◆ Networking at professional meetings

◆ Using advertising to emphasize you are the one

◆ Preparing to start actual program execution

The submission of your proposal is not the end of your marketing efforts; it's just a milestone as the process of getting this specific government contract goes on and on. The next major milestone is the contract award, but you can and should do some specific things between now and when the government decides the winner—actions to enhance your chances of being that winner.

The material in this chapter tells you how to influence the decision-makers, including the customer community as a whole, as it provides a checklist for actions to consider taking.

Let's be clear: this book does not advocate or suggest in any way that you overstep the bounds of acceptable business practice. Law, ethics, and regulations provide strict boundaries on your actions. You must know these boundaries and stay well within them. As you already know, this book contains no legal advice. Always rely on your legal counsel and other sources of guidance (as described in Chapter 3) if in doubt about what behavior is appropriate and legal.

Using back channels, professional networking opportunities, and advertising are several ways to market your company's capabilities. Let's take a look at each.

Use Back Channels

Back channels are the unofficial communications that take place independent of the formal communication modes. You need to know of these channels and use them to present your company and its subcontractors in the best possible light.

Red Flag

Throughout this chapter, the presumption is that you are the prime contractor, not a subcontractor. If you are a subcontractor, you need to know what your prime contract can and cannot do as well as what should be done to further the cause of the team. If you are the prime, then be aware that your subcontractors are subject to the same restrictions that apply to you as the prime contractor. It's a good idea to stay on top of your subcontractors and what they are doing to avoid stepping over the legal, ethical, and regulatory lines.

One way you can use back channels is to enhance the name and face recognition of the people you're offering for this opportunity. Chapter 12's discussion of the proposal drivers shows how important it is to ensure that the program manager-designate has positive name and face recognition with the customer. In the best circumstances, you have already achieved at least some modest success toward this goal. Now, using back channels gives you another opportunity to enhance that individual's standing with the customer.

What might a back channel look like? How about sponsoring a golf outing for your company, your subcontractors, and individuals from your customer? Or attending, in some numbers, the retirement ceremony for a senior member of the customer staff? If you're marketing to the military, the ceremonies marking any changes in command also offer great opportunities to get positive exposure. Using back channels can be helpful to your company, not only for this contract opportunity but also for future ones as well.

In terms of the rules of the FAR and ethics, you must be careful to remain well within the procurement rules. For example, avoid unseemly familiarity at critical times, especially with the individuals you know are in a position to influence directly the award decision. Staying within these lines while accomplishing your objective of promoting your company requires not only discretion, but also experience. When in doubt, refrain from anything you feel may be taken to be undue and inappropriate attempts to influence immediate decisions. And of course, consult competent and relevant legal advice.

Network at Professional Meetings

Nothing prevents you from seeking, or even making, opportunities to "show the flag" for your team's case. Professional meetings are a neutral ground on which to rub shoulders with your customer. But first, avoid the appearance of overstepping the bounds of regulation and ethics by simply asking a pre-emptive question.

Let's say you're at a meeting of the local chapter of an engineering society and you know that Wally Johnson is a government employee and an engineer at your customer's local facility. Before you embarrass yourself and Wally, open the conversation with, "Hey Wally. My company is in competition for the left-handed framazoid program at your agency. I want to make sure you're not involved in any way with that selection process. If you are, I know I can't really speak with you about the procurement." This, then, clears you to proceed with a conversation with Wally. It also establishes that you know the rules and have actively taken care to avoid breaking them.

With that out of the way (assuming you get a "No, I'm not" from Wally), you can go on to at least discuss how your company is approaching government work in general, what great people are there, and how well qualified your company is to meet the customer's needs.

In the nation's capital area, opportunities abound for all manner of professional meetings. Just about every interest group has a professional association. Some of these are primarily lobbying groups, and others are aimed at improving industry standards and practices. See Appendix B for a brief list of these. These are illustrative only. It's impractical, and even impossible, to begin to list all these groups. These groups exist throughout the country, and even throughout the world. A quick look at a search engine such as Google will yield professional associations in your area.

Beyond regular attendance, consider sponsoring a table at a banquet or committing to a booth at a trade show. All these keep your name and face in the mind of your customer, and all are perfectly legitimate under the procurement rules and regulations.

Advertising

In the Washington, D.C., area's media market, residents are accustomed to seeing lots of advertising for the various (usually the large) government contractors. This advertising falls into two categories: institutional advertising and opportunity-specific advertising.

The media these large companies use include mass transportation ads, newspaper ads, radio ads, and television ads (particularly cable TV, focusing on the local markets in Washington, D.C., Maryland, and Virginia).

> ### Beltway Buzz
>
> You may be at least curious about whether regional advertising in the mass media (buses, general circulation newspapers, regional cable TV, local over-the-air TV, and local radio stations) can possibly be effective for companies seeking government contracts. The answer is, it must be or the companies wouldn't use these media. You may question whether a Super Bowl ad is really worth $3 million for a 60-second spot. But those ads sell out year after year!

If you're a small business, you undoubtedly lack the budget to participate in anything similar in scope to the advertising described here. Just be aware that it's legal and ethical, and then adjust your thinking to cover advertising that's corresponding but is small enough for your company and its business partners to handle. If your target population is largely engineers, for example, consider buying a page in the local engineering society's newsletter or paying for an ad on their website. If your target is management personnel, do the same for their local society's publications.

Institutional Advertising

This type of advertising strives to place positive thoughts and images in the subconscious minds of its audience. These often stress the benefits of a company's work, especially those companies providing national defense products. The ads emphasize positive images, such as strength, safety, dedication to principle, and value for the government dollar. Institutional advertising does not focus on a specific opportunity, but on the good things your company and your subcontractors do. For example, if you sponsor a local basketball team or a summer recreation league softball team, put your logo on their uniforms and arrange for a picture of the team wearing these uniforms to appear in the local newspaper. The end-of-season banquet and awards ceremony is always a good photo opportunity.

Competition Advertising

Competition advertising is quite different from institutional. It's much more specific in that it sharply focuses on a single opportunity and especially on those opportunities with only two remaining competitors for a single award. The United States Air Force Tanker Refueling Program, the subject of an intense competition between two gigantic teams, each with a gaggle of super-large defense industry contractors, is a good example. Each team of giants touts the benefits of its solution, and by pointing out their differences, the undesirability of the competition's solution. This competition has been going on for years now and at one point seemed to have been over at long last. But the loser protested and had its protest upheld. So the competition remains open through at least another round of proposals, orals, and Best and Final Offers (BAFOs. If you're a betting soul, take the side that says when the competition heats up again, these ads will magically reappear.

Preparing to Start Program Execution

Part of a good post-submission marketing program is to proceed as if an award to you were imminent. This is the same optimistic philosophy that states, in your proposal plan attachment "02 Proposal Development Schedule" (see Chapter 12), you will end with the scheduled date for the victory party. Why create a plan unless it ends with a victory party? If you don't have a dream, how are you going to have a dream come true?

Government Insider

Any expenses you have before starting, even in preparation for starting, are not recoverable under most contracts. This is called "precontract cost recognition" and is typically specifically excluded from your allowable costs. Consider this yet another aspect of the cost of doing business development, which is, of course, not funded directly by the government.

Let's say you're the challenger in a recompete situation. Let's assume further that it's a support contract, and you'll need about 50 new employees for your team, not including the ones you've chosen who are already either on your payroll or committed to you by a letter of commitment. Your team is striving to unseat the incumbent contractor, and you know the time between award and contract start is very short. Here's where your preparations to begin actual program execution (sometimes called a "rolling start"), comes in with three good effects on your own team and on the customer community:

- Conduct a recruiting fair, posting an ad in the local newspaper or local website, looking for qualified technical and administrative folks to execute the contract.

- If you'll need certain equipment not furnished by the government on this contract, solicit bids on that equipment on a contingency basis, and have an escape clause on any orders you place in the event you are not the winner. These clauses are usually not difficult to get because suppliers realize you can't place an unconditional order. This activity sends a signal that you're serious about this contract, expect to win (without being arrogant), and are ready to assume responsibility with a minimum of schedule risk to the customer. You may expect the incumbent will hear about these solicitations, and this will perhaps strike fear in their collective hearts!

- If you're going to use a start-up specialist for help with your transition from being the bidder to being the program team (see Chapter 21), begin to interview candidates for that position. Also, let it be known in the contractor community that you're looking for someone with that skill. Just looking is a strong sign of your commitment to winning and achieving a smooth transition.

The Least You Need to Know

- Make every proper effort to signal to the customer community that you are serious about capturing this opportunity.

- Use targeted advertising to enhance the perception of your team's solution.

- Be prepared to start, and take actions to make the start-up low in all risks to the customer.

- Do all these things without appearing to be overconfident or arrogant.

Part 6

Starting and Remaining Strong After You Win (or Lose)

You've heard it a thousand times: be careful what you wish for. You work long and hard to develop a solution and pull together a proposal, and then, lo and behold, you actually win the contract! Your team is exhausted from the effort, but the work is only beginning. Living up to the promises you made in your proposal takes a smooth transition from proposal team to project team and from seeking a contract to living and breathing—executing on—a contract. Learn what to do in the first 45 to 60 days, how to communicate with the customer, and how to hold on to the business long into the future. What if you don't win? We also cover the importance of debriefing after an award is announced and learning from your mistakes.

Chapter 21

Executing a Tight Start-Up Plan

In This Chapter

- ◆ Making the most of post-award debriefings
- ◆ High-risk hand-off to your program team
- ◆ Start-up plans and their risks
- ◆ Your program manager's role

"Best begun is half done." Albert Einstein said it, but it's probably best remembered as something Mary Poppins said. And how true this is for your newly won program! You won the contract because you proved you were the best, but you're only half done. Getting off on the right foot with your new customer at the beginning of program implementation is the way to build a lasting and mutually beneficial relationship. On the other hand, stumbling badly in the first few days and weeks of your new contract can create a deep hole you may never get out of.

So here you learn how to get your new program off to a good start with some specific techniques to help get you through the difficult first few weeks and months by making the most of the important debriefings you have coming and to create and execute the start-up plan between the old way of doing business and the way required for your contract.

Post-Award Debriefings

Sad to say, you'd be surprised at the failure of even large and supposedly sophisticated companies to take full advantage of the government's requirement to conduct a meaningful debriefing of your proposal. But because you're reading this book, *you* know better and should make these suggestions a part of your standard policies and procedures.

Setting the Right Stage for Your Debriefings

The time to obtain a commitment to a meaningful debriefing is before you create the proposal, not after it. Your customer relationship staff should arrange for a face-to-face meeting with the government program manager or even a higher authority. (Your best guess at the Source Selection Authority—the person who is actually going to make the procurement decision—is a good start.) Of course, you must do this well before the curtain goes down on customer contact, at which point you can deal *only* with the government's Contracting Officer (KO). Typically, this is three months or maybe six weeks *before* the solicitation comes out.

In your pre-solicitation KO meeting, you should cover the following three points:

♦ You intend to bid on this job.

♦ You bid only to win, and therefore you're bidding with the expectation of winning.

♦ Win or lose, you expect, in return for your hard work in seeking the business, that the KO or some other authority will obtain a detailed, comprehensive, candid debriefing of how your proposal was evaluated highly and where they found it lacking.

Be sure you're planning to bid on a specific opportunity before you have this meeting. You can't claim to have firm plans to bid and not bid. Failing to keep

> **Beltway Buzz**
>
> You can obtain a debriefing from the KO, but you must ask for one within three days of being notified of a contract award. If you ask for one later, the KO is not required to give you one (FAR 15.506). Don't fail to promptly ask for one.

your word leaves a bad impression with your customer's own management and makes everything you say open to question. As in all dealings with your customer, be truthful, and make your word your bond.

Rules for All Debriefings

The government is good about doing debriefings even though there's a suspicion that the KOs would just as soon be doing almost anything other than performing this task. These two rules apply to all debriefings.

◆ Take along at least one designated listener/designated recorder. This ensures that at least someone on your debriefing team is taking careful notes, not only of what was said but also the body language of the debriefers. If the program manager-designate and the marketing manager are asking questions and probably emotionally involved (especially if you've lost a "must-win" competition), these people can't be good note-takers or objective observers.

◆ Document the results, and circulate them widely, even if the results are an embarrassment to some individuals. Yes, this is risky, and you must use some discretion, but the organization as a whole, and especially those proposal team members who labored long and hard in the trenches to create a winning proposal, deserve to hear the positive feedback that comes from a win and need to know the negative feedback from a losing proposal.

The only way to get better is to learn from your hits and misses. Insist on, and carry through with, debriefings.

Red Flag

So you've won, and you don't think you need to bother with a debriefing. *Wrong.* Even when you win, your proposal probably had some areas the evaluators did not rate highly. And just because you won doesn't mean you won for the reason you *think.* Some people assume they've won for their superior technical solution, when in fact the only reason they won was price, and the customer wasn't all that crazy about their technical solution. Knowing the proposal parts that were problems will help you during program execution. So don't think about skipping the debriefing, or you might find yourself behind the eight ball from the get-go.

The basic considerations are *when* should you obtain a debriefing, *who* should do it, *what data* should you ask for, and *how widely* should you disseminate these results within the organization.

The correct answers are, in short:

◆ When? Almost always.

◆ Who? The program manager, the proposal manager, and the relationship manager, plus someone as the designated listener. A good candidate for the designated listener is your own contracts manager, but it need not be.

◆ What data? As much as you can reasonably obtain, focusing on the technical aspects and the cost considerations that led the customer to his decision.

◆ How widely? In relation to common practices, very widely; if anyone can do his job better by having the results of a previous debriefing, that individual should have it.

Debriefing After a Loss—A Special Case

For single-award opportunities, only two grades are given: A and F. An important weakness in the proposal practices of many firms when the grade is F is the lack of a formal, recorded, and disseminated debrief by the customer as to why the firm's proposals lost. The practice may not exist at all or perhaps be focused on getting information to the proposal team, specifically to program manager and/or the proposal manager.

Sometimes, but not often, such debriefings are in the context of a potential protest or even an actual protest.

The Mind-Set for Debriefings After a Loss

Psychologically, a debriefing after losing a contract award is a tough task. The tendency is to perform various mental gymnastics to "make right" your proposal and your proposal team. The company has quite often invested what is a considerable amount of money, not to mention hopes and dreams, in bidding an opportunity. The proposal team members have devoted considerable personal and professional energy in the proposal effort—nights, weekends, travel—and extensions of their professional and organizational skills are typical. In the absence of hard data, all sorts of reasons may be manufactured to explain the loss. That is all the more reason to press on, to expend what some will claim is good money after bad to make a trip to the customer's place of business and obtain a thorough, professionally conducted debriefing.

Although debriefing after a loss can be painful, a thorough debriefing of proposal losses has value with the customer, can give valuable information about a competitor, and therefore result in better future proposals.

Benefit: Enhancing Your Image

The customer may cooperate in a debriefing for you, as a loser, only because he is required to do so. But your positive, professional conduct in a well-conducted debriefing can raise your company's image with the customer. Asking for a debriefing says several things to the customer on behalf of your company:

◆ You recognize and respect the authority of the evaluating organization and solicit its candid, thoughtful evaluation of your own organization and its capabilities. Remember the phrase "What do you, the customer, think of us, in relation to the competition?"

◆ You have lost this competition, but you will very likely be back again in the future to contend for this customer's business.

◆ You care about your money and your people. You care enough to want to do better in the future, even if it is painful to discuss your shortcomings now.

Let's take the opposite scenario: you fail to ask for a debriefing. What impression is left with the customer by a company that spends hundreds of thousands of dollars to submit a proposal and then doesn't care enough about the customer, and about its own work, to obtain a relatively inexpensive feedback session? The short answer is: the impression is *not* positive.

Benefit: Improving Future Proposals

The previous section may incorrectly indicate that debriefings are done primarily for cosmetic reasons, but that is not so. They can reveal major weaknesses in the proposals that are either not apparent at all or have a greater import on decision-making by the customer than you thought they would. Although the case considered here is a general case, if you knew you had a major weakness in a part important to the customer, why did you bid at all? That statement supports the proposition that your company collectively believed that the part was *not* a weakness or that the customer would overlook the weakness as relatively unimportant.

For example, the customer may tell you clearly that the technology proposal you thought was great was significantly inferior. Although this may bruise the ego of the technical guru who championed this solution, it is absolutely vital for you and your company to know this. This information influences your future bids with this customer. And you will then probably come to know the solution really favored by the customer and whether the winning company had that solution. So now you have two pieces of useful information: one on the customer and the other on the competition.

The careful listener may pick up on the customer's hopes, fears, and biases at a time when there is less reluctance than usual for the customer to reveal that information. The customer representative, a human being like you and your representatives, realizes the amount of effort and money that went into even the poorest proposal and probably wishes to encourage you to try again and to do better in the future. The customer, particularly in the current competition situation, has every incentive to encourage bidders and no incentive to discourage future proposals.

High-Risk Handoff to the Program Management Team

Once you get past the debriefing, it's time for the handoff between the proposal team—the authors of your winning proposal—and your newly minted program team. The proposal team has created a wonderful proposal. Well, maybe not wonderful but at least good enough to win. The proposal team has carried you and your company through all the post-submission activities: responded to customer questions, perhaps conducted an oral briefing for the customer, responded to the call for a Best and Final Offer (BAFO) with perhaps a better price, and waited, likely impatiently, for what seemed an eternity for the customer's decision on the contract award. Now that you've won, it's time to hand off the responsibility for the program from the proposal team to the program team.

Government Insider

Just as the customer's evaluators dislike risk of any kind, your own internal processes should recognize the existence of risks and plan to manage those risks. The second of two risk-risk times in the business development cycle occurs at the interface between the award and the early days of program execution. In this case, you should consider bringing in extra help for the program manager during this period, known as the transition, or start-up, period.

From Program Manager-Designate to Program Manager

In Chapter 14, you learned that the first high-risk time in the business development cycle is at the handoff between the relationship manager/capture manager and the proposal manager. At that handover, continuity of personnel makes all the difference—good continuity, low-risk handoff. Bad continuity is a high-risk handoff; it's all about relationships and continuity.

Now you face another high-risk handoff, and here's where the importance of having the program manager-designate as an integral part of the proposal team pays off. Because this individual has been present at the creation, it's now possible to make a (relatively) seamless transition from proposal to program activities. Because the program manager-designate knows the proposal inside-out, up, and down, the transfer is much easier than having a program manager not involved with the proposal begin program execution. In these circumstances, the newly designated program manager starts at a distinct disadvantage.

	ForeCastOpps					Pre-RFP							RFP							Post Award			
Time Period	Continuing Customer Contact	ID of Specific Opportunity	Qualify the Opportunity	Influence an Opportunity	Quality Win Potential	Commitment	Win Strategy/Differentiate You	Black Hat Review	Strategic Opportunity Partnerships	Notional Solution	Pre-RFP Submissions	Release of Solicitation	Validate Commitment	WIN Strategy	Teaming Agreements	Solution Development	Submission of Proposal	Post-Submission Activities	Contract Award !	Lessons Learned	Program Start-Up	Continuing Program Execution
Time Period	1	2										3					4	5	6		7	8
Relationship Management	X	X	X	X	X	X	X	X	X	X	X	X	X	X		X	X	X	X		X	X
Capture Management		X	X	X	X	X	X	X	X	X	X	X	X	X	X	X	X	X	X	X		
Top Management					X																	
Solutions Management		X								X	X	X				X	X	X	X	X		
Proposal Management		*										X				X	X	X	X			
Contracts and Price Analysis		*										X				X	X	X	X			
Submission Management																	X	X	X			
Discussions and Negotiations		*										*			X		*	X	X			
Award!																			X			
Start-Up Management																					X	
Continuing Program Management		*										*					*	*	*		*	X

High-risk times in the business development cycle.

Transitioning from proposal team to program team is one of two high-risk times in business development.

Program Plan Before and After Award

The most critical part of your proposal now becomes your program plan. On the basis of this plan, as modified, you will manage your program. In addition, your customer will "grade" your performance on that plan. So it's of the greatest importance and the greatest urgency that you meet with the customer to transform a proposal program plan into an executable program plan.

If you've planned correctly (and this instruction in the solicitation is difficult to miss), your proposal plan will show a meeting between you, the contractor, and the customer's program people to start honing in on the real program plan. This meeting is usually set for about the fifth day of the program, where the first day is the program start date. Clever name, don't you agree? This meeting is called the "Program Kickoff" or something similar. Starting with that meeting, you will have about five working days to make all the changes, negotiate out any differences, and present a revised and improved program plan, which is now subject to a final review by the customer and then approved as amended. This is the new baseline plan, the one that you're going to begin executing against.

Some government program managers don't clearly understand the difference between a) the program plan you submitted as a part of the winning proposal and b) the program plan you're now going to use during the program execution. The difference is that the program plan you've created now and which the government program manager has approved, is much more detailed. You've replaced generalities with specifics.

If your customer has a problem understanding the differences, you can preface your final program plan with the following explanation. Note that "our" or "we" means the winning contractor and "you" or "your" means the government customer.

Introduction to (Insert Program Name Here) Plan

In our winning proposal, we described how we accomplish first formulating and then executing program plans. These capabilities, in turn, provide a framework for answering your specific requirements for this program. As we are now the contract awardee, it's our task to formulate an executable program plan, very exactly tailored to your program.

Implicit in our approach to management plans are both a knowledge of how to do start-up planning for specific services *and* the certainty from our experience that such plans are best executed through collaboration with you, the customer, including all your end users. Therefore, our plans universally show a period at the beginning of plan execution which vets the plan as delivered with the winning proposal with your Subject Matter Experts (SMEs). This collaboration then verifies when we're right on target and when new data and new considerations allow us to modify those plans to be even better.

Other Plans Before and After Award

You probably submitted several plans with your proposal, including:

- ◆ Training Plan
- ◆ Risk Assessment Plan
- ◆ Security Plan
- ◆ Disaster Recovery Plan
- ◆ Operational Support Verification Plan
- ◆ Operational Services Support Change Management Plan
- ◆ Financial Status Plan

These are now subject to the same negotiations, revisions, and approval as the program plan. You always begin with the program plan, as it's the high-level one. All other plans depend, at least to some degree, on the program plan. Once the program plan is set, then the subordinate plans have what amounts to an effective anchor for their own delivery dates, for example.

So typically within the first 30 calendar days, you and your team will change not only the program plan but also all other subordinate and supplementary plans from "as proposed" to "ready for execution."

High-Risk Start-Up Plans

Getting started with your new contract is often the most difficult part. You have new members of your own team (including members of the subcontractors), and you have new individuals on the government side. Irrespective of any previous good relationships you've had with your own team members and the government program people, it takes a while to know how to operate, on a day-to-day basis, with this new group of people.

There are two different cases, which are related but distinctly different.

♦ Your company is replacing an existing operation, and the incumbent contractor is phasing out.

♦ This is brand-new work, and your company is starting to build a program team from the ground up.

Replacing an Incumbent Contractor

In this situation, you'll probably have some time to come up to speed in the operation. As you phase in, the outgoing contractor phases out. Here the personal relationships come to the fore. I advise you to develop very good interpersonal relationships with the outgoing contractor, because it's likely that the incumbent is disappointed about being an unsuccessful offeror to succeed itself in the position.

> **Beltway Buzz**
>
> Sometimes incumbents decide to no-bid because it's a small business set-aside and the incumbent is no longer a small business. Or the incumbent may know that the problems on the current contract make it impossible to win a re-compete.

Not often does the incumbent fail to bid any re-competitions, so you're going to have to deal with an incumbent still smarting from the loss. And many losers are also sore losers, perhaps with good reason. The outgoing crew may well be resentful and unhappy about losing. Further, the individuals may feel justified in taking out their disappointment on you and your company, with or without reason. So be it. Your job remains to strive for a smooth hand-off from them to you, and a smooth change is more likely if you strive for good interpersonal relationships.

Starting Up Brand-New Work

Case two is often easier. All you have to contend with is trying to start up a new program when you're probably at least to some extent dependent on the promised Government Furnished Equipment (GFE). For example, you're planning to use government-supplied office space and information technology infrastructure. What happens to your program if the required information technology (IT) equipment does not show up on time at the right place? What if it doesn't work as anticipated in your program plan? The cooperative answer is that you'll do a workaround to accomplish as much of your work as possible, even in the absence of the promised resources.

As in all such circumstances, you may have to do the best you can for a few days. If you do, and you're on a tight schedule, document any problems related to your government partner's failure to provide certain equipment. Don't do this documentation in a punitive way or for a cover-yourself reason. However, do keep a current record of exactly what happened, from your viewpoint, and be ready to ask for an equitable adjustment based on the government's revised requirements. Wandering too far from the contract terms, and especially the statement of work, is dangerous to you as the contractor. You are legally obligated to do the work described in the contract and only that work. If you routinely do work outside that prescribed scope, you are in danger of not being paid for that unauthorized work. Remember that the contract can be changed only through a formal change, as approved and supervised by the KO, and not as specified by the government program manager.

Using a Start-Up Plan Specialist

There are specialists in accomplishing smooth start-ups running transition plans, and you should carefully consider engaging an individual or a small team if your budget and the size of the program warrant such a specialist. For example, if you're taking over a large *support contract*, a cadre of individuals, who have done similar start-ups for years, can come onto your team (usually as short-term contractors) and apply specialized knowledge to get you through the first 45 to 60 days of the program.

The field of such people is limited to those individuals having extensive experience doing just that. These people are typically retired, or semi-retired. They are often very well qualified and anxious to take on the challenges of this role. Your best way to find them is usually by word of mouth among experienced program managers. Use your own sources first. If you're not successful, you can post your need for such a skill on Craig's List or other local job board. These people just seem to appear.

def•i•ni•tion

A **support contract** is an agreement wherein your company has near-absolute authority and responsibility to supply a level of manpower, usually at a government site. An example is operating all base operations at Ft. Dizzy (not a real place!) to include maintenance of the physical plant, the laundry, the phone system, and the heating and air conditioning.

Using a start-up specialist can be a great idea as it ensures you have the best chance at a smooth start-up. As an accompanying benefit, it takes the burden off the program manager at a time when that individual has plenty to do, even without worrying about achieving a smooth start-up.

Whether you call in a specialist or a team of specialists, never forget the role of program manager still takes precedence.

Your program manager-designate is no longer the designate. The new title and role is program manager, for real! This person now takes over the duties as described in your proposal. An important refinement (not a change, but a refinement) is that, if you bring on a start-up specialist, your (permanent) program manager should rely on the specialist to guide the special, nonrecurring tasks, such as hiring some of the incumbent contractor's people if that's part of the deal. All the while, the program manager should be the single point of contact with the government program manager in order to execute a tight, smooth start-up plan.

The Least You Need to Know

- Take full advantage of the post-award debriefings—win or lose.

- Go into any debriefings with a specific plan on who is going to do what, to whom, and why; this is not the time for freelancing.

- You may now fully appreciate the extra effort you made during the proposal by having the program manager-designate be an integral member of the proposal team.

- If you can justify a start-up specialist, use that person's specialized skills to achieve a smooth hand-off.

Chapter 22

Living Up to Your Promises

In This Chapter

- ◆ Doing what the contract says
- ◆ Understand contract deliverables
- ◆ Having one point of contact for the customer
- ◆ Dealing with problems as they arise
- ◆ Duties of top management

Getting a government contract was your first goal. Now, you must move beyond *getting* the government contract to *keeping* it. One of the nice features of having the government as your customer is that, once the customer identifies a need, that need tends to be a recurring need—year after year, decade after decade. The challenge is to keep the contract you have and use the net revenues from that contract to fund the getting of more contracts. Holding on to your own contracts is called defending your territory. For example, the local exchange carriers in the telecommunications business consider any services in their own territory (as defined by the old Bell System map) to be their own home territory and strive mightily to hold on to all that business.

Similarly, once the government awards you a contract, consider that contract *yours*, and defend it against all challengers. Do everything you can to avoid a termination, and begin preparing, from Day One, to defend that contract when it comes up for recompetition. This chapter offers guidelines and checklists to ensure that you are doing everything possible to hold on to your hard-fought gains.

"What *Do* the Contract Say?"

Yes, you read right. "What *do* the contract say" might be sloppy grammar, but there's nothing sloppy about how your contract lays out your obligations to the customer. The contract answers precisely the question of what counts as good in the eyes of the customer.

The contract is a serious, legal document which gives the answers to "What should I be doing?" Therefore, if you're the program manager, I strongly advise you to read the contract early and often during contract execution. Typically, the contract calls for specific deliverables (both products and services) as well as reports of your achievements and activities in many areas.

As the program manager, you will undoubtedly be faced—sooner or later—with the phenomenon known as *scope creep*. Sometimes slowly, sometimes quickly, the government program manager, or perhaps some other government employee, will hit you with a request to do something very reasonable but specifically not in the contract.

def•i•ni•tion

When a customer requests you and your staff to do something outside the bounds of the existing contract, your first reaction is probably to accommodate the customer by doing what he asks. We call this **scope creep**, as it can often occur slowly, small steps at a time, until you realize your activities are really far from the existing contract and your team is overextended.

Here's an example: the contract is for delivery of a particular product. Before you can deliver the product to the government and obtain an acceptable sign-off, the contract calls for a specific set of standards you must meet and pass. The acceptance and delivery triggers a chain of events that results in payment to you. But after the work has begun, the standard changes. So the customer test manager wants your testers to use the new standard. That request is perfectly reasonable and even the right thing to do in support of your customer. A new standard requires new acceptance tests.

Doesn't sound unreasonable, right? But, wait. Suppose the new standard is far more stringent, and therefore much more difficult to achieve an "accept" on the test. Now you're in a bind. Do you do what the customer's test manager—a perfectly wonderful person (undoubtedly, her mother and father love her, at least)—wants, or do you refuse and conform to the contractual standard? Well, "What *does* the contract say?"

The bottom line is that you are not obligated to use the new standard. You will need to take a close look at the implications to the obligations you would have under the new standard and compare those obligations with those now found in the contract. If there is a significant negative impact, in that you are now required to pass more stringent tests (therefore requiring you to do *more* work to pass the acceptance tests), then, in all fairness, you are allowed to ask for an adjustment in the price, schedule, or both. Correspondingly, if the new standard means *less* work and *lower* costs to you, then the government is allowed to negotiate for lower costs, to get delivery sooner, or both. The contracts in this case are an agreement about how, and under what circumstances, you and the KO will adjust the contract to fit new developments. In effect, it's an agreement to reach a new agreement, based on equity to each party.

The overarching rule here is to refrain from what may well be your natural instinct, which is to do just about anything to "please the customer." Pleasing the customer is a very good idea, but it must be within the confines of the contract of record. Examples of such out-of-the contract activities are: re-work of already accepted deliverables (unless such re-work is called for under the contract); creating deliverables helpful to the customer, but not specifically called out in the contract; and purchasing equipment from your own budget, when the contract requires the customer to supply that equipment.

Contract Deliverables

As you and your team toil away to meet the contract obligations, always track your progress through the creation of deliverables (CDRLs). These contract reports are not just busy work, but use them to report progress to the customer regarding how you're doing in relation to their goals and objectives. Having these reports ready on time and with a high degree of accuracy is of the utmost importance for two simple reasons: the reports are required contractually, and correctly reporting in accordance with the contract is a huge step forward in pleasing the customer.

To get an idea of the type and number of reports that may be required, here is a list of selected reports required under a multi-billion dollar GSA Networx Universal

Contract awarded to three large telecommunications companies in April 2007. They are available on the winning companies' websites.

Contract Reports

Monthly

Financial Status

Service Level Agreements Compliance

Program Status

Plans

Training

Risk Assessment

Program Management

Security

Disaster Recovery

Operational Support Verification

Operational Services Support Change Management

Others

Policy and Procedures

Data Dictionary Instructions

Inventory Management User Manual

Non-Domestic Providers

Beltway Buzz

A service level agreement (SLA) is a contract provision requiring that the supplied services or equipment meet certain performance standards. Examples of SLAs are system availability, and requirements to make system changes within a certain time.

Your contract may not have nearly as many deliverables as the ones listed in this sample; but whatever requirements your contract lists, you are contractually obligated to provide the reports. Reading the contract lets you know what the customer expects. Then actually doing those things means you are meeting the customer's expectations.

Often, one of the most serious contractual provisions is the program schedule. Typically, the contract spells out the important milestones, and the program manager has the responsibility to achieve those milestones, in accordance with the schedule.

One Point of Contact for the Customer

As you go about the business of delivering on the promise, you'll be in frequent communication with the customer. When you submitted an organization chart as part of your proposal, you clearly showed that the single point of contact for the government would be your program manager. So now that the project has kicked into action, the program manager should serve as that point of contact. The only exception to this is the "No Single Point of Failure Rule," which allows for an immediate fail-safe backup should the prior designated program manager not be able to fulfill the commitment.

> ### Beltway Buzz
>
> The "No Single Point of Failure Rule" applies to program execution as it did for proposal creation. Murphy's Law says, "Anything that can go wrong, will go wrong." So if your senior engineer *can* come down with the mumps, she *will*. Lacking a predetermined backup for her, you'll waste time and money trying to fill the gap. While not specifically required by the contract, this is still good operating policy.

The program manager encourages and allows contact between the government's people and the contractor's program people. For example, the quality representative from the government should work hand-in-glove with your quality people. The government engineers and your engineers work together to solve issues as they arise.

As program manager, you want to encourage peer-to-peer contact between the government personnel and your personnel. These contacts help solve day-to-day issues and problems. This contact is not contrary to the formal "single point of contact" process shown in your organization charts. It's necessary, though, to ensure that everyone concerned acknowledges that, in the final analysis, the formal line of communication is government program manager to you as the contractor program manager. Things can go along for weeks or months without a problem. But when problems that cannot be solved easily and quickly at the working level (for example, engineer-to-engineer) arise, the clear escalation path goes from the government program manager and you, as the program manager, upward in your organization to the next higher level of management.

Paving a Clear and Open Escalation Path

Chapter 17 shows the organization charts that apply to your program. In that chapter, Figure 17.2 shows the relationship between your program manager on this program and the balance of your own organization. The solid lines show the escalation path. The government program manager, therefore, knows exactly who is next in the escalation chain. There is no ambiguity.

We'd all like to believe that the government contracts we win go off without a hitch. Well, there's no such thing as the tooth fairy, and there's no such thing as a program without problems. The problems could be with technical performance, schedule variances, or cost overruns. In the worst case, it could be all three. So it's not a question of *will* things go wrong, because the fact is that things *will go wrong*. The important consideration is how you come to know that things are going wrong and then what you do to get back on track (for example, create and execute a catch-back plan).

What kinds of things can go wrong? The answer is just about anything shown in the management plan. Here's a short list of examples:

◆ The materials promised by your customer do not arrive as scheduled. This causes a slip in your schedule and extra costs to you because you have your engineers and technicians on the project with not enough to do, awaiting the promised materials.

◆ The testing due for completion in week 5 happens. But instead of two testing iterations, it takes four iterations and a week longer than planned, causing a ripple effect in the balance of the schedule.

◆ An emergency situation in another part of your company holds the critical team of three production planners three weeks longer than planned, delaying the finalizing of your own production plans.

Government Insider _____

When problems arise, turn to the management processes and procedures described in the management volume of your proposal. The way you described your management plan in the proposal is the way you must execute the program. In the best of circumstances, your team executes the program along the same parameters you used to describe the program in the proposal. If problems are arising, maybe someone is deviating from the plan.

A function of management is, among other things, the replacement of uncertainty with certainty. The way to do that and to show you're doing that is to develop a program plan (as in your winning proposal) and then follow that program plan during program execution. The best individual to author, or at least supervise, the creation of the management section is (not surprisingly) the program manager-designate. This person is the single person most likely to be concerned about the correctness of the plan.

Top Management Involvement

You've read it before: the number-one reason for losing competitions is the lack of top management (TM) involvement in the process. Correspondingly, an easy way (not the only way, but an easy way) to lose a customer is to give the impression that your top management is disengaged from your program execution. A TM who doesn't care enough to be accessible to the government program manager and that person's superiors is asking for the customer to become disenchanted. The customer quite properly says, "Hey, where is that top level of involvement that we, the government, saw throughout the competitive phase? Where is TM now, and why can't I get a prompt response to my issues with this program?"

The lesson is this: just as it was the responsibility of the proposal team (led by the three important functions: capture manager, proposal manager, and program manager-designate) to keep TM involved, it's now the program manager's responsibility, assisted by others as appropriate, to do the same during program execution.

The Least You Need to Know

- ◆ Getting contracts is difficult; keeping them can be just as difficult.

- ◆ Keeping government business depends on carefully living up to promises made in the proposal and obligations agreed to in the contract.

- ◆ Successful delivery of a program revolves around how you treat the customer.

- ◆ Take special care to execute the contract of record and to accompany any changes in your work with corresponding changes in the contract.

- ◆ Make the deliverables on your contracts living documents, and strive to use each deliverable to assist in the management of the program.

- Practice strict adherence to the lines of authority and responsibility as described in your organization charts and accompanying descriptions.

- Keep top management involved in any constructive way you can.

23

Preparing for the Recompetition

In This Chapter

♦ It's not over 'til it's over

♦ Start from day one to keep and grow the business

♦ Keep your customer happy

♦ Sometimes personnel and subcontractor changes are necessary

"Make new friends, and keep the old. One is silver, and the other gold." Government contracting is much like these old song lyrics. You're always looking for new business opportunities, but you don't want to lose the old ones. No matter how long a contract, it will eventually come to an end when the agreed-upon term ends. The contract then will likely be up for recompetition, meaning the customer will put the opportunity out for bid again. (The exception to this is when the need that led to your contract in the first place goes away and so the customer doesn't have any reason to open it up to recompetition.) All good things must end, including even your best, most profitable contracts. So you need both strategic and tactical plans to have the best chance to keep your customer when competition time comes again.

At the Contract's End, Tie Up All Loose Ends

The current contract isn't over until it's over. Just because you won quality awards in this program in years two, three, and four doesn't mean you're invincible after year six. Unfortunately, some government program managers have short memories. Or maybe there's a new program manager or a new customer's Contracting Officer (KO) since year four, and these new people have no memories of those glory days. From a recompete strategic perspective, it's more important that your company do well at meeting customer expectations toward the end of the program than at the beginning.

Your objective is to please the customer right on through the end of your contract and beyond. What's past is prologue. The customer has a right to expect, and does expect, to get the same level of performance in any new contract as you've delivered in the current contract. Your best bet is to start at a high level of performance and continue to the very end.

Start from Day One

Conventional wisdom says that retaining your current customers is only a fraction of the cost of getting new ones. Whether that fraction is 15 percent, 20 percent, 25 percent, or something higher, I advise you to invest heavily, and first, in keeping the customers you already have. You're already in place; you know this customer. You're making revenues and profits from this customer. In any recompetition, you have the high ground.

This is a tough point but a necessary one. Even in an eight-year contract, begin planning for the recompetition from Day One of the contract. This seems like a terrible idea, given that the first few days and weeks of a new contract are often fraught with unknown and perhaps unknowable problems. Yet the best circumstances are that you begin and end with a customer-focused mind-set.

> **Red Flag**
>
> It's never too early to start preparing for the recompetition, but it is possible to be too late in getting started. Just about the worst thing you can do is to take your customer for granted and then try to patch up the relationship near the end of the contract term so you will be in a good position to rewin the business. You must focus on satisfying the customer and strengthening the relationship from the beginning.

Keep This Customer Happy

At the highest conceptual level, your long-term success with a specific customer is wrapped up in a simple admonition: be customer-centric. What does this mean in operational terms? A simple test is this: you get what you want by helping the customer get what the customer wants. As long as you're helping the customer get what the customer wants and not getting what you want at the expense of the customer, you're on the right track. Achieving a win-win solution is always best. Avoid getting yourself backed into a corner where you have to help yourself, at the expense of and to the detriment of your customer.

It helps to be pro-active with your customer, rather than reactive. As you and your program staff sees problems, or potential problems, it helps both you and your customer if you expose those problems, and identify potential problems, early, rather than late. Unlike fine wine that gets better with age, problems don't. Hiding or ignoring problems can be a blueprint for disaster.

It's easiest to keep your customer happy by being forthright and truthful at all times. Regular (and short?) meetings with the customer create a forum for resolution of differences before these differences grow into major issues.

Be Willing to Change Personnel and Subcontractors

You really *do* want to keep this customer, so what are specific steps you can take to increase the probably that you will win the recompetition? Making personnel changes is often a step you have to take to inject new life into the solution you offer the customer and into the relationship with the customer.

Changes in personnel come it two flavors: management and staff. Each has its own, different considerations.

Management Changes

For purposes of this discussion, management means the program manager and anyone reporting to the program manager. This set of people is your program management team.

About a year or so before your current contract ends, your top management should make a focused effort to assess the state of your program management team, and especially its two or three or perhaps four most important individuals. The number will depend partly on the total program size and partly on how responsibilities break out between individuals. This smaller set will surely include the program manager. If you have a deputy program manager, that person will also be in this set. Next will be the chief technical person (chief engineer, senior engineer, technical team lead, or something like that). A fourth member could be the top person in administration.

It's a good idea to involve your own contract manager in any discussions with TM as well. While the program manager may have great insight on what is happening on-site, your contract manager may have other information that would benefit TM.

An important part of this year-ahead assessment is to have your top management meet with the customer's top management. This is best to target at least one if not two levels of authority above the government program manager. This should be a one-on-one meeting, preferably with the individual who in your judgment will be the source selection authority or someone close to that person.

If you're top management, don't take your program manager with you, but tell him about this meeting. He will undoubtedly find out about it anyway, so it's best to be candid with him.

The meeting should take place at the customer's place of business or perhaps a neutral site, such as a restaurant or private club. Always obey the ethics rules, of course, and refrain from appearing to offer anything of more than nominal value, such as springing for a lavish meal. The essence of the conversation should be clear, which is that you're there to assure the customer that your company fully intends to do an excellent job to the very end of the contract period. If you're planning to compete again (and you very likely will), you should say that, also. Then in a candid conversation, ask if there's anything you, as top management, can do to make the last few months of your contract be the best it can be. Depending on your comfort level with your host, you might even ask if there are any problems out of the ordinary, either in terms of individuals or processes or whatever, where you can be helpful. Then have the common sense to be quiet and listen.

> **Government Insider**
>
> Listening skills are crucial here. Be sensitive to body language, tone of voice, and things not said, as well as things said. You won't get any smarter by talking. Listening will do that. Be in receiving, not broadcasting, mode.

The worst thing you can do as the incumbent is to assume that everything is fine. If you don't confirm that things are fine, you're opening your company to a rude surprise when you lose the recompetition because of your failure to solve a problem you didn't know about.

Staff Changes

In some cases, changes in staff may be accomplished more easily and with less pain than management changes.

Particularly on a cost-type contract, where the government pays whatever your costs are, plus a fee, carefully guard against *grade creep*.

def•i•ni•tion

Grade creep is when the average length of service and average years of experience of your staff grows significantly over the life of a long contract. An unfortunate unintended consequence of this phenomenon is that the qualifications and the costs of the average person on the project exceed what is absolutely necessary to do the job. This excess gives a challenger an opportunity to bid less experienced people, at a lower cost, and win a price competition.

If you're successful, you'd like to continue the success by rewarding all your staff members with continued employment. Unfortunately, that may not be possible, given the competitive nature of the recompetition. During the last year or maybe last two of your contract, look for opportunities to move some of your more experienced people off and backfill their vacant slots with entry-level people or at least with people who have fewer years of experience and hence are probably lower cost.

This should not be done at the expense of performance on the current contract. However, and particularly on long contracts (say, five years), the average years of experience for individuals grows. This can (but not must) result in individuals who are overqualified to do the tasks required. For example, the person who started as an entry-level engineer five years ago, at the contract onset, now has almost five years of experience. That individual is now being paid much more than an entry-level engineer, but may be performing a task that could be done by someone with six months or a year of experience. So it's to the benefit of both the contract and the individual that you find more challenging work, perhaps on other projects, and back-fill the departing person with a new, entry-level engineer, at a considerably lower cost.

You can't do this suddenly three months before the end of your contract. Make any changes gradually, not precipitously. That's not fair to the staff, and it will be transparent to the customer that you're replacing staff just to achieve lower costs. If the changes are too obvious, the customer may worry that those replacements will be at the expense of performance.

Changing Subcontractors

There are also advantages in changing subcontractors. In the same way you solicited your customer's evaluations of your management team members, carefully consider the roles of your subcontractors. What does your customer think of each of them? Have the workers from your subcontractors helped the total team or have some of them been other than team players? If you have a problem subcontractor, the same careful winnowing out of the bad ones will help your bidding team. Don't hold on to the past, particularly if you can improve your team by doing so. Consider whether the subcontractor was a help to your small business goals on the current contract but is no longer a small business. If that's true, that subcontractor is certainly worth replacing with a new small business that can contribute to your small business goals. This is business, not a popularity contest, and you may have to discard some staff in favor of others.

Recompetitions as the Incumbent or the Challenger

Even in a hurricane, all the wind doesn't blow in the same direction. In fact, in a hurricane, changes in wind direction are inevitable. So it is with the question of whether it's better to be an incumbent or a challenger when going into a recompetition. There are advantages and disadvantages to each side.

The following two subsections show both considerations, whether you're the incumbent striving to keep this customer, or a challenger to an incumbent, attempting to take the business away for your own.

If You're the Incumbent

An industry myth holds that incumbents are always the heavy favorites to win any recompetitions. That's not necessarily so, and certainly not so for a specific recompetition. It depends greatly on the fine details of the circumstances. If you're the incumbent, consider these strategies to make yourself the favorite.

◆ Find out one or two things the customer would really like for you to change about your operation before the date of the release of the RFP, and make that change *now*, not later.

◆ For cost-type contracts, decrease your average hourly rate, appreciably, while remaining able to fill the customer's requirements. This decrease will be a strong signal to your customer of cost consciousness and discourage other competitive bidders. As the incumbent, don't allow your workforce to age significantly during the contract. The new hire from Year One is now the experienced one in Year Seven of an eight-year contract. So you should consciously seek new, cheaper employees such as recent college graduates. These then blend with the more experienced and more expensive workforce, driving down the average labor rate.

◆ Offer to team with potential rivals, with the idea of eliminating a potential competitor. However, be careful to avoid the actuality, or even the appearance, of collusion with the intention of completely eliminating the competition to which the government is entitled.

◆ There's such a thing as "incumbent-itis." No, this isn't "inflammation of the incumbent." It's that you, as the incumbent, have become complacent in your desire to please the customer. You may be familiar with "senior-itis," a malady striking scholars (at whatever level) during the final semester of a degree program. High school seniors get it. College seniors may get it. Correspondingly, your company may suffer an unintentional let-down toward the end of a contract. Don't let that happen. Be careful to avoid believing your own press releases, that you're the best contractor on earth, and that no one else could possibly do the great job you've been doing. With truly rare exceptions, it's just plain not true.

If You're the Challenger

Take heart. You actually *do* have a chance to unseat the incumbent, especially if you take heed of these considerations:

◆ Know the difference between having the customer whisper in your ear, "We want you to bid," and whispering, "We want you to win." The customer's motivation may be to create a *stalking horse* for the truly favored incumbent. KOs and program managers are in the business of encouraging competition, not discouraging it.

def•i•ni•tion

In this context, a **stalking horse** is a bid you're encouraged to make, with no real chance of winning the competition. Your bid will act only to assist the customer contracting officer (KO) in demonstrating there is real competition for this opportunity. But you really never have a chance, as the winner has been decided before the competition begins. Avoid playing this role, at all costs. Bid only when you have an excellent chance of winning.

♦ Your experience as a challenger may tell you the incumbent has an advantage that's difficult to overcome. But that's not necessarily true. The incumbents have the advantage that the present team knows the job better than any challenger possibly can. However, the good news for you as a challenger may be that the incumbent has seen the same problems, over and over, and has stock solutions to those problems. As a challenger, you may be able to cast fresh eyes over the customer's problems and come up with innovative, out-of-the-box solutions.

♦ You may actually have at least one clear advantage. Because you don't know everything about the job that the incumbent knows, you may be able to offer a simpler, less costly solution. Your ignorance becomes an advantage as you avoid the charge of deliberately underbidding, at a price you know or should know you cannot attain.

♦ Carefully analyze the current contract documents for signs of customer dissatisfaction; if you can't find much dissatisfaction, you are probably swimming upstream. Check the award fee results (on award fee contracts), and trust that data over the KO's urging you to bid. Facts win out over rumor and gossip.

♦ If there are more than about three challengers, including your company, there are probably too many. Somebody doesn't understand the procurement because there are probably not more than three or at most four companies with a meaningful chance of winning this job.

♦ If you're having trouble assembling a team using a draft RFP and feel you'll have a problem getting anyone to bid against a firmly entrenched incumbent, consider complaining to the KO that he won't get competition. Further suggest that the way to *get* competition is to break the job up into smaller pieces to attract both more and different bidders. You have a better chance to compete against a new configuration of competition than against a "brick wall" of the entrenched incumbent.

The Least You Need to Know

♦ Make tactical moves in both your management and staff in anticipation of the recompetition.

♦ For various reasons, it may be necessary to jettison some of your subcontractors.

♦ It's all about relationships; get and keep your customers by going the second mile.

Glossary

Acronyms

Government business is filled with abbreviations for common terms, and trying to decipher them can be frustrating. The list that follows contains common acronyms you'll hear as you do business with the government, as well as ones I have used throughout the book. For a definition of the term that follows each acronym, refer to the Terminology section of this glossary.

B&P (Bid and Proposal Dollars)

BA (Budget Authority)

BAA (Broad Agency Announcement)

BAFO (Best and Final Offer)

BOA (Basic Ordering Agreement)

BPO (Blanket Purchase Order)

CAGE (Commercial And Government Entity Code)

CBD (Commerce Business Daily)

CCR (Central Contractor Registration)

CDRL (Contract Document Requirements List)

CLIN (Contract Line Item Number)

COTR (Contracting Officer's Technical Representative)

COTS (Commercial Off the Shelf)

CPAF (Cost Plus Award Fee)

CPFF (Cost Plus Fixed Fee)

CPIF (Cost Plus Incentive Fee)

CR (Clarification Request)

DAR (Designated Agency Representative)

DR (Deficiency Reports)

DI (Discussion Items)

DUNS (Data Universal Numbering System)

FAR (Federal Acquisition Regulation)

FFP (Firm Fixed Price)

FOIA (Freedom of Information Act)

FSC (Codes Federal Supply Classification Codes)

GFE (Government Furnished Equipment)

GFP (Government Furnished Property)

GSA (General Services Administration)

GWAC (Government-wide Acquisition Contract)

HUBZone (Historically Underutilized Business Zone)

ICE (Independent Cost Estimate)

ID/IQ (Indefinite Delivery/Indefinite Quantity)

IFB (Invitation for Bid)

JIT training (Just-In-Time training)

JWOD (Javits Wagner O'Day Program)

KO (Contracting Officer) (on the government side)

LLC (Limited Liability Company)

MPIN (Marketing Partners Identification Number)

NAICS (North American Industry Classification System)

NDA (Nondisclosure Agreement)

NTE (Not to Exceed)

O&M (Operations & Maintenance)

OGE (Office of Government Ethics)

OMB (Office of Management and Budget)

OPM (Office of Personnel Management)

ORCA (Online Representations and Certifications)

P&P (Policies and Procedures Manuals)

PCO (Procuring Contracting Officer)

PDC (Proposal Development Center)

RAM (Responsibility Assignment Matrix)

RFI (Request for Information)

RFP (Request for Proposal)

ROM (Rough Order of Magnitude)

S&L (State and Local)

SAS (Single Award Schedule)

SBA (Small Business Administration)

SIC (Standard Industrial Classification)

SME (Subject Matter Experts)

SOO (Statement of Objectives)

SOR (Statement of Requirements)

SOW (Statement of Work)

SSA (Source Selection Authority)

SSEB (Source Selection Evaluation Board)

SSP (Source Selection Plan)

Ts & Cs (Terms and Conditions)

T&M (Time and Materials)

TIN (Taxpayer Identification Number)

TPIN (Trading Partners Identification Number)

TM (Top Management)

UCF (Uniform Contract Format)

Terminology

Dealing with the government can feel like traveling in a foreign country where you don't speak the local language. You will likely encounter the following terms and be expected to understand them.

Note that some of these words can have many different meanings if you look them up in a traditional dictionary, but the definitions offered here are within the context of government contracting or within the context of how I have used the term in this book. For example, "approach" can mean many different things, but here it refers to the way in which you plan to carry out a government project or specific aspect of a project, such as the management approach or the technical approach.

Be aware that out in the world of government contracting the meaning of some of these terms can vary depending on who is using the term and the context in which it's used. So if in doubt about any terminology, always try to clarify the exact meaning with the person or government entity that has used the term.

Ability One   This program sets aside certain government contracts for disabled persons, such as the blind. Formerly known as Javits Wagner O'Day Program (JWOD).

Anti-competition themes   Positive features of your own solution that differ from and are better than those of your competition.

Approach   How your organization plans to handle an aspect of the project you are proposing, such as the management approach or technical approach. Often used interchangeably with the terms "volume" or "part."

Appropriations Committee   Committee within the House and Senate that gives government agencies permission to draw down funds from the public treasury.

Authority to Proceed   Official approval given to the contractor by the customer after an award is made. May be delayed for various reasons including pending the resolution of a filed protest.

Authorizing Committee   Committee in the House and Senate that authorizes agencies to proceed with programs.

Award Fee contracts   Applies to cost-type contracts where the fee (over and above documented costs) is based on performance standards, as shown in the contract.

Basic Ordering Agreement (BOA)   Not a contract but a written instrument of understanding, negotiated between an agency, contracting activity, or contracting office and a contractor. (FAR 16.703(a))

Best and Final Offer (BAFO)   Final cost or price offer the customer requests before making final award decision.

Bid and proposal (B&P) dollars   Also referred to as B&P costs, the cost of preparing, submitting, and supporting bids and proposals to government agencies.

Bid/no-bid decisions   Decisions made as a result of periodic group meetings on whether to bid or not bid, a specific opportunity based on latest information.

Bidder *See* **Offeror.**

Black hat team   Review team that can review an approach/solution, especially just before or after the release of the final solicitation. The team compares its own strengths and weaknesses regarding technical management, past performance, and price range to those of the competitors.

Blanket Purchase Order (BPO)   A commitment to a supplier for certain goods or services for a predetermined period of time (usually a year or more) at predetermined prices. Eliminates the need for many individual small orders.

Boilerplate   Text and visuals used in a previous proposal or other presentation, for another purpose.

Bone-yard   Repository of materials from previously submitted bids, both winners and losers.

Broad Agency Announcement (BAA)   Used to communicate the needs and interests of a specific agency. Websites for major agencies list which announcements are open, with deadlines for submission for consideration of contract award.

Budget Authority (BA)   Authority provided by law to enter into obligations that will result in outlays of federal funds.

Budget execution   Actual spending of funds. Should be compared with budget formulation to assess whether actual funds expended match planned (formulated) funds.

Budget formulation   Spending plan for a program as specified in the proposal and then in the contract.

Burn barrel   Trash receptacle that segregates everyday waste paper and trash from those containing proprietary, confidential materials. Maintenance of barrels typically outsourced to a specialty vendor.

Capture   Transition point from seeking an opportunity to being awarded a contract.

Capture Manager   Active proposal team member who serves as liaison between proposal manager and top management to ensure proposal team is adequately resourced and strategic needs are met.

Capture Plan   A formal, written document containing evidence that the bidder has a good chance to win the procurement. Signatures on the plan indicate approval and commitment between line management and the proposal team.

Case   All positive aspects of the solution presented in a proposal, much like the case that attorneys build for their clients.

Case law   The body of legal opinions of various courts from individual legal actions, such as criminal and civil suits.

Central Contractor Registration (CCR)   The single place that all contractors with the government must have a listing in order to do business with the government.

Clarification Request (CR)   Government asks the offeror to explain more fully a certain part of a proposal under evaluation. Must be answered to remain under consideration.

Classified contracts   Contracts with the intelligence agencies, such as the Central Intelligence Agency (CIA), the National Security Agency (NSA), and other agencies doing work that must be hidden from public view. You can only learn about these contract opportunities when you have the proper government clearances.

Color Teams   Teams in the offering company that evaluate the solution and proposal at various points in the process. Color Teams are Black Hat, Green, Pink, Red, Purple, and Gold.

Commerce Business Daily (CBD)   A defunct publication documenting government contracting actions.

Commercial and Government Entity Code (CAGE Code)   Code that identifies a bidding company's name, address, socioeconomic data, and type of business. Only one code is needed for entire company.

Commercial Off the Shelf (COTS)   Products that are already commercially available, typically to both commercial and government customers. Examples include commercial software and hardware and items you might buy at The Home Depot.

Commitment Letter   A letter sent to the decision-maker at the customer organization with a proposal indicating commitment to the success of the program. Signed by top management.

Competitive Convergence   The point at which a company's solution becomes the preferred solution of the customer. Achieving this convergence before the solicitation comes out greatly enhances the probability of winning.

Competitive range   First step in the government's evaluation of a proposal; a determination of whether the proposal has a reasonable chance for an award. If it does have a chance, the evaluators will declare it in the competitive range; if not, it is deemed outside the competitive range.

Competitive Surveys   The customer, usually the KO, is required to go into the market to see what companies might be able to perform to a (preliminary) Statement of Work. This survey precedes the release of a draft or final solicitation.

Competitor   Another company seeking to get the same contract you want. Today's competitor may be tomorrow's bidding partner.

Compliant   A proposal judged to be compliant meets all requirements of a solicitation.

Contingency hires   If current staff is inadequate to perform all parts of a contract, employment offers may be extended to some critical individuals, contingent upon the award of the contract to your organization.

Contract   An agreement, enforceable by law, between two or more competent parties, to do or not to do something not prohibited by law.

Contract Data Requirements List (CDRL)   This list appears in many solicitations, especially those requiring the submission of many reports and other documents of record. Management Volume typically states who is responsible for each of these items and when.

Contract Line Item Number (CLIN)   Each item to be priced, per the requirements of Section B of a solicitation, has a specific number, the CLIN. This list is useful at program execution in tracking how you get paid for your work.

Contract Manager   Serves as the single point of contact with the customer Contracting Officer (KO).

Contracting Officer (KO) for the customer   The single person in the customer organization who offerors are allowed to contact after the solicitation has been released.

Contracting Officer's Technical Representative (COTR)   A government person provided to assist the KO in matters related to inspection, acceptance, and other duties; a person without specific authority acting as an extension of the KO at a specific duty station.

Cost Plus Award Fee (CPAF)   A cost-type contract having an award fee, calculated in accordance with the terms of the contract. The award fee is based on how well the contractor performs the contract.

Cost Plus Fixed Fee (CPFF)   A cost-type contract where the amount of fee is fixed and not directly tied to performance.

Cost Plus Incentive Fee (CPIF)   A cost-type contract where the amount of fee is dependent on performance as measured in ways described in the contract.

Cost/Price   How much you commit, with your offer (proposal) to perform the work described in your proposal. The proper term for cost-type offers is cost, and for fixed price offers is price, but the terms can be used interchangeably until confined to a specific circumstance.

Cost-type contract   Contracts based on the government paying a company its full costs, plus a margin (fee).

Customer   Encompasses a present customer and a potential customer depending on context in which the term is used in a particular chapter or section of this book. Customers award you contracts and eventually pay you for your work.

Data Universal Numbering System (DUNS)   A numbering system used to identify specific companies.

Debarment   Action taken by a debarring official to exclude a contractor from contracting and subcontracting for a reasonable, specified period.

Debriefing   At the conclusion of the competition for an opportunity, the KO is required, by the FAR, to grant requests from all offerors, including the winner, for an explanation of how the proposal of that company was evaluated—what was judged to be good, bad, or indifferent.

Deficiency Report (DR)   A report indicating that the evaluators see a part of a proposal as deficient in some way. If not changed, this may lead to disqualification.

Deliverable   The goods or services to be provided to the government as specified in the contract. The government requires specific acts to formally receive deliverables.

Designated Agency Representative (DAR)   A Designated Agency Representative (DAR) is a federal employee (not a contractor) authorized to order telecommunications services and equipment under the network services contracts managed by the General Services Administration (GSA).

Direct customer   If you are the prime contractor dealing directly with the government agency, then that agency is your direct customer. If you are a subcontractor, then your direct customer is the prime contractor.

Discussion Items (DIs)   Items the customer asks you to talk about. These typically are in the form of a question.

Down select   When many companies respond to a solicitation, the government may eliminate some offers even before making a final decision on the winner or winners. This prevents those companies whose offers have no chance of winning from wasting more money on this competition.

Equitable Adjustment   The compensation or price adjustment to which a contractor is entitled due to a constructive change to a contract or to a special event.

Evaluation Criteria   Factors upon which a proposal's quality and feasibility for an award are determined by the customer.

Evaluations   Also referred to as **Color Teams** and **Reviews,** a series of structured reviews of the strengths and weaknesses of the current versions of the proposal document.

Exit Strategy   The policy of having pre-established criteria for deciding to discontinue efforts you've started. Only by leaving some efforts can you have enough resources to pursue new, more appealing avenues.

Federal Acquisition Regulation (FAR) and the Agency supplements (DFAR, etc.)   This regulation applies to the procurement practices of most federal government agencies for most contracts. Your company should have at least one individual on staff or as a consultant who is familiar with this regulation.

Federal Supply Classification Codes (FSC Codes)   Identifies the specific item to be supplied.

Fee-for-Service Providers   These companies provide specialized services such as competition analysis, notices of impending solicitations, and how to obtain GSA schedule contracts.

Firm Fixed Price (FFP)   A commitment to deliver goods or services for a certain price without the necessity to provide cost data or justification. This type of contract can have great financial (cost) risks as you must deliver irrespective of your own costs.

First Team   The best a company has to offer. First team members are analogous to the starting lineup for sports teams.

Framazoid   A mythical device of questionable origin and unknown use that is cited throughout this book to illustrate various points concerning products one might sell to the government. Not a real product!

Freedom of Information Act (FOIA)   Opened government records to the public.

Frontispiece   The inside front cover of the Executive Summary that contains the four to seven most important themes and answers the customer's implicit question, "Why should I choose *you*?"

General Services Administration (GSA)   A government agency providing vehicles for federal, state, and local government entities to buy services and products to meet their needs. The majority of GSA schedule contracts at this time are for services rather than products.

General Services Administration Schedule Contracts   Opportunities that are typically open (no cutoff date for submitting applications for contracts) and are generally for a long term (for example, for five years).

Gold Team   Important individuals who have the authority to approve submission of a proposal.

Government contracts   Products or services delivered by a company via the terms of a legal agreement (contract) to an organization within some type of public agency: federal, state, and local governments.

Government-Furnished Equipment (GFE)   Any equipment purchased directly by the government, rather than through a contractor, and used on the program.

Government-Furnished Property (GFP)   Similar to GFE, but a broader category. It can be something other than equipment, such as services.

Government-Wide Acquisition Contract (GWAC)   A task-order or delivery-order contract that is for information technology and is established by one agency (for example, the Department of Commerce) for use throughout the government.

Grade creep   When the average length of service and years of experience of program staff grows significantly over the life of a long contract, resulting in the need to bring on less-experienced people, at a lower cost, to win a price competition.

Graphics   Graphics is a standard industry term, but this book uses the alternate term visuals, which is a slightly broader term for anything in a proposal that is not words (text). *See also* **Visuals.**

Graybeard reviews   Reviews conducted by individuals who tend to be highly experienced, and sometimes significantly older, than the average proposal team member.

Green Team   Evaluators who focus on the financial, cost, and price aspects of the proposal, looking for opportunities to cut costs while still meeting specifications.

Head   Government jargon for an individual person. A head may carry out one or multiple roles on a proposal or project team.

Historically Underutilized Business Zone   The SBA may designate a place as a HUBZone if it is in certain census tracts, in a nonmetropolitan area with low-income people, or is on the boundary of an Indian reservation. These areas are eligible for set-aside contracts.

Hot buttons   Those issues causing the customer to become anxious and uneasy. These may or may not be reflected in the solicitation of record.

Incumbent   The company or team now holding the contract, currently supplying the government with products or services.

Indefinite Delivery/Indefinite Quantity (ID/IQ)   These contracts enable agencies to purchase products and services using the baseline contract as a starting point. At the time of contract award, the delivery dates and quantities are unknown, but there will surely be some demand for the items listed in the contract.

Independent Cost Estimate (ICE)   The government may ask for or produce an estimate of what the opportunity should cost. This establishes either single point estimation or a range of estimates of what the opportunity will cost. If the costs are too high for the funds available, the procurement will be postponed or down-scaled to get within the available funds.

Integration (horizontal vs. vertical)   Vertical integration means that you're trying to sell to a current customer products different from your current ones. Horizontal integration means, in the same situation, you now want to sell a different customer those same products.

Intermediate documents   These are documents used by the proposal team in the preparation of the proposal but not delivered to the customer.

Invitation for Bid   A solicitation for bids, at a fixed price.

JIT (Just In Time) Training   Training delivered to users (trainees) just before the trainees have a need to use the knowledge gained from the training.

Javits Wagner O'Day Program (JWOD)   *See* **Ability One**.

Kickoff Meeting   The first formal team meeting held within five days of the release of the solicitation. All team members attend.

Limited Liability Company   A form of legal entity advantageous for small business.

Line item   Contracts contain line items, typically in Section B of the solicitation, and therefore in the contract. Each line item specifies a specific deliverable (a product or service) and a cost/price associated with it.

Marketing manager   The chief marketing person on a specific opportunity.

Marketing Partners Identification Number (MPIN)   A number created by you when you register with the Central Contracts Registration website.

Marketing plan   Describes the market you're striving to capture. It may be broad or narrow but is not opportunity-specific. Once you have identified a specific opportunity, then you create a capture plan for that opportunity, but the capture plan must be consistent with the marketing plans.

Multiple-Award Contracts   Contracts awarded to more than one contractor.

Negotiated Acquisition Process   Contracting through the use of either competitive or other-than-competitive proposals and discussion. Any contract awarded without using sealed bidding procedures.

Niche   A market so specialized and, in some cases, so small that other potential offerors are not attracted to that line of products or services and do not bid.

Non-Disclosure Agreement (NDA)   An agreement between two companies to refrain from disclosing to other parties the proprietary data that may be acquired as a result of working together on a specific opportunity.

Noncompliant   If your proposal does not conform to all the instructions in the solicitation, your offer may be declared noncompliant and eliminated from further consideration.

Nonresponsive   *See* **Responsive.**

North American Industry Classification System Codes (NAICS Codes)   The standard used by federal statistical agencies in classifying business establishments for the purpose of collecting, analyzing, and publishing statistical data related to the U.S. business economy. Supervised by OMB and administered by the U. S. Bureau of the Census.

Not to Exceed (NTE)   A maximum price that you may not exceed while negotiations are underway to establish a final price. Enables you to perform the contract while negotiations are being conducted and protects the government from excessive expenditures.

Offeror   The party making a legally binding promise to enter into an agreement if the offer is accepted. Offers are made in response to RFPs, and bids are made in response to IFBs. This book uses "offeror" to cover both and avoids the awkward "offer or bid." *See also* **Bidder.**

Office of Government Ethics   Established in 1978 by the Ethics in Government Act as part of the Office of Personnel Management (OPM), but the Office of Government Ethics Reauthorization Act of 1988 made it a separate agency. The OGE's charter is to prevent conflicts of interest by government employees and to resolve those conflicts when they do happen.

Office of Management and Budget (OMB)   A part of the Executive Office of the President, this office evaluates agency budget requests and does the staff work in support of creating the President's budget.

Office of Personnel Management   The government's personnel office. Matches qualified candidates for government employment with open requisitions and handles other personnel matters. Replaced the former Civil Service Commission.

Office of Small and Disadvantaged Business Utilization (OSADBU)   An element of the procurement system whose mission is to encourage increased small business participation.

One voice   A proposal with a one-voice quality reads as if all parts were written by a single person, when in fact, a proposal is the creation of many people.

Online Representations and Certifications (ORCA)   Your registration (updated annually) commits your company to the terms and conditions of certain contracts. This eliminates the requirement to recertify to each individual contract.

Operations and Maintenance (O&M)   A type of support contract commonly used to acquire a broad spectrum of equipment, supplies, and services at a specific location.

Opportunity   A government entity identifies a need it has for a specific product or service and seeks offers from suppliers who could fulfill that need. That need is an opportunity for those who wish to secure a contract to provide the product or service.

Partners   As used in this book, this is not in the legal sense of creating a partnership agreement. The term loosely describes the creation of a common interest. The legal relationship is prime/subcontractor.

Past Performance   The citations of contracts you've performed are evaluated by the customer to see how well you did this work. If you're new to government contracting, commercial work can be cited if the work is similar.

Pink Team   This team conducts a review about 15 days after the solicitation release, and its members are typically in-house people at your organization but not members of your main proposal team for this effort. This team's review is at the storyboard, or outline, level.

Point of Influence   Times during the procurement cycle when it's allowable (under the FAR and other restrictions) to influence the process to your advantage.

Policies and Procedures (P&P) Manuals   Documents describing, often in detail, how to go about routine support operations, such as employee hiring, maintenance, and employee travel.

Pre-Solicitation postings   Notices to potential offerors that an agency has identified a need and that there is a possibility that the agency will issue a solicitation.

Precipitating Event   A specific reason that the procurement activity will result in an actual award of a contract to do work. In the absence of a precipitating event (for example, a schedule or cost driver), there may be a solicitation and several proposals written and submitted, but there might not be an award.

Pricing Manager   Creates a responsive, winning solution regarding cost and price to carry out a program.

Prime contractor   Any company with a direct contract with the government.

Procurement   The complete action or process of acquiring products and services. This is the total circumstance of the buying activity and not just the acquisition documents proper.

Procuring Contracting Officer (PCO)   The government agent designated by warrant having the authority to obligate the government. This may or may not be the CO of an opportunity.

Production facility   The place where final versions of the proposal are produced, it often doubles as a support facility for any other documents created in support of project work.

Program Manager-Designate   He helps the proposal team describe to the customer how they will manage the program if the contract is won, and he will be in charge of the program upon receiving the contract award.

Project Manager-Designate   *See* **Program Manager-Designate.**

Proposal   A written offer by you, as a seller (or bidder or offeror), describing the offering terms. Proposals may be issued in response to a specific request (for example, a Request for Proposal or RFP).

Proposal Development Center (PDC)   Also referred to as a war room, an area reserved for the exclusive use of the proposal team to develop major proposals.

Proposal Drivers   The answers to four critical questions: What are our win themes? What past performances will we offer? Why is our approach better than the competition? What is our staffing plan?

Proposal Evaluators (for your company)   These are individuals you engage to simulate the evaluation done ultimately by the customer. Your evaluators review versions of your proposals before they go to the customer, as members of a Pink Team, Red Team, or the other color teams.

Proposal manager   Team member with two main responsibilities: discovering the best case that can be made in this competition for your company and communicating that case.

Purple Team   The top management reviewers who review the proposal concurrently with the Red Team to evaluate it just before the final version is created.

Recompetition   All contracts have a termination date. If the customer still needs that type of product, law requires that customer to hold another competition for that product—a recompetition.

Red Team   A group charged with the responsibility of verifying or refuting that the proposal team has complied with the instruction of the solicitation and has produced a good response.

Referenceable   Your previous contracts (government or commercial) are referenceable if you are certain that, when asked, your past or current customer will give you a favorable rating in response to an inquiry by the customer evaluators.

Relationship manager   The relationship manager interacts directly with the customer, cultivating relationships with the important people in the customer organization.

Reps & Certs   Section K of a solicitation, it requires you to make many statements about your company to verify that you are a responsible offeror.

Request for Information   Issued by a CO to aid in the development of a solicitation. It is often to your advantage to respond to those requests, to ensure you will be included on any list of companies to receive the resulting solicitation.

Request for Proposal (RFP)   A solicitation for you to submit a proposal in anticipation of subsequent awarding of a contract through negotiations and discussions.

Response   The material that you, as an offeror, provide to the customer, consistent with the customer's description of what is required of offerors. The responses from all offerors are evaluated and a contract awarded (or not), in accordance with the terms of the customer's solicitation. This book more often uses the alternate term "solution."

Responsible   Your company must be able to handle the work you're seeking, must be responsible according to GSA criteria. You can be found nonresponsible if you've been debarred, have a questionable history of contract terminations, etc.

Responsibility assignment matrix (RAM)   Document containing the outline of your proposal, as driven by the Section L instructions, and assigning responsibilities for each piece of the outline to an individual.

Responsive   Your proposal will be judged responsive if you have complied with all the terms and conditions of the solicitation according to GSA criteria.

Reviews   *See* **Evaluations**.

Rough Order of Magnitude (ROM)   A nonbinding guess at how many or how much of something will be required to do something. The KO may ask you for this as a help to properly size an upcoming procurement.

S&L governments   State and local governments. This is shorthand for the nonfederal governments you wish to have as your customers.

Scope creep   When a customer requests you and your staff to do something that is outside the bounds of the existing contract.

Sealed Bidding Process   The government evaluates all bids for acceptability, not including price offered. Then all bids are opened, simultaneously and publicly, and the low bidder is the awardee.

Set-Asides   Competitions specifying that only a certain class of offerors can be awarded a contract.

Shelfware   A pejorative term for documents that are created, often with great fanfare and cost, and then ignored. Proposal process manuals sometime fall into this category.

Should Cost   The government's estimate of what the contract should cost the government.

Single Award Schedule (SAS)   Contracts made with one, and only one, supplier for delivery in one geographic area.

Single Point of Contact   On either side, government or contractor, this is the single individual (or group of people in one function in a large organization) who speaks for that side.

Single Point of Failure   If a single individual is the only person in your organization capable of performing a task, you are vulnerable to a catastrophic failure should that person be unable to perform. An example of such failure is your contract manager's responsibilities to communicate with the customer KO. If your manager is out and you miss critical messages from the KO, you will be in serious trouble.

Small Business Administration (SBA)   An independent agency of the federal government with the charter to help Americans start, build, and grow businesses.

Sole proprietorship   A business structure in which an individual and his or her company are considered a single entity for tax and liability purposes.

Sole Source   Under certain circumstances, agencies may award contracts without having a competition. Typically, KOs have the right to award contracts, especially but not exclusively, to small businesses on a sole source basis. That means the KO has determined that a specific company and only that company can perform the work.

Solicitation   A document requesting or inviting offerors to submit offers. A formal announcement of an opportunity. Solicitations typically include a draft contract and provisions on preparing and submitting offers.

Solution   An alternative to the other industry standard term, response. Solution tells how your company plans to solve the customer's problem.

Source Selection Authority (SSA)   The ultimate decision-maker for a government contract award.

Source Selection Evaluation Board (SSEB)   Performs the staff work analysis and often makes a recommendation to the SSA on which offerors or bidders should be awarded the contract.

Source Selection Plan (SSP)   The top-level plan to make a selection of the source (the winner).

Sources Sought   This is often the first step, by the KO, in determining the capability of industry to meet a specific, identified need. This is in essence a market survey.

Stalking horse   A bid you're encouraged to make with no real chance of winning the competition. Your bid will act only to assist the KO in demonstrating that there is real competition for this opportunity.

Standard Industrial Classification (SIC)   A list of five-digit codes, managed by the Office of Management and Budget, to classify all industries in the United States.

Statement of Objectives (SOO)   The part of the solicitation and the contract that states the broad description of the government's required performance objectives.

Statement of Requirements (SOR)   A Statement of Requirements document is written at the outset of a new project to define the project's requirements.

Statement of Work (SOW)   The part of the solicitation and the contract that describes the actual work to be done and specifies requirements, quantities, performance date, and a statement of required quality.

Stuckee   The individual or individuals having the responsibility to respond to a specific action item under the "06 Action Items."

Subchapter S Corporation   A closely-held corporation with special tax advantages. Allows the protection of a corporation without some of the reporting requirements.

Subcontractor   A formal relationship between prime offeror and a company that provides services or products under the terms of the contract and entrepreneurial skills to the proposal team.

Subject Matter Expert (SME)   A person having the in-depth knowledge of an expert on a given subject.

Supplier   *See* **Vendor**.

Task order   After the government has awarded a contract, whether a multiple-award or single-award, and the customer wants a specific task to be done under that contract, the KO issues a request to respond to a Task Order. This may be competitive (multiple award) or not (single award).

Taxpayer Identification Number (TIN)   A number issued by the Internal Revenue Service that identifies an entity for tax purposes. For individuals this is the Social Security number; for corporations it's a number assigned by the IRS.

Technical and Marketing Interchange   A meeting at the customer's place of business that involves your technical and management people and their counterparts in the customer organization.

Technical arrogance   An attitude that evidences that you know better what the customer really needs to buy than the government's specifications.

Technical Champion   The individual with the technical skills to carry out the program; he often guides the critical sections of the technical part of a solution.

Termination for Convenience (of the government)   If the government KO decides it is in the best interest of the government to end a contract, or a part of a contract, that right is granted by the terms and conditions section of the contract.

Termination for Default   Terms and Conditions (Ts and Cs)   If the Government KO determines that the contractor has failed to perform under the contract, the KO may terminate all or parts of the contract.

Tiger Team   A small group of individuals created to solve an important problem, the team acts for a short duration and has a specific charter to accomplish a task or solve a problem.

Time and Materials (T&M)   The type of contract featuring a fixed hourly rate, including overhead and profit, plus material at cost plus handling fee. Used when a detailed definition of the task is difficult or impossible.

Top Management (TM)   This person or persons is at the level within the company having the greatest business interest in getting a specific contract.

Trade Study   More formally known as a trade-off study, this is a classical operations research term for the formal analysis of reasonable alternative solutions for the purpose of comparing and contrasting these alternatives by important characteristics.

Trading Partners Identification Number (TPIN)   A number assigned to your company upon completed registration at CCR. This is a password that enables you to access your records on CCR.

Transmittal letter   A brief letter that responds directly to any customer concerns as expressed in a solicitation. The contracts manager signs the letters.

Uniform Contract Format (UCF)   The format (Sections A through M) that must be used for invitations for bids (IFBs) and requests for proposals (RFPs).

Vendor (same as Supplier)   A company on your bidding team that supplies only price and availability data and does not contribute entrepreneurial skills to the team. Vendors often participate on many teams in a competition.

Visuals   Anything that is not text; includes charts, graphs, tables, illustrations, photographs, and more. *See also* **Graphics.**

Volume   A part of a proposal, as in technical volume.

White Paper   Typically argues a specific position or solution to a problem, especially a government problem.

Win Themes   These answer the customer's implicit question, "Why should I, the customer, choose your solution?"

Word Problem   Evaluation criteria are often stated as word problems like those students experience.

You-Gotta-Do-Better-Than-That   A negotiation technique wherein one party places the parties on the opposite side of the negotiations against each other in an effort to extract the most favorable terms from the eventual winner.

Resources

For more detailed advice and information on various topics covered in this book, turn to the resources listed here. Included are websites with guidance on many aspects of government contracting or business development, service providers offering expertise in areas where you and your team might be lacking in skills or experience, professional associations for networking with potential or current customers, tools for producing proposals or enhancing project team communications, and recommended books to read.

Government Resources

Federal Business Opportunities
www.fedbizopps.gov, or more simply: www.fbo.gov
This is the federal government's primary site for posting and tracking opportunities to get contracts with the federal government.

Small Business Administration
www.sba.gov
This is the federal government's first-line resource for small business help, including financing.

General Services Administration
www.gsa.gov
This is the federal government real estate agent, and source of many contracts for use by agencies throughout the federal government. In recent years, other government agencies (state and local) have access to many of the same contracts previously available only to federal agencies.

Executive Office of the President, Office of Management and Budget
202-395-3080 (information and directory)
www.whitehouse.gov/omb
Publishes A-10, A-76, and many others in this series.

Service Providers

This list of selected service providers has at least two in each category. The appearance on this list does not constitute an endorsement, nor does the absence of a service provider indicate a failure to endorse.

These companies charge for their services. Their fees vary widely, as do the depth and breadth of those services. It's up to you to choose a service provider matching both your needs and your budget. Or go it alone. *Caveat emptor!* (Let the buyer beware.)

Competition Information

CAISISCo
www.caisisco.com
301-840-5959

Federal Sources, Inc.
www.federalsources.com
Local: 703-610-8700 Toll-free: 1-800-210-6326

Input
www.input.com
Phone: 703-707-3500
"The authority on government business, provides market intelligence, analysis, consulting, and events & training to help companies develop government business and public sector organizations achieve their objectives."

GSA Schedule Contracts

Federal Schedules, Inc.
www.fedsched.com
703-709-8700

EZ GSA Schedules, Inc.
www.ezgsa.com
local: 301-913-5000; toll-free: 1-800-991-6848

Government Sales Consultants, Inc.
www.govt-sales.com
West Coast: Patti Reardon; patti.reardon@att.net; 619-421-5487
East Coast: Sue Dobyns; 703-793-9690; 703-421-5180

B2G Institute
www.B2Ginstitute.com
1-800-809-1289 X 11200
jjustus@B2GInstitute.com

Staff Supplementations, Proposal Consultants, Proposal Support

Proposal Leadership, Inc.
www.proposalleadership.com
www.gettinggovtcontracts.com
www.gettinggovcontracts.com
John C. Lauderdale III; 703-629-1166

Organizational Communications, Inc.
www.ociwins.com
Russell Smith; 703-689-9600

DataWrite, Inc.
www.datawrite.com
Chet Shinaman; 727-215-6688

360 Ink
www.360ink.com
Maggie Mestraud; 703-266-8119

Graphics (Visuals) Support

24 Hour Company
www.24hrco.com
Dennis Fitzgerald; 703-533-7209

Strategic Proposal Services, Inc.
www.strategicproposalservices.com
Keith D. Lee; 240-232-0193

Orals Coach

Head First Consulting
Jack Harris
www.headfirstconsulting.com
Phone: 321-729-9955

An experienced professional, specializing in coaching teams in oral presentations.

Professional Associations

These are not-for-profits you may find useful for both recruiting personnel and providing specialized training for your staff.

Society of Competitive Intelligence Professionals (SCIP)
www.scip.org
703-739-0696

Association of Proposal Management Professionals (APMP)
www.apmp.org

National Contract Management Association (NCMA)
www.ncmahq.org
571-382-0082

National Association of Government Contractors (NAGC)
governmentcontractors.org
1-800-979-NAGC

Coalition for Government Procurement (CGP)
thecgp.org
202-331-0975

Software

These companies provide specialized software to help you manage your proposal activities.

Privia by SpringCM
www.springcm.com
1-877-362-7273 (PT)

SharePoint
www.microsoft.com/sharepoint

Recommended Reading

Altman, Evie, and Scott Orbach. *Getting a GSA Schedule: A Step by Step Guide*. Bethesda, MD 20824 : EZGSA Publications, Inc., 2008.

APMP Glossary, www.apmp.org.

Desktop Guide to Basic Contacts Terms, Sixth Edition, Revised and Expanded. McLean, VA 22102: NCMA, 2006.

Stanberry, Scott A. *Federal Contracting Made Easy, Third Edition*. Vienna, VA 22182: Management Concepts, 2009.

Following are various CDs from the National Association of Government Contractors. Representative titles are:

> *An Introduction to Government Contracting*
>
> *A Guide to the General Services Administration (GSA) Schedule*
>
> *A Guide to Marketing to Government Agencies*
>
> *Guide to 8(a) and Small Disadvantaged Business Certification with Forms*
>
> *A Guide to Subcontracting Opportunities*
>
> *A Guide to Facility and Personal Security Clearances*

Win Government Contracts for your Small Business, Third Edition, by John DiGiacomo and James Kleckner. Riverwoods, IL 60015, CCH Tax and Accounting, 2005.

Winning Government Contracts by Malcolm Parvey and Deborah Alston. Franklin Lakes, NJ 07417, The Career Press, 2008.

Glossaries, Acronyms, and Codes

These government publications are the most authoritative source on the subjects they cover.

DOD Dictionary of Military Terms:
www.dtic.mil/doctrine/jel/doddict

Glossary of Acquisition Terms (Federal Acquisition Institute)
www.fai.gov/pdfs/glossary.pdf

North American Industry Classification System (for NAICS codes)
www.naics.com

Appendix

Sample Capture Plan

A capture plan is one of the documents critical for effective proposal planning, as it contains information the team needs to use to help it decide whether or not to bid on an opportunity. And if you do go ahead with a bid, the capture plan data can help your team craft a strong response.

The capture plan is a structured approach to developing a clear understanding of the customer, their environment, and their needs. It ensures that you have a thorough understanding of the competitive landscape and the solutions the competition is offering, especially as matched against your company's suite of products and services. The capture plan helps you turn all that understanding into a strategy for winning the contract through a combination of produce, price, and performance offering.

The capture plan is created and maintained (updated and revised) by a member of your proposal team, usually the capture manager, who presents each evolution of the document at a team meeting, sharing the information as a written report and/or as a PowerPoint presentation. These correspond with the bid decision points discussed in Chapters 4, 8, 14, and 15.

On the following pages, you'll find a sample capture plan that you can adapt as a template for your own company's use. This document contains no real names or data. WooNoo is a fictitious government entity (the customer) offering a fake opportunity. Consolidated Amalgam is a fictitious company trying to capture (bid on and win) that opportunity. Everything else about the document is realistic, in that the questions or topics posed and the data filled in next to those questions or topics is what you might expect to see in a real capture plan.

In this sample capture plan, the text in **bold** represents the standard questions to be answered. The data supplied by the presenter (usually the capture manager) is in normal typeface.

The text in *italics* shows that the presenter knows the answer is not satisfactory, meaning the answers at this time are incomplete. Those items are therefore on the presenter's action item list, which means the presenter needs to fix the problems. The good news is that sometimes others on the review team either can supply the right answer or can offer to help get the right information in cooperation with the presenter.

Here are a few final tips before you read the actual document:

♦ Your capture plan is a living document, so it's up to the presenter to keep the capture plan current by replacing old data with the very latest available.

♦ The sample plan provided here is only an example. It will not fit your business precisely, so think of this as a template you can tailor to fit your own company's needs.

♦ Once you've adapted this sample to fit your needs, use that template for all capture plans across the company and across opportunities to ensure a consistent format—and make everyone's job easier.

Now, let's look at the sample capture plan ....

Capture Plan

Next Big Procurement

WooNoo, Orlando, FL

For Training throughout CONUS

September   November 2013

Consolidated Amalgam

Arlington, VA

Prepared by John C. Lauderdale III
Proposal Leadership, Inc.
Herndon, VA
703-629-1166

Table of Contents

A. Data Summary Sheet

B. Marketing Questions and Answers

C. Background and History

      Bid/No-Bid Results/Template

D. The Technology

E. The Competition

      Opportunity evaluation

F. Why We Can Win

      Discriminators

G. Objections and Barriers

      Win Strategy

H. Proposal Outline

      1. Technical Approach

            Technical Risk

            Schedule for Delivery of Products

      2. Management Approach

            Schedule Risk

      3. Cost Approach

            Cost Risk; Should-Cost Estimate

A. Data Summary Sheet

Customer: WooNoo, out of Orlando, FL

Key customer personnel: Contracting Officer: (KO): Lisa Williams /Deputy KO: Derrick Abercrombie

Product or service to be procured: For Lot II, this is technology-based training material

Location of customer and location of work performance: various locations throughout CONUS

Our key technical staff: To Be Supplied (TBS). This is an action item for the next review.

Contract duration and best estimate of target cost: Total contract ceiling is $4.5 B over 9 years; contracts officers' estimate of currently-identified total needs is approximately $1.2B; Split between Lot I (not of interest to Consolidated Amalgam) and Lot II (we're bidding as prime) is unknown at this time ….

Source and amount of customer's funds: Routine operating funds will be used for this contract; no extraordinary or unusual funding requirements that are likely to be interrupted by external events. This money is earmarked in the entire forward planning documents of the Navy. We expect no significant increases or decreases in the funding available.

Critical, or precipitating, event: Expiration of existing contracts; desire of the customer to have a vehicle to attract a limited number of well-qualified suppliers, capable of successfully performing these tasks, under a variety of contract types, each reflecting the degree of risk to the successful bidders.

Relation of this procurement to our own long-range or strategic plans (that is, how important is this procurement to the firm's future?): As one of several incumbents, Consolidated Amalgam is not only well positioned to win one of the two small business contracts, but winning these, as a prime, is also important to us as an independent company. Failure to win, as a prime, will surely be a severe blow to our growth possibilities in this, an important marketplace for Consolidated Amalgam.

B. Marketing Questions and Answers

Question 1: Who will make the procurement decision (that is, who is the Source Selection Authority, and who is likely to be on the Source Selection Evaluation Board)?

Answer 1: *(Not available at this time. This is an Action Item to be closed no later than the release of the final solicitation.)*

Question 2: What criteria will be used to pick the winner?

Answer 2: This is a "best value" award, based on Technical (Instructional Systems Development) & (Management), Past Performance, and Price. We suspect that, during the selection process, at least three and perhaps four small businesses will be judged "technically acceptable," and from there it will be a cost/price shootout to determine the two winners.

C. Background and History

1. The players

Individuals: Robert Beurlot, WooNoo Program Manager; Steve Larton, Deputy WooNoo Program Manager; Lisa Williams, KO

Institutions: No outside institutions are relevant to this competition.

Customer: Some elements outside of WooNoo will be supplying evaluators for this competition. Their organizations are only partially known at this time. We will endeavor to identify those organizations and factor their own interests into our discussions in our proposal.

Competition: The important personnel from all competing teams are well known to us. And we are known to them.

2. **Customer's motivation:** No special considerations. This is the re-competition of existing work but with a slightly different mix of small and large businesses to win some of these ID/IQ contracts.

Cost savings? No more than usual.

Risk reduction? No. Customer views this as a low-risk program.

Other? Not known, but probably none.

3. **Our motivation and interests**

Pre-RFP contact and RFP influence: Consolidated Amalgam, and XMX of our business partners (subcontractors) took advantage of the customer's invitation for a 1-hour meeting, in Orlando, during August. Consolidated Amalgam has influenced the solicitation in the following way(s):

Follow-on, spin-off considerations: This is a continuation of our mainline business. Winning this would position us to compete for the new work from this command coming up in about two years.

D. The Technology

1. Describe the technology to be applied to the customer's problems:

This is a low-technology application. Most of the work is the creation of PowerPoint presentations.

There is, however, some research work required regarding high-technology equipment. The equipment manufacturers usually provide some modest amount of documentation with their equipment when delivered. However, it quickly becomes obsolete, and documentation downloadable from their websites tends to be inadequate to outright wrong. Therefore, an important part of this task is to improve that documentation to be fully usable. In addition, when the individual pieces of equipment become part of a total system, the interfaces are complex and not documented at all.

2. Relate this technology to competing technologies and why we've decided this particular technology is the best one:

We expect the instructional approach and the technical solution to be largely the same by all offerors, whether for the free and open competition or the small business competition. The differentiators among offerors should be in the XMX niche market for handling the interface problem as discussed above. As a subcontractor to us incumbent and on the basis of similar work that XMX has done for the command not only in CONUS, but OCONUS, XMX represents a significant and sustainable competitive advantage for our team.

E. The Competition

Describe all competitors, probably including the two SHADOW competitors, 0 and 00. (This is for Lot II only and small-business competition only):

> **0. Do nothing, or defer a procurement decision for the indefinite future.** Not realistic as the procurement is required by law and regulation.
>
> **00. Perform the tasks in-house (or under other contract vehicles).** Again, not realistic. The customer has very little, if any, capability to do this job.
>
> **1. Us (Team Consolidated Amalgam):** Consolidated Amalgam is prime; subcontractors are XMX, Cisco, and YERS (a certified 8(a) company with a sterling reputation with this customer).
>
> **2. Team CCRS** (subcontractors unknown)
>
> **3. Team Northern Bamff** (subcontractors only from other divisions of Bamff)
>
> **4. Team ArkansasOttes** (subcontractors unknown)
>
> **5. Possibly another team, but we have not been able to get definitive information on it.**

(General Note: If there are more than about three or four, try to be realistic about your chances of winning. You should either be able to reduce the list to three or four or consider getting out of the competition.)

Eliminating the Competition

1. Can some competitors be neutralized by offering them a subcontractor status? Only Team ArkansasOttes is a good candidate for that move. Preliminary discussions have taken place, but there is a problem between our two teams, as there is too much overlap to make a sensible team.

2. What does a list of competitors tell us about what the customer wants? These are the usual players, and we can discern nothing special about this list.

F. Why We Can Win

(Why Us?)

1. Describe the advantages that we possess over the competition; these will become the discriminators or themes in the proposal. Are we singularly well qualified or just "me-too"? We are at least as well qualified as our primary competition, Team CCRS. We believe this may well be a price shootout among equally compliant and attractive technical solutions.

2. Discuss what you believe to be necessary (price: waiver of rights; deviation from corporate policy; strongest subcontractor or associate relationships) to win this work. Any price concessions will have to come in the last two weeks of the competition. But in light of the answer to 1 above, we need to be ready to sharpen our pencils during those last two weeks.

3. What subcontractors or suppliers have been chosen to support this effort? Why were they chosen? Are they committed to us? Exclusively? Signed a non-disclosure agreement? Signed an agreement not to compete? Both of our subcontractors have been with us for the last 18 months. All NDAs and other agreements have been in place for over a year.

4. Have we influenced the RFP, thereby achieving Competitive Convergence (between our views and theirs)? Is the RFP likely to reflect our input? Are some firms now discouraged from competing or placed at a distinct disadvantage because of our skillful interfaces with the customer? We've done the best we can. We know the competition has also been in to see this customer, as have we and both our team members.

G. Objections and Barriers

List all of the objections a skeptical, critical, informed management team might make to proceeding with this business development. Overcome or discount these objections, using verifiable facts and/or judgments.

There are no significant existing objections. Those objections raised at the last review have all been addressed and are no longer operative.

Executive Summary Outline and Template

This appendix gives additional details about the executive summary, as introduced in Chapter 12. This is the third document in the proposal plan attachments, appearing as 03 Executive Summary. The executive summary is an unusual document because you use it not only extensively during the proposal creation process but also—potentially—as a deliverable to the customer as a part of your proposal submission.

If a solicitation requires an executive summary, then you must follow the instructions of the solicitation and deliver the summary exactly as required. More often, however, you're not required to submit an executive summary, but it's a good idea to create one anyway, both for your internal use and for your customer.

Here is a detailed layout of a typical executive summary. First you have an outline of the sections of the summary; then I've provided a template showing the format and structure of a typical summary. Keep in mind that these are only suggestions that you can adapt to fit your company's needs. When you do adapt it, remember to use this template for all executive summaries across your company and across opportunities as appropriate. This ensures that everyone in your organization is using a consistent format—one that best serves your company and makes everyone's job easier.

Executive Summary Outline

1. Purpose

Positively influence the customer's decision-maker(s) to understand why you should win the competition.

2. Uses

2.1   communicates your case to the customer;

2.2   focuses your own top management on their own task and forces their own decisions;

2.3   communicates with the proposal team (including teammates) about the most important aspects of the competition.

3. Elements

3.1   logos;

3.2   photos of your people actually performing the customer's work (in support of the customer's product);

3.3   inside front cover of themes & discriminators (Why You??);

3.4   commitment letter (addressed to the customer Decision Maker from his counterpart in your own organization);

3.5   Schedule for Delivery of Products (most folks call it a "Schedule" or a "Program Schedule," but this name is more accurate and better), demonstrating that you know what is to be delivered and when it is to be delivered. That's the really important thing to the customer: "When do I get my stuff?"

3.6   flow diagram, demonstrating your knowledge of the customer's important business processes or demonstrating how you're going to achieve product deliveries on time and within budget;

3.7   photographs of your key people, reinforcing name & face recognition (but never *introducing* key people; if you have to introduce key people at proposal submission time, it's too late!!);

3.8   special appeals to "hot buttons," which are the critical concerns expressed by the customer;

3.9   reference to the Precipitating Event, the one that led to this procurement;

3.10   schematic or photo of place the work is to be done;

3.11   map or other graphic, demonstrating geographic disbursement, if that is important, or proximity to the customer if that is important.

4. Creation Methods

    4.1   templated

    4.2   archived

    4.3   abstracted from other, submitted materials (past and present)

    4.4   develops as elaborate a document as the procurement warrants

    4.5   uses action captions

    4.6   incorporates anti-competition themes wherever possible, and you're sure you can make those themes stick. Avoid like the plague any anti-competition themes you're unsure about.

Executive Summary Format Template

1. Cover page

features customer's logo (may have to obtain permission from customer for use; usually doesn't require approval from United States government agencies).

photographs or other representations of *your* people performing the customer's work, conveying the concept that "You're already working on your program."

2. Inside cover

employs the 4–7 win themes to answer the question, "Why You?"
themes are of three types: garden variety, discriminating, and anti-competition.

3. Commitment Letter

combined with the cover page and the inside cover, it causes the reader to breathe a sigh of relief and think: "Good ole John came through for me!"

addresses crisply the important discriminators—particularly good anti-competition themes—without lapsing into meaningless, generalized sales slogans

is addressed to the decision-maker, from his/her counterpart in your own organization.

4. Schedule for Delivery of Products (Program Schedule)

shows deliverables, de-emphasizes activities;

contains enough detail to demonstrate technical competence;

ideally, provides the customer with a better program summary in visual than is available from any other source.

(Customers, particularly federal government customers, are especially unskilled in their graphics ability.)

5. Organization Charts

re-enforces name and face recognition with people the customer needs to have confidence in;

shows simplicity of reporting relationships;

speaks to the customer's desires, not your own internal organization. Simple is better.

6. Product Flow Diagrams

shows, visually, that you really know the sequence of steps which occur in delivering the customer's products and services;

7. Material Addressing Customer's Known "Hot Buttons"

overcomes any uncertainties you know the customer has about:

dealing with you;

accomplishing the task on time, within budget; etc.

re-enforces the idea that you understand what the customer really *wants* to buy.

Training Your Team

Likely many, if not all, of your proposal team members, whether part of the prime or subcontractor groups, will need training on some aspect of the process. Effective training on best policies and practices can help you focus on getting the job done and winning more business.

Now you may be thinking that if it's so important, why am I addressing the topic of training in an appendix rather than as a chapter? Well, many companies seeking government contracts prefer to have an outside source provide training, so they don't need to know the information I cover here. They prefer to call in the hired guns to handle training and be done with it.

However, there's a danger in relying on outside sources for training. The wrong training, at the wrong time, is bad for two reasons: the training may be misguided or misapplied, and such training gives the appearance of progress, when in fact there is none. So this appendix provides information on how the typical outsourced, usually two-day format, training should be conducted. And I also describe an alternative to outsourcing—the Just-In-Time (JIT) in-house training approach.

The Advantages of JIT Training

The most effective training for getting government contracts is done in the context of a specific proposal effort. This JIT is given to the team members, including the prime and all subcontractors, as an integral part of the kickoff meeting.

Here are questions you're likely to have if you are involved in conducting or coordinating this training, along with brief answers to each question. The rest of the appendix explores these answers in more detail.

Q: Who is to be trained?

A: Your staff assigned as members of your proposal team.

Q: What is important to such training but often not clearly stated by all?

A: The instructional objective must be firmly established and understood.

Q: What is the role of the trainees?

A: The trainees must be active participants in their own training with no "I'm only here because I have to be" attitudes.

Q: Why is the training taking pace at this specific time?

A: It's time to get to work, as the solicitation is now out and the clock is ticking on developing a solution and proposal.

Q: Other than presentation of the materials, what does this process gain?

A: If properly conducted, it either begins or enhances team building among the trainees, who are also proposal team members.

Q: Are there standards for this training?

A: Yes, and they appear in a seven-item checklist in this appendix.

Q: Are there particularly good days of the week to hold this training to benefit both you, the customer, and the training faculty?

A: Yes; it's called the Fri-Sat For-Mat and is described below.

Q: Is there a way to ensure that the training delivered is relevant to the solicitation in hand?

A: Yes; it's called the vetting of instructional materials and happens on Thursday before the training on Friday and Saturday.

Setting the Stage for Effective JIT

Let's proceed on the hypothesis that we have only adults here. These adults arrive at the training with some, but not all, of the prerequisite skills and interests to perform the tasks they will be performing in creating a winning proposal. Further, the training is delivered by platform instruction. The term used here for the platform instructor or instructors is "faculty." The trainees are able to hear and see clearly the materials the faculty presents.

So let's begin with the right way to do training with the instructional objective of improving your proposals and getting a high win rate as a result. Here's a step-by-step walk-through:

- Start with the Instructional Objective. Simply stated, an instructional objective is the answer to, "What do you wish to accomplish?" This sounds so simple, and yet much training of proposal team members is without a clear and simple instructional objective. If you don't know where you're going, any road will take you there.

- Choose the right trainees. The best circumstance is that the trainees are prepared, by their previous education and work experience, to absorb the training. There's nothing worse than having a percentage of the attendees be lost from the first moments of the training experience. This is frustrating to the "lost," and their frustration presents a challenge to the remainder of the participants, as well as to the faculty.

- Begin the training with the expectation that those in attendance will not only be physically present, occupying a seat, but be participants in their own training. Encourage the participants to ask questions and even challenge the faculty as questions come up. Of course, the participants should ask questions in a constructive way, and the faculty should be expected to keep the training on track, to achieve the instructional objectives.

- The training is delivered to your proposal team, in the context of a planned response to a specific solicitation. This training is typically done very shortly after the solicitation has been released; that's why it's called "Just-In-Time" (JIT) training. This has the critical advantage that the participants have an opportunity to put to work immediately the concepts and processes taught in the course. Virtually no learning is lost because of a gap between their exposure to the materials and actual use.

- The entire proposal team is included in the same training session. So there is not only the chance for collaboration on this specific opportunity but also almost a necessity to do so because of the time pressure to deliver a proposal within the allowed time. All trainees have a clear and present motivation to not only understand the material presented but also cooperate with each other toward their common goal of winning the competition.

Checklist of Performance Standards

All types of training should be required to meet specifications and have performance standard. Following is a checklist of training course specifications and performance standards. These apply to all training, and specifically to the training in proposal creation:

❏ Course sessions will begin and end faithfully at the announced times.

❏ Written materials supporting specific instruction blocks will be available in advance of that block, so as to avoid any distracting shuffling of papers.

❏ All images (such as PowerPoint slides) used during the course will be available at the beginning of the course. This allows participants to take notes during the presentations on the materials themselves and will greatly increase the value of the written materials to the participants. If the training budget allows, materials will be bound in a quality notebook, suitable for placement on a shelf of professional reference materials, and will carry the identification and telephone number of the author(s).

❏ Feedback during the course will be encouraged. Faculty will answer all questions courteously and completely, consistent with the time available and the necessity for meeting the needs of the class as a whole.

❏ Formal, written evaluation of the course will be obtained from all participants. The faculty will give a diploma or certificate of attendance to each participant in exchange for the evaluation forms. Evaluations will be compiled and summarized to draw valid conclusions about how to improve the course.

❏ Faculty will dress in appropriate professional attire and use careful language and restrained mannerisms.

❏ If training funds allow, faculty will provide a set of supplementary materials. These materials will enhance or expand upon some topics in the seminar and introduce new subjects which time does not allow to be covered. Materials could include machine-readable templates, formats, and supplementary materials on any related subjects.

The Fri-Sat For-Mat

The most popular form of proposal training in the industry is not JIT but The Fri-Sat For-Mat, a two-day session for members of your company, with representatives of all the roles in your process.

Customer Reasons

The major cost of most training is not what you would expect. It's not hotel rooms, airline tickets, rental cars, meals, training materials, faculty fees, or facilities charges. It's personnel costs—personnel being those on your team who must participate in the training.

The Friday-Saturday sequence just about cuts the personnel cost in half because (virtually) all the employees are professional (exempt from overtime pay). Although there may be some exceptions, professionals are if not happy, at least understanding, to trade one of their normally off-days in exchange for being included in training because they realize such training is important to their career development. In addition, individuals doing this work are accustomed to being required to work long hours in the weeks and days before the due date for large proposals. These individuals therefore have a greater acceptance of giving up a single Saturday, if it means the training will result in a more efficient proposal-creation process in the future. If the training cannot eliminate the last-minute push and long hours, it can at lease reduce those long hours.

The Fri-Sat For-Mat is not a requirement, and is only a suggestion. It is wise to test the waters with the population of potential trainees, and gain their buy-in for this scheduling. Trainees must understand where each fits in to the objectives of the training. It's important that all trainees have a positive attitude; negative attitudes are contagious, and not at all helpful. Better to schedule during the normal work week than to impose overtime hours to an unwilling group of trainees.

The learning environment is better on Saturdays when there is no major threat of interruptions from frantic "emergency" phone calls or meetings associated with the normal business day. Especially for on-site training, the temptation for participants to drop out of the class for a few minutes or hours is almost irresistible.

Because of cost savings available to the faculty for such an arrangement, the fee is typically lower than it would be for other days.

Faculty Reasons

Assuming that faculty is coming in from out of town expressly for this training course, the following conditions exist:

- ◆ Saturdays are often not billable, and therefore the faculty converts a day not normally billable into a billable one.

- ◆ Weekend hotel rates are typically half the weekday rate.

- ◆ Many advance-purchase deep-discount airfares require a Saturday stay-over. By not being in a hurry and leaving on the red-eye after midnight Saturday or early Sunday morning, the faculty saves a bundle on airfares. Faculty can even afford to bring spouses or significant others along for the price you'd normally pay for just one individual.

- ◆ The training is more likely to involve the top management (TM) of your company. His or her presence will add greatly to the level of attention and the consequent learning. The downside is that this could blow up if the faculty holds and advocates views that are far different from the TM's; the risk is minimal, however, and it's possible to mitigate that risk via the Thursday afternoon meeting.

The Thursday Meeting with Top Management

If you agree that the Fri-Sat For-Mat makes sense to meet a specific instructional objective, then you should know that an important part of the pre-training preparation is the opportunity for the (outsourced) faculty to meet with your top management.

An important part of the Fri-Sat For-Mat training plan is the Thursday afternoon meeting with your Top Management. At this meeting, Top Management has an opportunity to describe in detail the specific needs of this set of trainees. This enables the trainers to tailor the course materials and meet the specific needs of the trainees. If this is truly in the context of the response to a specific solicitation, the faculty can address the peculiarities of that solicitation, and therefore make the training even more relevant and useful. This presupposes that the faculty members have signed a Non-Disclosure Agreement (NDA) with the sponsoring company.

This type of training, JIT and for all proposal team members, allows the proposal team management (proposal manager, capture manager, program manager-designate) to proceed in the belief that all members have at least been exposed to the right material. This translates into relatively high expectations for adherence to the processes and standards taught during the course.

Index

N